Getting Along in

ITALIAN

A

HOLIDAY

MAGAZINE

LANGUAGE SERIES

edited by MARIO PEI

Getting Along in French

Getting Along in Italian

IN PREPARATION:

Getting Along in German

Getting Along in Spanish

Getting Along in Portuguese

Getting Along in Russian

Getting Along in

ITALIAN

A

HOLIDAY
MAGAZINE
LANGUAGE BOOK

---

by
MARIO PEI
Professor of Romance Philology, Columbia University
with the editorial collaboration of

EMILIO PERUZZI
Assistant Professor of Romance Languages, Rutgers University

and

GINO BIGONGIARI
Assistant Professor of Italian, Columbia University

Harper & Brothers ⚜ *Publishers, New York*

Contents

Getting Along in
ITALIAN

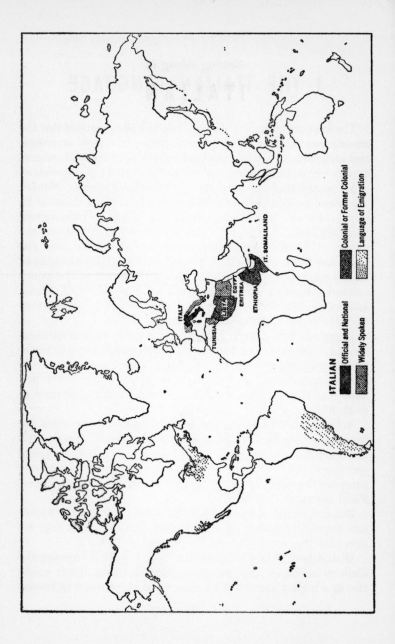

ITALIAN

Official and National ▓

Widely Spoken ▨

Colonial or Former Colonial ▨

Language of Emigration ░

ITALY

TUNISIA LIBYA EGYPT

ERITREA

ETHIOPIA

IT. SOMALILAND

I THE ITALIAN LANGUAGE

The keynote to Italy is variety. You become aware of this the minute you set foot on Italian soil. There is variety of artistic and architectural forms, variety of landscape, variety of cuisine, variety of physical types, and, above all, variety of expression.

No world traveler who has seen Rome, Florence, Naples, Turin and Bologna will ever be tempted to confuse them, as he might confuse Chicago, Philadelphia, Boston, Indianapolis and Cincinnati. No gourmet who has tasted the *ossobuco con risotto* of Milan, the *polenta cogli osei* of Venice, and the *pasta con sarde* of Sicily will ever deny the infinite diversity of Italian gastronomy. No tourist who has listened to the multicolored cadences and intonations of the North, Tuscany, Latium and the South can really bring himself to believe that they are facets of the same tongue.

There are two things, however, that most Italian speakers hold in common. One is the gestural accompaniment that seems an idle redundancy when applied to a language so apparently endless in its forms of vocal expression. The other is the animation of the speakers, which foreigners often misinterpret as excitability.

Actually, the Italian is not *unduly* excitable; he does not speak *too* fast; he is not *over*generous with his gestures. All you have to do to prove this to yourself is to attend a typical sporting event in Italy (say the race of the *palio* in Siena) and compare the behavior of the spectators with that of an Ebbets Field crowd in Brooklyn.

But the Italian is normally more animated than his American opposite number, and he carries this animation into his everyday life, not just to the sports arena.

Watch two Italian businessmen taking a stroll through the *Galleria* in Naples and discussing their problems. Their voices rise to a higher, shriller pitch than would be normal in Rocke-

1

feller Plaza; but at times they sink to an almost inaudible whisper. One of the speakers suddenly stops, forcing the other to do likewise. He joins his hands, then throws them out wide, fingers apart. You don't have to hear what he says. His meaning is crystal clear: "How in the world could I accept a proposition like that?"

The other energetically nods assent as he cuts into his friend's rapid flow of talk. He raises his right hand, cupping thumb and fingers together, tips uppermost, and shakes it repeatedly up and down. "How in the world could he have expected you to accept it?" the gesture says just as clearly as if you could hear the words—which indeed you can, for they are loud enough even if you don't understand them.

After witnessing these scenes a few times, you begin to acquire a misplaced confidence. "After all," you say, "I don't really have to learn this language. I can get along with gestures!"

Undeceive yourself. The gesture language of Italy is fully as complicated as a spoken tongue with its grammar. Furthermore it, too, has dialectal varieties; the gestures used in Naples are not quite identical with those of Venice. And, in any case, they are misleading, since we, too, use gestures.

Try, for example, giving the American "come here" gesture: palm up, fingers crooked and moved back and forth with tips upward. The Italian will interpret that as "Good-by." Reverse your gesture, with palm and fingertips down. Now you have an American "Good-by" and an Italian "Come here." It can get to be very confusing.

So perhaps it is better to learn a few words of the spoken tongue, just to carry you through difficult spots. It is not too hard if you go about it the right way, for Italian is a tongue of smooth sounds and comparatively easy spelling, and of all the Romance languages it is the one that generally comes closest to its ancestral Latin, which has contributed so much to our own vocabulary.

To offset these advantages, Italian has a grammar that presents complications, at least at the outset. It also has more bewildering dialects than practically any other language on earth. The northern dialects, for instance, are distinguished by their lack of the characteristic Italian double consonant sounds and by the fall of many vowel endings (*fatto,* for example, may appear as *fato, fat, fait*). In the northwest, but not in the northeast, you will hear sounds that make you think you are listening to French (French *u* and *eu,* and French nasals). If you move just south of Rome, on the other hand, you will hear a heavy stress that is completely at variance with the clear, staccato pronunciation of the North, along with a prolongation of accented vowels and a general deadening of final vowels to the sound of *e* in *the,* with a singsong cadence that faintly reminds you of Chinese. In the toe of the Italian boot and in Sicily you become aware of a predominance of *ee* and *oo* sounds, along with a sharp, explosive pronunciation. It is only in the central part of Italy, from Florence to Rome, that you hear the beautiful, clear sounds of the literary tongue, at least in the mouths of the entire population.

But the tourist can bypass some of these difficulties. The dialects are taken care of by the fact that just about everybody with whom he is likely to have contacts can speak the standard language. The grammar can be learned partly by indirection (that is, by learning phrases and expressions to the point where the grammatical pattern becomes natural), partly by concentrating on a few main points which we have provided in our grammatical outline (see pages 132–151).

Take the matter of sounds and spellings first. There is no Italian sound that does not have a counterpart, identical or fairly close, in English. The *written* vowels are five: *a, e, i, o, u.* For three of them, there is no trouble whatsoever: whenever you see a written *a,* use the *ah*-sound of "father"; for the written Italian *i,* use the *ee* of "meet"; for the Italian *u,* use the *oo* of "food." The written Italian *e* is sometimes open (as in "met"; let us use *eh* to indicate this sound); sometimes closed, like the *ay* of "maybe," or better yet, our colloquial "mebbe"; we can use *ay* for this, but let us remember to make the *ay* short and clipped, not drawled. Italian written *o* sometimes has the sound of *aw* in "awful," but short and clipped (if you can

3

imitate a Britisher, use the British *o* of "pot"); at other times it sounds like the initial part of our exclamation "oh!" but again short and clipped.

Let's train on the vowels, and at the same time learn a few easy, one-letter or one-syllable words:

a (AH) to
è (EH) is
e (AY) and
di (DEE) of
ho (AW) I have
o (OH) or
su (SOO) on

Italian does not use the written letters *y* and *w*, but replaces them with *i* and *u*:

piano (PYAH-noh) piano, slowly, softly
qua (KWAH) here
buono (BWAW-noh) good
guerra (GWEHR-rah) war

At this point, we can leave off sounds for a while, and learn some common greetings. (From here on, small capitals will be used to indicate stressed syllables or words.)

buon giorno (BWAWN JOHR-noh) good day, good morning, good afternoon
buona sera (BWAW-nah SAY-rah) good evening
buona notte (BWAW-nah NAWT-tay) good night
arrivederci (ahr-ree-vay-DAYR-chee) good-by (this literally means "to again seeing each other"; if you want to be more polite, shift to *arrivederla* [ahr-ree-vay-DAYR-lah], "to again seeing you"). *Addio* (ahd-DEE-oh) literally means "to God," and is more of a farewell. *Ciao* (CHAH-oh) is popular and familiar for both "hello" and "good-by." "Hello" on the phone is usually *pronto* (PROHN-toh), literally "Ready!"
Come sta? (KOH-may STAH?) is "How are you?" Less formal is *Come va?* (KOH-may VAH?), "How goes it?" The normal reply is:

4

Bene, grazie, e Lei? (BEH-nay, GRAH-tsyay, ay LEH-ee?), "Well, thanks, and you?"

Most Italian consonant sounds are almost the same as in English. But there are a few spelling peculiarities. For instance, written Italian *ch* is *always* pronounced like a *k*:

chi (KEE) who, whom
che (KAY) what

C before *e* or *i* is *always* like English *ch* in "church":

cena (CHAY-nah) supper
amici (ah-MEE-che) friends

G before *a, o, u* or a consonant is like the *g* of "God," but before *e* or *i* it is like English *j*:

largo (LAHR-goh) wide
gesto (JEHS-toh) gesture

Sc before *a, o* or *u* is pronounced *sk*, but before *e* or *i* it is pronounced *sh*:

scala (SKAH-lah) stair, ladder
scuro (SKOO-roh) dark
pesce (PAY-shay) fish
sciopero (SHAW-pay-roh) strike

Sch (used only before *e* and *i*) is pronounced *sk*:

scherzo (SKAYR-tsoh) joke
schizzo (SKEE-tsoh) sketch

The only other sound-and-spelling combinations apt to give trouble are *gl* (usually like *lli* in "million"; we'll use LY for this); *gn* (like *ni* in "onion"; NY is our transcription); *h* (always silent); *r* (trilled as in British "very"); and *z* (sometimes TS, sometimes DZ):

meglio (MEH-lyoh) better
aglio (AH-lyoh) garlic
legno (LAY-nyoh) wood

5

agnello (ah-NYEHL-loh) lamb
ho (AW) I have
hanno (AHN-noh) they have
raro (RAH-roh) rare
roba (RAW-bah) stuff, things
grazie (GRAH-tsyay) thanks
zucchero (DZOOK-kay-roh) sugar

Politeness plays a big role in Italian conversation. Here are a few of the many polite expressions in current use. A friendly smile helps, too.

per favore, per piacere (payr fah-VOH-ray, payr pyah-CHAY-ray) please
grazie mille (GRAH-tsyay MEEL-lay) thanks a lot
prego (PREH-goh) don't mention it
scusi (SKOO-see) excuse me, pardon me, I beg your pardon
permesso? (payr-MAYS-soh?) may I come in?, may I pass?
avanti! (ah-VAHN-tee!) come in!
sì (SEE) yes
no (NAW) no
volentieri (voh-layn-TYEH-ree) gladly

The last important point in Italian pronunciation is the double consonant. In English, the fact that a consonant is written double usually makes no difference in the pronunciation. In Italian it does. A consonant that is written double is pronounced over a longer period of time than if it is written single. In the case of some consonants (particularly *t, d, c, g, p, b*) there is no way to lengthen the period of time when the consonant actually comes out; what you do instead is to stretch the holding period before you release the consonant. Take two words, *fato* (fate) and *fatto* (done). In *fato*, you pronounce FAH-, then go on to toh. In *fatto*, you pronounce FAHT- getting your tongue in position for *t*, but not releasing it; the release comes a fraction of a second later, when you say toh.

Try a few words where the single or double consonant makes a lot of difference in the meaning:

eco (EH-koh) echo
ecco (EHK-koh) here is, here are

6

ala (AH-lah) wing
alla (AHL-lah) to the

caro (KAH-roh) dear, expensive
carro (KAHR-roh) cart

nono (NAW-noh) ninth
nonno (NAWN-noh) grandfather

poso (PAW-soh) I lay down
posso (PAWS-soh) I can

cade (KAH-day) he falls
cadde (KAHD-day) he fell

The tourist almost invariably "wants" something. Here are a few useful "wanting" expressions, preceded by the questions that bring them on:

in che posso servirla? (een KAY PAWS-soh sayr-VEER-lah?) may I help you?

che (or *cosa,* or *che cosa*) *vuole* (or *desidera*)? (KAY, KAW-sah, kay KAW-sah vwaw-lay, day-SEE-day-rah?) what do you wish? (often the entire expression is cut down to *desidera?*)

The answers:

voglio (VAW-lyoh) I want
vorrei (vohr-REH-ee) I should like
mi dia (or *mi favorisca*) (mee DEE-ah, mee fah-voh-REES-kah) give me
vuol darmi (or *vuol favorirmi*)? (VWAWL DAHR-mee, VWAWL fah-voh-REER-mee?) will you give me?
mi porti (mee PAWR-tee) bring me

Now to try a few of these out:

Vorrei un pacchetto di sigarette. (vohr-REH-ee oon pahk-KAYT-toh dee see-gah-RAYT-tay.) I should like to have a pack of cigarettes.

Vuol darmi un pezzo di sapone? (VWAWL DAHR-mee oon PEH-tsoh dee sah-POH-nay?) Would you give me a piece of soap?

7

Mi porti una bottiglia di birra. (mee PAWR-tee OO-nah boht-TEE-lyah dee BEER-rah.) Bring me a bottle of beer.

A few other shopping terms are:

mi faccia vedere (mee FAH-chah vay-DAY-ray) show me
quanto? (or *quanto costa?*) (KWAHN-toh, KWAHN-toh KAWS-tah?) how much?
troppo (TRAWP-poh) too much
altro? (AHL-troh?) anything else?
nient'altro (nyehn-TAHL-troh) nothing else

Numerals are extremely important, because they appear in price tags and on restaurant checks. You will find the complete list of numerals on pages 101–103, and also on pages 138–139. Try them with *lire,* the plural of *lira,* the Italian unit of currency (you can't buy anything for one *lira;* it's less than two mills, and have you ever tried to spend a mill?). Here are a few samples of their use:

Questo vestito costa quindicimila cinquecento lire. (KWAYS-toh vays-TEE-toh KAWS-tah kween-dee-chee-MEE-lah cheen-kway-CHEHN-toh LEE-ray.) This suit costs 15,500 lire.
Quant'è il conto? Seimila quattrocento cinquanta lire (kwahn-TEH eel KOHN-toh? seh-ee-MEE-lah kwaht-troh-CHEHN-toh cheen-KWAHN-tah LEE-ray.) How much is the bill? Six thousand four hundred fifty lire.

Finding one's way is important, too. Here are a few inquiries and possible replies:

sa dirmi? (SAH DEER-mee?) can you tell me?
dov'è? (doh-VEH?) where is?
dove va? (DOH-vay VAH?) where are you going?
dove andiamo? (DOH-vay ahn-DYAH-moh?) where are we going?
da che parte si trova? (dah KAY PAHR-tay see TRAW-vah?) which way is?
ecco (EHK-koh) here is, here are
di qua (dee KWAH) this way
di là (dee LAH) that way

8

a destra   (ah DEHS-trah)   to the right
a sinistra   (ah see-NEES-trah)   to the left
vada dritto   (VAH-dah DREET-toh)   go straight ahead
venga con me   (VEHN-gah kohn MAY)   come with me

Let's try a few of these in combination:

Scusi, sa dirmi dov'è il Duomo?   (SKOO-see, SAH DEER-mee doh-VEH eel DWAW-moh?)   Pardon me, can you tell where the cathedral is?

Da che parte si trova l'ascensore?   (dah KAY PAHR-tay see TRAW-vah lah-shayn-SOH-ray?)   Which way is the elevator?

Dove posso trovare un salone di bellezza?   (DOH-vay PAWS-soh troh-VAH-ray oon sah-LOH-nay dee bayl-LAY-tsah?)   Where can I find a beauty parlor?

Directional signs are of importance, even if they do come only in written form. You will find a fairly complete list on pages 125–131, but here are a few samples:

Vietato fumare   (vyay-TAH-toh foo-MAH-ray)   No smoking
Vietato l'ingresso   (vyay-TAH-toh leen-GREHS-soh)   No admittance
Entrata, uscita   (ayn-TRAH-tah, oo-SHEE-tah)   Entrance, exit
Signori, or *uomini*   (see-NYOH-ree, WAW-mee-nee)   Gentlemen, men
Signore, or *dame,* or *donne*   (see-NYOH-ray, DAH-may, DAWN-nay)   Ladies, women (Watch out for this, for it can be extremely embarrassing; *signore* is "gentleman," "sir," "Mr." (singular); it has a plural *signori*. But *signore* is also the plural of *signora,* "lady." If you, a male, see *signore* on a rest-room door, don't figure it means "Mr." and go in. Watch for the telltale *-i*).

Speaking is an important activity, even if you can't participate in it to the full. Here are a few phrases:

Parla italiano (inglese, francese, tedesco, spagnuolo)?   (PAHR-lah ee-tah-LYAH-noh, een-GLAY-say, frahn-CHAY-say, tay-DAYS-koh, spah-NYWAW-loh?)   Do you speak Italian (English, French, German, Spanish)?

9

Un pò. (oon PAW.) A little.

Molto poco. (MOHL-toh PAW-koh.) Very little.

Parli più lentamente. (PAHR-lee PYOO layn-tah-MAYN-tay.) Speak more slowly. (This is terribly important; the Italian is not speaking fast, by his standards; it only seems so to you, because you are not familiar with the language. If you can get him to do a slow-motion speech, you may be able to figure him out.)

Capisce? (kah-PEE-shay?) Do you understand?

Non capisco. (nawn kah-PEES-koh?) I don't understand.

Cosa vuol dire? (KAW-sah VWAWL DEE-ray?) What do you mean?

Come si chiama questo in italiano? (KOH-may see KYAH-mah KWAYS-toh een ee-tah-LYAH-noh?) What do you call this in Italian?

Sono americano (*americana* if you are a woman). (SOH-noh ah-may-ree-KAH-noh, ah-may-ree-KAH-nah.) I'm an American.

Siamo americani (*americane* if you are all women). (SYAH-moh ah-may-ree-KAH-nee, ah-may-ree-KAH-nay.) We are Americans. (These expressions cover a multitude of sins, for the Italians generally like us.)

You may need or have to send for someone. Here is how to do it:

ho bisogno di (AW bee-SAW-nyoh dee) I need

faccia chiamare (FAH-chah kyah-MAH-ray) send for

il direttore (eel dee-rayt-TOH-ray) the manager

un agente di polizia (oon ah-JEHN-tay dee poh-lee-TSEE-ah) a policeman

un medico (oon MEH-dee-koh) a doctor

un facchino (oon fahk-KEE-noh) a porter

un interprete (oon een-TEHR-pray-tay) an interpreter

il console americano (eel KAWN-soh-lay ah-may-ree-KAH-noh) the American consul

In combination:

Ho bisogno di un medico. (AW bee-SAW-nyoh dee oon MEH-dee-koh.) I need a doctor.

10

Faccia chiamare un agente di polizia! (FAH-chah kyah-MAH-ray oon ah-JEHN-tay dee poh-lee-TSEE-ah!) Send for a policeman!

The whole world, not Americans alone, likes to discuss the weather. It's the easiest way to strike up an acquaintance, both at home and abroad.

Piove. (PYAW-vay.) It's raining.

Fa bel (cattivo) tempo. (FAH BEHL, kaht-TEE-voh, TEHM-poh.) It's fine (bad) weather.

Fa caldo (freddo). (FAH KAHL-doh, FRAYD-doh.) It's warm (cold).

Ho caldo (freddo). (AW KAHL-doh, FRAYD-doh.) I'm warm (cold).

Here are a few important verbs. You can put *vorrei* (I should like) in front of most of them, an appropriate noun after them, and have a complete sentence:

vorrei (vohr-REH-ee) I should like

comprare (kohm-PRAH-ray) to buy
vedere (vay-DAY-ray) to see
parlare (pahr-LAH-ray) to speak
visitare (vee-see-TAH-ray) to visit
domandare or *chiedere* (doh-mahn-DAH-ray, KYEH-day-ray) to ask, ask for
pagare (pah-GAH-ray) to pay, pay for
mangiare (mahn-JAH-ray) to eat
bere (BAY-ray) to drink
fare un bagno (una doccia) (FAH-ray oon BAH-nyoh, oo-nah DOH-chah) to take a bath (shower)
lavarmi le mani (lah-VAHR-mee lay MAH-nee) to wash my hands
andare (ahn-DAH-ray) to go
prendere (PREHN-day-ray) to take
sapere (sah-PAY-ray) to know (a fact), know how
conoscere (koh-NOH-shay-ray) to know (a fact or a person), to meet

11

trovare   (troh-VAH-ray)   to find

fare   (FAH-ray)   to do, make (*fare* followed by another verb means "to have something done": *far stirare* [FAHR stee-RAH-ray] to have pressed; *far pulire* [FAHR poo-LEE-ray] to have cleaned; *far riparare* [FAHR ree-pah-RAH-ray] to have repaired; *far lavare* [FAHR lah-VAH-ray] to have washed; *vorrei farmi fare la barba* [vohr-REH-ee FAHR-mee FAH-ray lah BAHR-bah] I should like to get a shave; *vorrei farmi tagliare i capelli* [vohr-REH-ee FAHR-mee tah-LYAH-ray ee kah-PAYL-lee] I should like to get a haircut)

essere   (EHS-say-ray)   to be

avere   (ah-VAY-ray)   to have

Only a few points of grammar need be discussed here (if you really want to know how Italian grammar works, see the Grammatical Outline on pages 132–151).

If a noun or adjective ends in *-a* in the singular, it usually changes *-a* to *-e* in the plural (*la sigaretta, le sigarette*). If it ends in *-e* or *-o* in the singular, shift to *-i* in the plural (*il giornale, i giornali; il sigaro, i sigari*).

Verbs have mostly been given in the infinitive form (*parlare,* to speak), but they change the *-are, -ere, -ire* ending of the infinitive to a variety of other endings, according to person, number, tense, etc. During the war, the American G.I.s used a Pidgin Italian in which all verbs appeared in the infinitive, and they discovered that they could be easily understood (*Noi parlare italiano*—We to speak Italian. *Voi dove andare?* —You where to go? for Where are you going?). This practice is not recommended by the schools of language, but it has been found to work in a number of instances.

To learn the full grammar of any foreign tongue so that you handle it with complete fluency and correctness requires years of study followed by years of practice. But why be tongue-tied in the name of perfectionism, when you can make yourself understood with a few hours' study? So, by all means, *andiamo in Italia e parliamo italiano!*

II PHRASES

1. PASSPORT

What is your name?
Come si chiama? *or* Il Suo nome? *or* Nome, cognome e paternità.
koh-may see KYAH-mah? Eel soo-oh NAW-may? NAW-may, koh-NYAW-may ay pah-tayr-nee-TAH.

Note: the last of these three expressions implies that what is wanted is your first name, your family name, and the name of your father; for the last, use *di* (DEE) if your father is living, *fu* (FOO) if he is dead: John Smith di James, John Smith fu James.

Your first (family) name?
Il Suo nome di battesimo (famiglia)?
Eel soo-oh NAW-may dee baht-TAY-see-moh (fah-MEE-lyah)?

My name is ——
Mi chiamo ——
Mee KYAH-moh ——

What is your nationality?
Qual'è la Sua nazionalità?
Kwah-LEH lah soo-ah nah-tsyoh-nah-lee-TAH?

I am an American.
Sono americano (americana).
soh-noh ah-may-ree-KAH-noh (ah-may-ree-KAH-nah).

Where were you born?
Dov'è nato (nata)?
Doh-VEH NAH-toh (NAH-tah)?

I was born in the United States.
Sono nato (nata) negli Stati Uniti.
soh-noh NAH-toh (NAH-tah) NAY-lyee STAH-tee oo-NEE-tee.

13

What is your address in Italy?
Qual'è il Suo indirizzo in Italia?
Kwa-LEH eel soo-oh een-dee-REE-tsoh een ee-TAH-lee-ah?

My address is ——
Il mio indirizzo è ——
Eel MEE-oh een-dee-REE-tsoh EH ——

Are you alone?
È solo (sola)?
EH SOH-loh (SOH-lah)?

Yes, I am alone.
Sì, sono solo (sola).
SEE, SOH-noh SOH-loh (SOH-lah).

No, I am traveling with my husband (wife).
No, viaggio con mio marito (mia moglie).
NAW, VYAH-joh kohn MEE-oh mah-REE-toh (MEE-ah MOH-lyay).

How many of you are there?
In quanti sono?
Een KWAHN-tee SOH-noh?

There are five of us.
Siamo in cinque.
SYAH-moh een CHEEN-kway.

Have you your passport?
Ha il Suo passaporto?
AH eel soo-oh pahs-sah-PAWR-toh?

Here is my passport.
Ecco il mio passaporto.
EHK-koh eel MEE-oh pahs-sah-PAWR-toh.

Where is your vaccination certificate?
Dov'è il Suo certificato di vaccinazione?
Doh-VEH eel soo-oh chayr-tee-fee-KAH-toh dee vah-chee-nah-TSYOH-nay?

Here it is.
Eccolo
EHK-koh-loh.

14

May I see your landing permit?
Mi fa vedere il Suo permesso di sbarco?
Mee FAH vay-DAY-ray eel soo-oh payr-MAYS-soh dee ZBAHR-koh?

Here is my permit.
Ecco il mio permesso.
EHK-koh eel MEE-oh payr-MAYS-soh.

Here are my documents.
Ecco i miei documenti.
EHK-koh ee MYAY doh-koo-MAYN-tee.

Here they are.
Eccoli.
EHK-koh-lee.

2. CUSTOMS

Where is the customs office?
Dov'è l'ufficio dogana?
Doh-VEH loof-FEE-choh doh-GAH-nah?

Here is the customs office.
Ecco l'ufficio dogana.
EHK-koh loof-FEE-choh doh-GAH-nah.

Where is your baggage?
Dove sono i Suoi bagagli?
DOH-vay SOH-noh ee swoy bah-GAH-lyee?

Here is my baggage.
Ecco i miei bagagli.
EKH-koh ee MYAY bah-GAH-lyee.

Those are my bags.
Quelle sono le mie valigie.
KWAYL-lay SOH-noh lay MEE-ay vah-LEE-jay.

I cannot find my baggage.
Non posso trovare i miei bagagli.
Nohn PAWS-soh troh-VAH-ray ee MYAY bah-GAH-lyee.

Have you anything (else) to declare?
Ha niente (nient'altro) da dichiarare?
AH NYEHN-tay (nyehn-TAHL-troh) dah dee-kyah-RAH-ray?

I have nothing (else) to declare.
Non ho niente (nient'altro) da dichiarare.
Nohn AW NYEHN-tay (nyehn-TAHL-troh) dah dee-kyah-RAH-
ray.

Is that all?
È tutto?
EH TOOT-toh?

That is all.
È tutto.
EH TOOT-toh.

Anything else?
C'è altro?
CHEH AHL-troh?

Nothing else.
Non c'è altro.
Nohn CHEH AHL-troh.

Must I pay duty on this?
C'è da pagar dogana per questo?
CHEH dah pah-GAHR doh-GAH-nah payr KWAYS-toh?

Must I open this bag?
Devo aprire questa valigia?
DAY-voh ah-PREE-ray KWAYS-tah vah-LEE-jah?

How much must I pay?
Quanto devo pagare?
KWAHN-toh DAY-voh pah-GAH-ray?

You must pay 500 lire.
Deve pagare cinquecento lire.
DAY-vay pah-GAH-ray cheen-kway-CHEHN-toh LEE-ray.

I cannot open this valise (this trunk).
Non posso aprire questa valigia (questo baule).
Nohn PAWS-soh ah-PREE-ray KWAYS-tah vah-LEE-jah (KWAYS-
toh bah-OO-lay).

I have lost the key.
Ho perso la chiave.
AW PEHR-soh lah KYAH-vay.

16

Where can I have a new key made?
Dove posso farmi fare un'altra chiave?
DOH-vay PAWS-soh FAHR-mee FAH-ray oo-NAHL-trah KYAH-vay?

Is there a locksmith close by?
C'è un magnano da queste parti?
CHEH oon mah-NYAH-noh dah KWAYS-tay PAHR-tee?

Please be careful.
Faccia attenzione.
FAH-chah aht-tayn-TSYOH-nay.

Please help me close this bag.
Per favore, mi aiuti a chiudere questa valigia.
Payr fah-VOH-ray, mee ah-YOO-tee ah KYOO-day-ray KWAYS-tah
vah-LEE-jah.

This is (not) dutiable.
Questo (non) è soggetto a dogana.
KWAYS-toh (nohn) EH soh-JEHT-toh ah doh-GAH-nah.

I am on a pleasure trip.
Sono in viaggio di piacere.
SOH-noh een VYAH-joh dee pyah-CHAY-ray.

These articles are for personal use.
Questi sono effetti personali.
KWAYS-tee SOH-noh ayf-FEHT-tee payr-soh-NAH-lee.

These are gifts.
Questi sono regali.
KWAYS-tee SOH-noh ray-GAH-lee.

Must I fill out this form?
Devo riempire questo modulo?
DAY-voh ree-aym-PEE-ray KWAYS-toh MAW-doo-loh?

Please fill out this form.
Per favore, riempia questo modulo.
Payr fah-VOH-ray, ree-AYM-pyah KWAYS-toh MAW-doo-loh.

Have you any foreign currency?
Ha valuta estera?
AH vah-LOO-tah EHS-tay-rah?

17

I have three hundred dollars.
Ho trecento dollari.
AW tray-CHEHN-toh DAWL-lah-ree.

May I close the bag (trunk) now?
Posso chiudere la valigia (il baule) ora?
PAWS-soh KYOO-day-ray lah vah-LEE-jah (eel bah-OO-lay) OH-
rah?

You may close it.
Può chiudere.
PWAW KYOO-day-ray.

3. BAGGAGE

This is my bag.
Questa è la mia valigia.
KWAYS-tah EH lah MEE-ah vah-LEE-jah.

These are our bags.
Queste sono le nostre valigie.
KWAYS-tay SOH-noh lay NAWS-tray vah-LEE-jay.

This is my trunk.
Questo è il mio baule.
KWAYS-toh EH eel MEE-oh bah-OO-lay.

These are our trunks.
Questi sono i nostri bauli.
KWAYS-tee SOH-noh ee NAWS-tree bah-OO-lee.

This is not my baggage.
Questi non sono i miei bagagli.
KWAYS-tee nohn SOH-noh ee MYAY bah-GAH-lyee.

I want a porter.
Vorrei un facchino.
vohr-REH-ee oon fahk-KEE-noh.

I want to insure (check) my baggage.
Vorrei assicurare (lasciare in deposito) i miei bagagli.
Vohr-REH-ee ahs-see-koo-RAH-ray (lah-SHAH-ray een day-PAW-
see-toh) ee MYAY bah-GAH-lyee.

18

I should like to check this trunk to Florence.
Vorrei spedire questo baule come bagaglio appresso a Firenze.
Vohr-REH-ee spay-DEE-ray KWAYS-toh bah-oo-lay KOH-may bah-
  GAH-lyoh ahp-PREHS-soh ah fee-REHN-tsay.

I want to leave the bags here.
Vorrei lasciar qui in deposito le valigie.
Vohr-REH-ee lah-SHAHR KWEE een day-PAW-see-toh lay vah-
  LEE-jay.

I want to take out my bag.
Vorrei ritirare la mia valigia.
Vohr-REH-ee ree-tee-RAH-ray lah MEE-ah vah-LEE-jah.

Where is the baggage room?
Dov'è il deposito bagagli?
Doh-VEH eel day-PAW-see-toh bah-GAH-lyee?

Must I wait?
Devo aspettare?
DAY-voh ahs-payt-TAH-ray?

Must I pay excess weight?
Devo pagare peso in eccesso?
DAY-voh pah-GAH-ray PAY-soh een ay-CHEHS-soh?

Shall I pay now or later?
Devo pagare ora o in seguito?
DAY-voh pah-GAH-ray OH-rah oh een SAY-gwee-toh?

Please do not break the seals.
Per favore, non rompa i sigilli.
Payr fah-VOH-ray, nohn ROHM-pah ee see-JEEL-lee.

Carry that bag carefully.
Faccia attenzione con quella valigia.
FAH-chah aht-tayn-TSYOH-nay kohn KWAYL-lah vah-LEE-jah.

Take it to a taxi.
La porti a un tassì.
Lah PAWR-tee ah oon tahs-SEE.

Call me a taxi.
Mi chiami un tassì.
Mee KYAH-mee oon tahs-SEE.

Bring it over here.
La porti qua.
Lah PAWR-tee KWAH.

Put them over there.
Li metta laggiù.
Lee MAYT-tah lah-JOO.

Take me to the hotel.
Mi porti all'albergo.
Mee PAWR-tee ahl-lahl-BEHR-goh.

Here are my baggage checks.
Ecco i miei scontrini.
EHK-koh ee MYAY skohn-TREE-nee.

What is the rate per bag?
Qual'è la tariffa per collo?
Kwah-LEH lah tah-REEF-fah payr KAWL-loh?

How many pieces of baggage?
Quanti colli?
KWAHN-tee KAWL-lee?

Give me a receipt.
Mi dia la ricevuta.
Mee DEE-ah lah ree-chay-voo-tah.

Here is a tip.
Ecco una mancia.
EHK-koh OO-nah MAHN-chah.

4. TICKETS

Where is the ticket office?
Dov'è l'ufficio biglietti?
Doh-VEH loof-FEE-choh bee-LYAYT-tee?

    the station master
    il capo stazione
    eel KAH-poh stah-TSYOH-nay

    the waiting room
    la sala d'aspetto
    lah SAH-lah dahs-PEHT-toh

the men's room
il gabinetto uomini
eel gah-bee-NAYT-toh WAW-mee-nee

the ladies' room
il gabinetto per signore
eel gah-bee-NAYT-toh payr see-NYOH-ray

I want a ticket to Rome.
Vorrei un biglietto per Roma.
Voh-REH-ee oon bee-LYAYT-toh payr ROH-mah.

one way
di sola andata
dee SOH-lah ahn-DAH-tah

round trip
d'andata e ritorno
dahn-DAH-tah ay ree-TOHR-noh

first, second, third class
di prima, di seconda, di terza classe
dee PREE-mah, dee say-KOHN-dah, dee TEHR-tsah KLAHS-say

I want a timetable.
Vorrei un orario.
Vohr-REH-ee oon oh-RAH-ryoh.

a reserved seat
un posto prenotato
oon PAWS-toh pray-noh-TAH-toh

a seat in the center of the coach
un posto nel centro del vagone
oon PAWS-toh nayl CHAYN-troh dayl vah-GOH-nay

a lower berth
una cuccetta inferiore
oo-nah koo-CHAYT-tah een-fay-RYOH-ray

an upper berth
una cuccetta superiore
oo-nah koo-CHAYT-tah soo-pay-RYOH-ray

21

a compartment
una cabina letto
oo-nah kah-BEE-nah LEHT-toh

travel insurance
assicurazione di viaggio
ahs-see-koo-rah-TSYOH-nay dee VYAH-joh

Where do you want to go?
Dove vuol andare?
DOH-vay VWAWL ahn-DAH-ray?

I want to go to Padua.
Voglio andare a Padova.
VAW-lyoh ahn-DAH-ray ah PAH-doh-vah.

Where is the railroad station?
Dov'è la stazione ferroviaria?
Doh-VEH lah stah-TSYOH-nay fayr-roh-VYAH-ryah?

How do you reach it from here?
Come ci si può andare da qua?
KOH-may chee see PWAW ahn-DAH-ray dah KWAH?

Where can I get the train to Turin?
Dove posso prendere il treno per andare a Torino?
DOH-vay PAWS-soh PREHN-day-ray eel TREH-noh payr ahn-DAH-ray ah toh-REE-noh?

I want to take the 9:30 train.
Vorrei partire col treno delle nove e mezza.
Vohr-REH-ee pahr-TEE-ray kohl TREH-noh DAYL-lay NAW-vay ay MEH-dzah.

How much is the ticket to Leghorn?
Quanto costa il biglietto per Livorno?
KWAHN-toh KAWS-tah eel bee-LYAYT-toh payr lee-VOHR-noh?

How long is the ticket good for?
Per quanto tempo è valido il biglietto?
Payr KWAHN-toh TEHM-poh EH VAH-lee-doh eel bee-LYAYT-toh?

Ten days.
Per dieci giorni.
Payr DYEH-chee JOHR-nee.

Where can I buy a ticket?
Dove potrei comprare un biglietto?
DOH-vay poh-TREH-ee kohm-PRAH-ray oon bee-LYAYT-toh?

The ticket window is on the right.
La biglietteria è a destra.
Lah bee-lyayt-tay-REE-ah EH ah DEHS-trah.

At what time does the train for Naples leave?
A che ora parte il treno per Napoli?
Ah kay OH-rah PAHR-tay eel TREH-noh payr NAH-poh-lee?

It leaves at six o'clock.
Parte alle sei.
PAHR-tay AHL-lay SEH-ee.

It leaves in twenty minutes.
Parte fra venti minuti.
PAHR-tay frah VAYN-tee mee-NOO-tee.

I should like to go by way of Mantua.
Vorrei andare per via di Mantova.
Vohr-REH-ee ahn-DAH-ray payr VEE-ah dee MAHN-toh-vah.

May I stop over at Bologna?
Potrei fare una fermata intermedia a Bologna?
Poh-TREH-ee FAH-ray OO-nah fayr-MAH-tah een-tayr-MEH-dyah
ah boh-LAW-nyah?

Do I have to change trains?
Devo cambiar treno?
DAY-voh kahm-BYAHR TREH-noh?

Yes, change at Perugia.
Sì, cambi treno a Perugia.
SEE, KAHM-bee TREH-noh ah pay-ROO-jah.

**I want to change my reservation from the 10:30 to the 4:30
train.**
Desidero cambiare la mia prenotazione dal treno delle dieci e
trenta a quello delle quattro e trenta.
Day-SEE-day-roh kahm-BYAH-ray lah MEE-ah pray-noh-tah-
TSYOH-nay dahl TREH-noh DAYL-lay DYEH-chee ay TREHN-tah
ah KWAYL-loh DAYL-lay KWAHT-troh ay TREHN-tah.

23

5. TRAVEL BY BOAT

When does the boat leave?
A che ora parte il piroscafo?
Ah kay OH-rah PAHR-tay eel pee-RAW-skah-foh?

At 5:45 p.m.
Alle cinque e quarantacinque del pomeriggio.
AHL-lay CHEEN-kway ay kwah-rahn-tah-CHEEN-kway dayl poh-may-REE-joh.

May visitors go on board?
È permesso ai visitatori recarsi a bordo?
EH payr-MAYS-soh AH-ee vee-see-tah-TOH-ree ray-KAHR-see ah BOHR-doh?

I feel seasick.
Ho il mal di mare.
AW eel MAHL dee MAH-ray.

Have you a remedy against seasickness?
Ha un rimedio contro il mal di mare?
AH oon ree-MEH-dyoh KOHN-troh eel MAHL dee MAH-ray?

Take me to my stateroom.
Mi accompagni in cabina.
Mee ahk-kohm-PAH-nyee een kah-BEE-nah.

I'm going on deck.
Vado sopra coperta.
VAH-doh SOH-prah koh-PEHR-tah.

I want to rent a deck chair.
Desidero prendere in affitto una sedia a sdraio.
Day-SEE-day-roh PREHN-day-ray een ahf-FEET-toh OO-nah SEH-dyah ah ZDRAH-yoh.

At what time are meals served?
A che ora si servono i pasti?
Ah KAY OH-rah see SEHR-voh-noh ee PAHS-tee?

Breakfast 7 to 9, lunch 12 to 2, dinner 6 to 9.
Prima colazione dalle sette alle nove, seconda colazione dalle dodici alle due, pranzo dalle sei alle nove.

PREE-mah koh-lah-TSYOH-nay DAHL-lay SEHT-tay AHL-lay NAW-vay, say-KOHN-dah koh-lah-TSYOH-nay DAHL-lay DOH-dee-chee AHL-lay DOO-ay, PRAHN-dzoh DAHL-lay SEH-ee AHL-lay NAW-vay.

Where is the dining room (lounge)?
Dov'è la sala da pranzo (il salone)?
Doh-VEH lah SAH-lah dah PRAHN-dzoh (eel sah-LOH-nay)?

On Deck B.
Sul ponte B.
Sool POHN-tay BEE.

Where are the lifeboats (life preservers)?
Dove sono le scialuppe (i salvagente)?
DOH-vay SOH-noh lay shah-LOOP-pay (ee sahl-vah-JEHN-tay)?

I should like to speak to the captain (purser, deck steward).
Vorrei parlare col capitano (col commissario di bordo, col cameriere di coperta).
Vohr-REH-ee pahr-LAH-ray kohl kah-pee-TAH-noh (kohl kohm-mees-SAH-ryoh dee BOHR-doh, kohl kah-may-RYEH-ray dee koh-PEHR-tah).

I should like to sit at the captain's (doctor's, first mate's) table.
Vorrei sedere al tavolo del capitano (del medico, del primo ufficiale).
Vohr-REH-ee say-DAY-ray ahl TAH-voh-loh dayl kah-pee-TAH-noh (dayl MEH-dee-koh, dayl PREE-moh oof-fee-CHAH-lay).

Is there a swimming pool on board?
C'è una piscina a bordo?
CHEH OO-nah pee-SHEE-nah ah BOHR-doh?

The boat sails from the company's pier.
Il piroscafo salpa dal molo della campagnia di navigazione.
Eel pee-RAW-skah-foh SAHL-pah dahl MAW-loh DAYL-lah kohm-pah-NYEE-ah dee nah-vee-gah-TSYOH-nay.

Where are you landing?
Dove sbarca?
DOH-vay ZBAHR-kah?

I am landing in Genoa.
Sbarco a Genova.
ZBAHR-koh ah JEH-noh-vah.

All visitors off the boat!
I visitatori son pregati di scendere! *or* Visitatori a terra!
Ee vee-see-tah-TOH-ree SOHN pray-GAH-tee dee SHAYN-day-ray!
or Vee-see-tah-TOH-ree ah TEHR-rah!

6. TRAVEL BY TRAIN OR PLANE

On what track does the Rome train leave?
Da che binario parte il treno per Roma?
Dah KAY bee-NAH-ryoh PAHR-tay eel TREH-noh payr ROH-mah?

Where are the first- (second-) class cars?
Dove sono i vagoni di prima (di seconda)?
DOH-vay SOH-noh ee vah-GOH-nee dee PREE-mah (dee say-KOHN-dah)?

Ahead (behind).
Avanti (dietro).
Ah-VAHN-tee (DYEH-troh).

Please put my baggage in my compartment (on the train, on the plane).
Favorisca mettermi i bagagli nel mio scompartimento (nel treno, nell'aeroplano).
Fah-voh-REES-kah MAYT-tayr-mee ee bah-GAH-lyee nayl MEE-oh skohm-pahr-tee-MAYN-toh (nayl TREH-noh, nayl-lah-ay-roh-PLAH-noh).

Will you put this bag on the rack?
Vuol mettermi questa valigia sulla rete?
VWAWL MAYT-tayr-mee KWAYS-tah vah-LEE-jah SOOL-lah RAY-tay?

Is this seat taken?
È occupato questo posto?
EH ohk-koo-PAH-toh KWAYS-toh PAWS-toh?

26

No, it's free.
No, è libero.
NAW, EH LEE-bay-roh.

Where are you going?
Dove va?
DOH-vay VAH?

I'm going by train (plane) to Bari.
Vado in treno (in aeroplano) a Bari.
VAH-doh een TREH-noh (een ah-ay-roh-PLAH-noh) ah BAH-ree.

All aboard!
Partenza! or Tutti in carrozza!
Pahr-TEHN-tsah! or TOOT-tee een kahr-RAW-tsah!

All visitors off the train!
Visitatori a terra!
Vee-see-tah-TOH-ree ah TEHR-rah!

Which is the train (plane) to Milan?
Qual'è il treno (l'aereo) per Milano?
Kwah-LEH eel TREH-noh (lah-EH-ray-oh) payr mee-LAH-noh?

Track number seven.
Binario (linea) numero sette.
Bee-NAH-ryoh (LEE-nay-ah) NOO-may-roh SEHT-tay.

Runway number four.
Pista numero quattro.
PEES-tah NOO-may-roh KWAHT-troh.

Does this train stop at Pavia?
Si ferma a Pavia questo treno?
See FAYR-mah ah pah-VEE-ah KWAYS-toh TREH-noh?

How long does it stop?
Per quanto tempo si ferma?
Payr KWAHN-toh TEHM-poh see FAYR-mah?

When do we arrive at Monza?
Quando si arriva a Monza?
KWAHN-doh see ahr-REE-vah ah MOHN-dzah?

27

At five ten.
Alle cinque e dieci.
AHL-lay CHEEN-kway ay DYAY-chee.

In half an hour.
Tra mezz'ora.
Trah MEH-dzoh-rah.

Is the train on time?
È in orario il treno?
EH een oh-RAH-ryoh eel TREH-noh?

We are fifteen minutes late.
Siamo in ritardo di quindici minuti.
SYAH-moh een ree-TAHR-doh dee KWEEN-dee-chee mee-NOO-tee.

Why are we stopping?
Perchè ci fermiamo?
Payr-KAY chee fayr-MYAH-moh?

What is the matter?
Che c'è?
KAY CHEH?

May I open the window?
Posso aprire il finestrino?
PAWS-soh ah-PREE-ray eel fee-nays-TREE-noh?

Please close the window.
Per favore, chiuda il finestrino.
Payr fah-VOH-ray, KYOO-dah eel fee-nays-TREE-noh.

There is a draft.
C'è corrente.
CHEH koh-REHN-tay.

Please call me at seven.
Per favore, mi svegli alle sette.
Payr fah-VOH-ray, mee ZVAY-lyee AHL-lay SEHT-tay.

Shall I prepare your berth?
Le preparo il letto?
Lay pray-PAH-roh eel LEHT-toh?

28

Please prepare it early.
Me lo prepari presto.
May loh pray-PAH-ree PREHS-toh.

Here is the railroad station (the airport).
Ecco la stazione ferroviaria (l'aeroporto).
EHK-koh lah stah-TSYOH-nay fayr-roh-VYAH-ryah (lah-ay-roh-PAWR-toh).

Where is the dining car?
Dov'è il vagone ristorante?
Doh-VEH eel vah-GOH-nay rees-toh-RAHN-tay?

Five cars ahead (back).
Cinque vagoni più avanti (addietro).
CHEEN-kway vah-GOH-nee PYOO ah-VAHN-tee (ahd-DYEH-troh).

Where is the smoker?
Dov'è lo scompartimento fumatori?
Doh-VEH loh skohm-pahr-tee-MAYN-toh foo-mah-TOH-ree?

Last car on the train.
È nell'ultimo vagone.
EH nayl-LOOL-tee-moh vah-GOH-nay.

Is there a sleeping car on this train?
C'è un vagone letto in questo treno?
CHEH oon vah-GOH-nay LEHT-toh een KWAYS-toh TREH-noh?

Are you the conductor?
È Lei il controllore?
EH LEH-ee eel kohn-trohl-LOH-ray?

No, I'm the sleeping-car porter.
No, sono l'addetto ai vagoni letto.
NAW, SOH-noh lahd-DAYT-toh AH-ee vah-GOH-nee LEHT-toh.

First call for dinner (breakfast, lunch)!
Vagone ristorante prima serie!
Vah-GOH-nay rees-toh-RAHN-tay PREE-mah SEH-ree-ay!

Is there time to get a bite?
C'è tempo di mangiare un boccone?
CHEH TEHM-poh dee mahn-JAH-ray oon bohk-KOH-nay?

29

At the next stop you can get a sandwich or a lunch basket.

Alla prossima fermata potrà comprare un panino imbottito o un cestino da viaggio.

AHL-lah PRAWS-see-mah fayr-MAH-tah poh-TRAH kohm-PRAH-ray oon pah-NEE-noh eem-boht-TEE-toh oh oon chays-TEE-noh dah VYA-joh.

I have a reserved seat (a reserved compartment) for Reggio Calabria.

Ho un posto prenotato (una cabina letto prenotata) per Reggio Calabria.

AW oon PAWS-toh pray-noh-TAH-toh (oo-nah kah-BEE-nah LEHT-toh pray-noh-TAH-tah) payr REH-joh kah-LAH-bryah.

Where is the airlines office?

Dov'è l'ufficio delle aviolinee?

Doh-VEH loof-FEE-choh DAYL-lay ah-vyoh-LEE-nay-ay?

Is there motor service to the airport?

C'è servizio di autobus per l'aeroporto?

CHEH sayr-VEE-tsyoh dee ow-toh-boos payr lah-ay-roh-PAWR-toh?

Where is the stewardess?

Dov'è la hostess?

Doh-VEH lah OH-stess?

I am the stewardess.

Sono io la hostess.

SOH-no EE-oh lah OH-stess.

Is this an express or a local train?

Questo treno è diretto o accelerato

KWAYS-toh TREH-noh EH dee-REHT-toh oh ah-chay-lay-RAH-toh?

Wait for me at the gate.

Mi aspetti all'entrata dei treni.

Mee ahs-PEHT-tee ahl-layn-TRAH-tah day TREH-nee.

7. TRAVEL BY BUS OR STREETCAR

Does this bus (streetcar) go to Fiesole?

Quest'autobus (questo tram) va a Fiesole?

Kways-TOW-toh-boos (KWAYS-toh TRAHM) VAH ah FYEH-soh-lay?

30

Yes, wait at the bus stop (car stop).
Sì, aspetti alla fermata degli autobus (fermata tramviaria).
SEE, ahs-PEHT-tee AHL-lah fayr-MAH-tah DAY-lyee ow-toh-boos
(fayr-MAH-tah trahm-VYAH-ryah).

How much is the fare to St. Peter's Square?
Quant'è la corsa fino a Piazza San Pietro?
Kwahn-TEH lah KOHR-sah FEE-noh ah PYAH-tsah SAHN PYEH-
troh?

Where can I get a bus to the Cascine?
Dove potrei prendere un autobus per andare alle Cascine?
DOH-vay poh-TREH-ee PREHN-day-ray oon ow-toh-boos payr
ahn-DAH-ray AHL-lay kah-SHEE-nay?

Driver, will you please tell me where to get off?
Conducente, mi vuol dire dove devo scendere?
Kohn-doo-CHEHN-tay, mee VWAWL DEE-ray DOH-vay DAY-voh
SHAYN-day-ray?

Get off at the next stop (corner).
Scenda alla prossima fermata (traversa).
SHAYN-dah AHL-lah PRAWS-see-mah fayr-MAH-tah (trah-VEHR-
sah).

I want to go to the Pincio.
Vorrei andare al Pincio.
Vohr-REH-ee ahn-DAH-ray ahl PEEN-choh.

Is it very far from here?
È molto distante?
EH MOHL-toh dees-TAHN-tay?

Please let me off at Villa Borghese.
Per favore, mi faccia scendere a Villa Borghese.
Payr fah-VOH-ray, mee FAH-chah SHAYN-day-ray ah VEEL-lah
bohr-GAY-say.

Get off here.
Scenda qui.
SHAYN-dah KWEE.

Do I need a transfer?
Devo prendere la coincidenza?
DAY-voh PREHN-day-ray lah coh-een-chee-DEHN-tsah?

31

Yes, take the No. 5 bus.
Sì, prenda l'autobus numero cinque.
SEE, PREHN-dah LOW-toh-boos NOO-may-roh CHEEN-kway.

Do I have to buy a token?
Devo comprare un gettone?
DAY-voh kohm-PRAH-ray oon jayt-TOH-nay?

When does this bus return from the shrine?
A che ora torna dal santuario quest'autobus?
Ah KAY OH-rah TOHR-nah dahl sahn-too-AH-ryoh kways-TOW-toh-boos?

8. TRAVEL BY TAXI OR OTHER HIRED CONVEYANCE

Driver (coachman), what is your rate to Pozzuoli?
Autista (vetturino), qual'è la Sua tariffa per andare a Pozzuoli?
Ow-TEES-tah (vayt-too-REE-noh), kwah-LEH lah soo-ah tah-REEF-fah payr ahn-DAH-ray ah poh-TSWAW-lee?

What is the hourly (daily) rate?
Qual'è la tariffa oraria (per tutta la giornata)?
Kwah-LEH lah tah-REEF-fah oh-RAH-ryah (payr TOOT-tah lah johr-NAH-tah)?

This bag is extra.
Questa valigia è in eccesso.
KWAYS-tah vah-LEE-jah EH een ay-CHEHS-soh.

Take the shortest way.
Segua la via più breve.
SAY-gwah lah VEE-ah PYOO BREH-vay.

Where to?
Dove si va?
DOH-vay see VAH?

Drive around the city (through the shopping, theater, district).
Faccia il giro della città (del centro dei negozi, dei teatri).
FAH-chah eel JEE-roh DAYL-lah cheet-TAH (dayl CHAYN-troh day nay-GAW-tsee, day tay-AH-tree).

32

Stop here; I want to get out.
Fermi qui; voglio scendere.
FAYR-mee KWEE; VAW-lyoh SHAYN-day-ray.

Show me the points of interest.
Mi faccia vedere i punti interessanti.
Mee FAH-chah vay-DAY-ray ee POON-tee een-tay-rays-SAHN-tee.

Let's take a horse carriage and go on an excursion.
Prendiamo una carrozzella e andiamo a fare una gita.
Prayn-DYAH-moh oo-nah kahr-roh-TSEHL-lah ay ahn-DYAH-moh
ah FAH-ray oo-nah JEE-tah.

Please wait for me.
Mi aspetti, per favore.
Mee ahs-PEHT-tee, payr fah-VOH-ray.

I'm not allowed to wait here.
Non mi è permesso aspettare qua.
NOHN mee EH payr-MAYS-soh ahs-payt-TAH-ray KWAH.

Drive more slowly (faster, more carefully).
Vada più adagio (più presto, con più attenzione).
VAH-dah PYOO ah-DAH-joh (PYOO PREHS-toh, kohn PYOO aht-
tayn-TSYOH-nay).

That's not the price we agreed upon (showing on the meter).
Questo non è l'ammontare convenuto (che segna il tassametro).
KWAYS-toh noh-NEH lahm-mohn-TAH-ray kohn-vay-NOO-toh
(kay SAY-nyah eel tahs-SAH-may-troh).

Thanks for a pleasant ride.
Grazie di avermi fatto fare una bella gita.
GRAH-tsyay dee ah-VAYR-mee FAHT-toh FAH-ray oo-nah BEHL-lah
JEE-tah.

9. DRIVING YOUR OWN CAR

How much a liter?
Quanto costa al litro la benzina?
KWAHN-toh KAWS-tah ahl LEE-troh lah bayn-DZEE-nah?

Fill her up!
Faccia il pieno!
FAH-chah eel PYEH-noh!

Give me thirty liters, please.
Me ne dia trenta litri, per favore.
May nay DEE-ah TREHN-tah LEE-tree, payr fah-VOH-ray.

Do I need oil (water, air)?
Ho bisogno d'olio (d'acqua, d'aria)?
AW bee-SAW-nyoh DAW-lee-oh (DAHK-kwah, DAH-ryah)?

Have you a road map?
Ha una carta stradale?
AH OO-nah KAHR-tah strah-DAH-lay?

Please check the tires (oil, battery, water, spark plugs).
Per favore, dia un'occhiata alle gomme (all'olio, all'accumula-
tore, all'acqua, alle candele).
Payr fah-VOH-ray, DEE-ah oo-nohk-KYAH-tah AHL-lay GOHM-may
(ahl-LAW-lee-oh, ahl-lahk-koo-moo-lah-TOH-ray, ahl-LAHK-
kwah, AHL-lay kahn-DAY-lay).

How far is the next gas station?
Dov'è il distributore di benzina più vicino?
Doh-VEH eel dees-tree-boo-TOH-ray dee bayn-DZEE-nah PYOO
vee-CHEE-noh?

Go four blocks and turn left.
Vada fino alla quarta traversa, poi giri a sinistra.
VAH-dah FEE-noh AHL-lah KWAHR-tah trah-VEHR-sah, POY JEE-ree
ah see-NEES-trah.

Is this the way to Rimini?
È questa la via giusta per andare a Rimini?
EH KWAYS-tah lah VEE-ah JOOS-tah payr ahn-DAH-ray ah REE-
mee-nee?

Turn right at the next crossroad (stop light).
Giri a destra al primo incrocio (semaforo).
JEE-ree ah DEHS-trah ahl PREE-moh een-KROH-choh (say-MAH-
foh-roh).

Which is the road to Viterbo?
Qual'è la strada per andare a Viterbo?
Kwah-LEH lah STRAH-dah payr ahn-DAH-ray ah vee-TEHR-boh?

Turn left after you pass the bridge, then go straight.
Giri a sinistra dopo aver passato il ponte, poi vada sempre
dritto.
JEE-ree ah see-NEES-trah DOH-poh ah-VAYR pahs-SAH-toh eel
POHN-tay, POY VAH-dah SEHM-pray DREET-toh.

Is there a good hotel (restaurant) in Orvieto?
C'è un buon albergo (ristorante) a Orvieto?
CHEH oon BWAWN ahl-BEHR-goh (rees-toh-RAHN-tay) ah ohr-
VYEH-toh?

Is the highway good?
È buona l'autostrada?
EH BWAW-nah low-toh-STRAH-dah?

Where is the garage?
Dov'è l'autorimessa?
Doh-VEH low-toh-ree-MAYS-sah?

May I leave my car here?
Posso lasciar qui la macchina?
PAWS-soh lah-SHAHR KWEE lah MAHK-kee-nah?

Where may I park?
Dove potrei posteggiare?
DOH-vay poh-TREH-ee pohs-tay-JAH-ray?

Will you change the oil?
Mi vuol cambiar l'olio?
Mee VWAWL kahm-BYAHR LAW-lee-oh?

Light, medium or heavy?
Fluido, semidenso, o denso?
FLOO-ee-doh, say-mee-DEHN-soh, oh DEHN-soh?

Please grease the car.
Per favore, m'ingrassi la macchina.
Payr fah-VOH-ray, meen-GRAHS-see lah MAHK-kee-nah.

35

Tighten the brakes.
Mi aggiusti i freni.
Mee ah-JOOS-tee ee FRAY-nee.

Adjust the carburetor (clutch).
Mi aggiusti il carburatore (la frizione).
Mee ah-JOOS-tee eel kahr-boo-rah-TOH-ray (lah free-TSYOH-nay).

Wash the car.
Mi lavi la macchina.
Mee LAH-vee lah MAHK-kee-nah.

Put water in the battery (radiator).
Metta acqua nella batteria (nel radiatore).
MAYT-tah AHK-kwah NAYL-lah baht-tay-REE-ah (nayl rah-dyah-TOH-ray).

This car doesn't run well (doesn't go).
Questa macchina non funziona bene (non va).
KWAYS-tah MAHK-kee-nah nohn foon-TSYOH-nah BEH-nay (nohn VAH).

Can you tow me?
Può prendermi a rimorchio?
PWAW PREHN-dayr-mee ah ree-MAWR-kyoh?

The battery is dead.
La batteria è scarica.
Lah baht-tay-REE-ah EH SKAH-ree-kah.

There is a grinding (noise, rattle, squeak).
C'è una sgranatura (un rumore, un battito, un cigolio).
CHEH oo-nah zgrah-nah-TOO-rah (oon roo-MOH-ray, oon BAHT-tee-toh, oon chee-goh-LEE-oh).

The engine overheats (stalls).
Il motore riscalda troppo (si arresta).
Eel moh-TOH-ray rees-KAHL-dah TRAWP-poh (see ahr-REHS-tah).

I have a flat; can you change (fix) it?
Ho una gomma a terra; me la può cambiare (accomodare)?
AW oo-nah GOHM-mah ah TEHR-rah; may lah PWAW kahm-BYAH-ray (ahk-koh-moh-DAH-ray)?

36

Help me jack up the car.
Mi aiuti a sollevare la macchina col cricco.
Mee ah-YOO-tee ah sohl-lay-VAH-ray lah MAHK-kee-nah kohl
  KREEK-koh.

Have you a spare?
Ha una gomma di ricambio?
AH OO-nah GOHM-mah dee ree-KAHM-byoh?

Where is the key?
Dov'è la chiave?
Doh-VEH lah KYAH-vay?

Is there a mechanic here?
Qui c'è un meccanico?
KWEE CHEH oon mayk-KAH-nee-koh?

How much are the repairs?
Quanto costano le riparazioni?
KWAHN-toh KAWS-tah-noh lay ree-pah-rah-TSYOH-nee?

Can you fix it?
Me la può riparare?
May lah PWAW ree-pah-RAH-ray?

I can fix it for the time being.
Gliela posso riparare temporaneamente.
LYAY-lah PAWS-soh ree-pah-RAH-ray taym-poh-rah-nay-ah-
  MAYN-tay.

How long will it take?
Quanto tempo ci vorrà?
KWAHN-toh TEHM-poh chee vohr-RAH?

I can't do it today.
Oggi non posso farlo.
AW-jee nohn PAWS-soh FAHR-loh.

I have to send for parts.
Devo mandare a cercare i pezzi di ricambio.
DAY-voh mahn-DAH-ray ah chayr-KAH-ray ee PEH-tsee dee ree-
  KAHM-byoh.

I need a bulb.
Ho bisogno di una lampadina.
AW bee-SAW-nyoh dee OO-nah lahm-pah-DEE-nah.

a bumper
un paraurti
oon pah-rah-OOR-tee

a door handle
una maniglia
oo-nah mah-NEE-lyah

a fan
un ventilatore
oon vayn-tee-lah-TOH-ray

a fan belt
una cinghia del ventilatore
oo-nah CHEEN-gyah dayl vayn-tee-lah-TOH-ray

a fender
un parafango
oon pah-rah-FAHN-goh

a bolt
un bullone
oon bool-LOH-nay

a nut
un dado
oon DAH-doh

a fuel pump
una pompa di alimentazione
oo-nah POHM-pah dee ah-lee-mayn-tah-TSYOH-nay

a headlight
un fanale
oon fah-NAH-lay

a horn
un clacson
oon KLAHK-sohn

an inner tube
una camera d'aria
oo-nah KAH-may-rah DAH-ryah

38

a tail light
un fanalino posteriore
oon fah-nah-LEE-noh pohs-tay-RYOH-ray

a windshield wiper
un tergicristallo
oon tehr-jee-krees-TAHL-loh

a jack
un cricco
oon KREEK-koh

a wrench
una chiave inglese
oo-nah KYAH-vay een-GLAY-say

a screwdriver
un cacciavite
oon kah-chah-VEE-tay

a hammer
un martello
oon mahr-TEHL-loh

a pair of pliers
un paio di tenaglie
oon PAH-yoh dee tay-NAH-lyay

There's something wrong with the exhaust.
Non funziona bene lo scappamento.
Nohn foon-TSYOH-nah BEH-nay loh skahp-pah-MAYN-toh.

the gears
la marcia
lah MAHR-chah

the gear shift
il cambio di velocità
eel KAHM-byoh dee vay-loh-chee-TAH

the radiator
il radiatore
eel rah-dyah-TOH-ray

the starter
l'avviamento
lahv-vyah-MAYN-toh

the steering wheel
il volante
eel voh-LAHN-tay

the gas tank
il serbatoio
eel sayr-bah-TOH-yoh

the trunk compartment
il portabagagli
eel pawr-tah-bah-GAH-lyee

the ignition
l'accensione
lah-chayn-SYOH-nay

the hood
il cofano
eel KAW-fah-noh

I have a breakdown.
Ho un guasto al motore.
AW oon GWAHS-toh ahl moh-TOH-ray.

Please check my tires.
Mi verifichi i pneumatici.
Mee vay-REE-fee-kee ee pneu-MAH-tee-chee.

This is a violation.
Lei è in contravvenzione.
LEH-ee EH een kohn-trahv-vayn-TSYOH-nay.

10. HOTEL, BOARDINGHOUSE, APARTMENT

Where is a good (the best) hotel?
Dove si trova un buon (il miglior) albergo?
DOH-vay see TRAW-vah oon BWAWN (eel mee-LYOHR) ahl-BEHR-goh?

40

Here it is, in the center of the town, close to the station.
Eccolo, nel centro della città, vicino alla stazione.
EHK-koh-loh, nayl CHAYN-troh DAYL-lah cheet-TAH, vee-CHEE-noh AHL-lah stah-TSYOH-nay.

Is it very expensive?
È molto caro?
EH MOHL-toh KAH-roh?

It is quite expensive.
È abbastanza caro.
EH ahb-bahs-TAHN-tsah KAH-roh.

It is not very expensive.
Non è molto caro.
Nohn EH MOHL-toh KAH-roh.

Have you a single (double) room with private bath (shower, running water)?
Ha una stanza singola (per due) con bagno particolare (doccia, acqua corrente)?
AH OO-nah STAHN-tsah SEEN-goh-lah (payr DOO-ay) kohn BAH-nyoh pahr-tee-koh-LAH-ray (DOH-chah, AHK-kwah kohr-REHN-tay)?

I want a front (back) room with twin beds.
Vorrei una stanza davanti (di dietro) con due letti.
Vohr-REH-ee OO-nah STAHN-tsah dah-VAHN-tee (dee DYEH-troh) kohn DOO-ay LEHT-tee.

I want a suite near the elevator (stairs).
Vorrei un appartamentino vicino all'ascensore (alle scale).
Vohr-REH-ee oon ahp-pahr-tah-mayn-TEE-noh vee-CHEE-noh ahl-lah-shayn-SOH-ray (AHL-lay SKAH-lay).

I want a boardinghouse (furnished apartment, furnished room).
Vorrei una pensione (un appartamento ammobiliato, una camera ammobiliata).
Vohr-REH-ee OO-nah payn-SYOH-nay (oon ahp-pahr-tah-MAYN-toh ahm-moh-bee-LYAH-toh, OO-nah KAH-may-rah ahm-moh-bee-LYAH-tah).

41

I want a living room, bedroom and kitchen.
Vorrei salotto, camera da letto e cucina.
Vohr-REH-ee sah-LAWT-toh, KAH-may-rah dah LEHT-toh ay koo-
CHEE-nah.

Are these rooms for rent?
Si affittano queste stanze?
See ahf-FEET-tah-noh KWAYS-tay STAHN-tsay?

Have you a reservation?
Ha prenotato?
AH pray-noh-TAH-toh?

I made a reservation two weeks ago.
Ho prenotato due settimane fa.
AW pray-noh-TAH-toh DOO-ay sayt-tee-MAH-nay FAH.

How long are you staying?
Quanto tempo si tratterrà qui?
KWAHN-toh TEHM-poh see traht-tayr-RAH KWEE?

Overnight.
Fino a domani.
FEE-noh ah doh-MAH-nee.

I shall be here till Saturday.
Mi tratterrò fino a sabato.
Mee traht-tayr-RAW FEE-noh ah SAH-bah-toh.

Will you please sign the register (fill out the registration blank)?
Vuol aver la gentilezza di firmare il registro (di riempire la dichiarazione di soggiorno)?
VWAWL ah-VAYR lah jayn-tee-LAY-tsah dee feer-MAH-ray eel
ray-JEES-troh (dee ree-aym-PEE-ray lah dee-kyah-rah-TSYOH-
nay dee soh-JOHR-noh)?

How much is it by the day (week, month)?
Quanto è alla giornata (alla settimana, al mese)?
KWAHN-toh EH AHL-lah johr-NAH-tah (AHL-lah sayt-tee-MAH-
nah, ahl MAY-say)?

On what floor is it?
A che piano si trova?
Ah KAY PYAH-noh see TRAW-vah?

On the third floor.
Al terzo piano.
Ahl TEHR-tsoh PYAH-noh.

I should like to see the room.
Vorrei vedere la stanza.
Vohr-REH-ee vay-DAY-ray lah STAHN-tsah.

I (don't) like this room.
(Non) mi piace questa stanza.
(Nohn) mee PYAH-chay KWAYS-tah STAHN-tsah.

It has no view.
Non ha visuale.
Nohn AH vee-soo-AH-lay.

It faces the courtyard.
Dà sul cortile.
DAH sool kohr-TEE-lay.

Have you something better (cheaper, larger)?
Ha niente di meglio (di meno caro, di più grande)?
AH NYEN-tay dee MEH-lyoh (dee MAY-noh KAH-roh, dee PYOO
    GRAHN-day)?

It is too small (large, noisy, hot, cold).
È troppo piccola (grande, rumorosa, calda, fredda).
EH TRAWP-poh PEEK-koh-lah (GRAHN-day, roo-moh-ROH-sah,
    KAHL-dah, FRAYD-dah).

There is no rug (radio, radiator) in this room.
Non c'è tappeto (radio, termosifone) in questa stanza.
Nohn CHEH tahp-PAY-toh (RAH-dyoh, tehr-moh-see-FOH-nay)
    een KWAYS-tah STAHN-tsah.

Are meals included?
Sono compresi i pasti?
SOH-noh kohm-PRAY-see ee PAHS-tee?

Only breakfast.
Solo la prima colazione.
SOH-loh lah PREE-mah koh-lah-TSYOH-nay.

How much is the room without meals?
Quant'è la stanza senza pasti?
Kwahn-TEH lah STAHN-tsah SEHN-tsah PAHS-tee?

How much do you charge American plan? For breakfast and one other meal?
Quanto fanno pagare per la pensione completa? Per la mezza pensione?
KWAHN-toh FAHN-noh pah-GAH-ray payr lah payn-SYOH-nay kohm-PLEH-tah? Payr lah MEH-dzah payn-SYOH-nay?

May I see your passport (identification)?
Mi fa vedere il Suo passaporto (i Suoi documenti d'identità)?
Mee FAH vay-DAY-ray eel soo-oh pahs-sah-PAWR-toh (ee SWOY doh-koo-MAYN-tee dee-dayn-tee-TAH)?

Can I reserve a room?
Potrei prenotare una stanza?
Poh-TREH-ee pray-noh-TAH-ray oo-nah STAHN-tsah?

May I leave my baggage here until Friday?
Potrei lasciar qui i miei bagagli fino a venerdì?
Poh-TREH-ee lah-SHAHR KWEE ee myay bah-GAH-lyee FEE-noh ah vay-nayr-DEE?

Let me have my key, please.
Mi vuol favorire la chiave?
Mee VWAWL fah-voh-REE-ray lah KYAH-vay?

Here is my (your) key.
Ecco la mia (Sua) chiave.
EHK-koh lah MEE-ah (soo-ah) KYAH-vay.

What is your room number?
Qual'è il numero della Sua stanza?
Kwah-LEH eel NOO-may-roh DAYL-lah soo-ah STAHN-tsah?

Please send another pillow to my room.
Favorisca mandarmi in camera un altro cuscino.
Fah-voh-REES-kah mahn-DAHR-mee een KAH-may-rah oon AHL-troh koo-SHEE-noh.

another blanket
un'altra coperta
oo-NAHL-trah koh-PEHR-tah

another clothes hanger
un altro attaccapanni
oo-NAHL-troh aht-tahk-kah-PAHN-nee

44

some soap
del sapone
dayl sah-POH-nay

some toilet paper
della carta igienica
DAYL-lah KAHR-tah ee-JEH-nee-kah

an ash tray
un portacenere
oon pawr-tah-CHAY-nay-ray

Please send up a bellboy (waiter).
Per favore, mi mandi il cameriere.
Payr fah-VOH-ray, mee MAHN-dee eel kah-may-RYEH-ray.

the maid
la cameriera
lah kah-may-RYEH-rah

ice
del ghiaccio
dayl GYAH-choh

ice water
dell'acqua ghiacciata
dahl-LAHK-kwah gyah-CHAH-tah

Where is the bathroom?
Dov'è la sala da bagno?
Doh-VEH lah SAH-lah dah BAH-nyoh?

the phone
il telefono
eel tay-LEH-foh-noh

the lavatory
il gabinetto
eel gah-bee-NAYT-toh

the dining room
la sala da pranzo
lah SAH-lah dah PRAHN-dzoh

45

the electric switch
l'interruttore
leen-tayr-root-TOH-ray

the outlet
la presa di corrente
lah PRAY-sah dee kohr-REHN-tay

the closet
l'armadio
lahr-MAH-dyoh

the lamp
la lampada
lah LAHM-pah-dah

the sink
il lavandino
eel lah-vahn-DEE-noh

the faucet, tap
il rubinetto
eel roo-bee-NAYT-toh

Please draw the curtains.
Per favore, tiri le tendine.
Payr fah-VOH-ray, TEE-ree lay tayn-DEE-nay.

close the shutters
chiuda le imposte
KYOO-dah lay eem-PAWS-tay

Is there a hook here?
C'è un uncino?
CHEH oo-noon-CHEE-noh?

When may I have a bath?
Quando potrei fare un bagno?
KWAHN-doh poh-TREH-ee FAH-ray oon BAH-nyoh?

I should like a bath tonight.
Vorrei farmi un bagno stasera.
Vohr-REH-ee FAHR-mee oon BAH-nyoh stah-SAY-rah.

46

You must provide your own soap and facecloth.

Deve provvedere per conto Suo il sapone e la pezzuola da bagno.

DAY-vay prohv-vay-DAY-ray payr KOHN-toh SOO-oh eel sah-POH-nay ay lah pay-TSWAW-lah dah BAH-nyoh.

I want my shoes shined; shall I leave them outside the door?

Vorrei farmi lucidare le scarpe; le lascio fuor della porta?

Vohr-REH-ee FAHR-mee loo-chee-DAH-ray lay SKAHR-pay; lay LAH-shoh fwawr DAYL-lah PAWR-tah?

Send these things to the laundry (cleaner's). When do I get them back?

Mandi questa roba alla lavandaia (a far pulire a secco). Quando potrò riaverla?

MAHN-dee KWAYS-tah RAW-bah AHL-lah lah-vahn-DAH-yah (ah FAHR poo-LEE-ray ah SAYK-koh). KWAHN-doh poh-TRAW ree-ah-VAYR-lah?

Have this suit pressed. I want it back tonight.

Mi faccia stirare questo vestito. Vorrei riaverlo stasera.

Mee FAH-chah stee-RAH-ray KWAYS-toh vays-TEE-toh. Vohr-REH-ee ree-ah-VAYR-loh stah-SAY-rah.

There are mosquitoes on the wall (ceiling). Please spray.

Ci sono zanzare sul muro (sul soffitto). Per favore, spruzzi un po' d'insetticida.

Chee SOH-noh dzahn-DZAH-ray sool MOO-roh (sool sohf-FEET-toh). Payr fah-VOH-ray, SPROO-tsee oon PAW deen-sayt-tee-CHEE-dah.

Let me have a mosquito net (a bath mat).

Mi faccia avere una zanzariera (uno scendibagno).

Mee FAH-chah ah-VAY-ray OO-nah dzahn-dzah-RYEH-rah (OO-noh shayn-dee-BAH-nyoh).

What is that for?

A che serve quello?

Ah KAY SEHR-vay KWAYL-loh?

There is no lock.

Non c'è serratura.

Nohn CHEH sayr-rah-TOO-rah.

47

Open the window.
Apra la finestra.
AH-prah lah fee-NEHS-trah.

Close the door.
Chiuda la porta.
KYOO-dah lah PAWR-tah.

May I come in?
Permesso?
Payr-MAYS-soh?

Come in!
Avanti!
Ah-VAHN-tee!

Who is there?
Chi è?
KEE EH?

Wait a minute!
Aspetti un istante!
Ahs-PEHT-tee oon ees-TAHN-tay!

Do not disturb.
Non disturbare.
Nohn dees-toor-BAH-ray.

Call me at 6:00 a.m.
Mi faccia chiamare alle sei del mattino.
Mee FAH-chah kyah-MAH-ray AHL-lay SEH-ee dayl maht-TEE-noh.

Please change the sheets (pillowcases, towels).
Per favore, mi cambi le lenzuola (le federe, gli asciugamani).
Payr fah-VOH-ray, mee KAHM-bee lay layn-TSWAW-lah (lay FEH-day-ray, lyee ah-shoo-gah-MAH-nee).

The water is not hot.
L'acqua non è calda.
LAHK-kwah nohn EH KAHL-dah.

I'd like to speak to the manager.
Vorrei parlare col direttore.
Vohr-REH-ee pahr-LAH-ray kohl dee-rayt-TOH-ray.

48

Put this package on the table (chair, armchair, sofa).
Metta questo pacco sul tavolo (sulla sedia, sulla poltrona, sul
sofà).
MAYT-tah KWAYS-toh PAHK-koh sool TAH-voh-loh (SOOL-lah
SEH-dyah, SOOL-lah pohl-TROH-nah, sool soh-FAH).

Are there any letters (packages) for me?
Ci sono lettere (pacchi) per me?
Chee SOH-noh LAYT-tay-ray (PAHK-kee) payr MAY?

Ask the doorman.
Chieda al portiere.
KYEH-dah ahl pohr-TYEH-ray.

Here is a letter for you.
Ecco una lettera per Lei.
EHK-koh OO-nah LAYT-tay-rah payr LEH-ee.

There is no mail.
Non c'è posta.
Nohn CHEH PAWS-tah.

I want an interpreter (an English-speaking guide, secretary).
Vorrei un interprete (una guida, una segretaria che parli inglese).
Vohr-REH-ee oon een-TEHR-pray-tay (OO-nah GWEE-dah, OO-nah
say-gray-TAH-ryah kay PAHR-lee een-GLAY-say).

Page Mr. Bianchi in the lobby.
Faccia cercare il Signor Bianchi nell'atrio.
FAH-chah chayr-KAH-ray eel see-NYOHR BYAHN-kee nayl-LAH-
tryoh.

Please give me stamps (writing paper, envelopes, post cards).
Mi favorisca dei francobolli (della carta da lettere, delle buste,
delle cartoline).
Mee fah-voh-REES-kah day frahn-koh-BOHL-lee (DAYL-lah KAHR-
tah dah LAYT-tay-ray, DAYL-lay BOOS-tay, DAYL-lay kahr-toh-
LEE-nay).

Did anyone call me?
Mi ha telefonato nessuno?
Mee AH tay-lay-foh-NAH-toh nays-SOO-noh?

Did anyone come for me?
È venuto nessuno a cercarmi?
EH vay-NOO-toh nay-soo-noh ah chayr-KAHR-mee?

No one called.
Non ha telefonato nessuno.
Nohn AH tay-lay-foh-NAH-toh nays-soo-noh.

No one came.
Non è venuto nessuno.
Nohn EH vay-NOO-toh nays-soo-noh.

There is a gentleman (lady) to see you.
C'è un signore (una signora) che vuol vederla.
CHEH oon see-NYOH-ray (oo-nah see-NYOH-rah) kay VWAWL
vay-DAYR-lah.

If someone calls, I'll be back at three.
Se telefona qualcuno, dica che sarò di ritorno alle tre.
Say tay-LAY-foh-nah kwahl-KOO-noh, DEE-kah kay sah-RAW
dee ree-TOHR-noh AHL-lay TRAY.

I'm expecting someone; tell him to wait.
Aspetto qualcuno; gli dica di attendermi.
Ahs-PEHT-toh kwahl-KOO-noh; lyee DEE-kah dee aht-TEHN-dayr-
mee.

I'm checking out at six.
Lascio la stanza alle sei.
LAH-shoh lah STAHN-tsah AHL-lay SEH-ee.

Please prepare my bill.
Mi prepari il conto.
Mee pray-PAH-ree eel KOHN-toh.

Is everything included?
Tutto compreso?
TOOT-toh kohm-PRAY-soh?

The service and tax are included.
Il servizio e la tassa di soggiorno sono compresi.
Eel sayr-VEE-tsyoh ay lah TAHS-sah dee soh-JOHR-noh SOH-noh
kohm-PRAY-see.

50

Forward my mail to this address.
Faccia inoltrare la mia corrispondenza a quest'indirizzo.
FAH-chah ee-nohl-TRAH-ray lah MEE-ah kohr-rees-pohn-DEHN-
tsah ah kways-teen-dee-REE-tsoh.

11. MONEY, BANK, MEASURES

Where can I change dollars into lire?
Dove potrei cambiare dollari in lire?
DOH-vay poh-TREH-ee kahm-BYAH-ray DAWL-lah-ree een LEE-
ray?

At the bank (hotel, exchange office).
Alla banca (all'albergo, dal cambiavalute).
AHL-lah BAHN-kah (ahl-lahl-BEHR-goh, dahl kahm-byah-vah-
LOO-tay).

Where is the bank?
Dov'è la banca?
Doh-VEH lah BAHN-kah?

I have no money (change).
Non ho danaro (spiccioli).
Nohn AW dah-NAH-roh (SPEE-choh-lee).

Can you change a twenty-dollar bill?
Può cambiarmi un biglietto da venti dollari?
PWAW kahm-BYAHR-mee oon bee-LYAYT-toh dah VAYN-tee
DAWL-lah-ree?

Let me have some small change.
Mi favorisca degli spiccioli.
Mee fah-voh-REES-kah DAY-lyee SPEE-choh-lee.

Can I borrow money at the bank?
Potrei prendere in prestito danaro alla banca?
Poh-TREH-ee PREHN-day-ray een PREHS-tee-toh dah-NAH-roh
AHL-lah BAHN-kah?

Perhaps they will lend you some money.
Può darsi che Le prestino del danaro.
PWAW DAHR-see kay lay PREHS-tee-noh dayl dah-NAH-roh.

51

Do you accept traveler's checks?
Accetta assegni di viaggio?
Ah-CHEHT-tah ahs-SAY-nyee dee VYAH-joh?

We (do not) accept them.
(Non) li accettiamo.
(Nohn) lee ah-chayt-TYAH-moh.

What is the (best) rate today?
Qual'è il (miglior) cambio della giornata?
Kwah-LEH eel (mee-LYOHR) KAHM-byoh DAYL-lah johr-NAH-tah?

Six hundred twenty lire to the dollar.
Seicento venti lire per dollaro.
Say-CHEHN-toh VAYN-tee LEE-ray payr DAWL-lah-roh.

Can you cash this check (international money order, telegraphic money order)?
Mi può pagare quest'assegno (questo vaglia internazionale, telegrafico)?
Mee PWAW pah-GAH-ray kways-tahs-SAY-nyoh (KWAYS-toh VAH-lyah een-tayr-nah-tsyoh-NAH-lay, tay-lay-GRAH-fee-koh)?

We cannot take a personal check.
Non possiamo pagare un assegno personale.
Nohn pohs-SYAH-moh pah-GAH-ray oon ahs-SAY-nyoh payr-soh-NAH-lay.

Is this check made out to you?
Quest'assegno è all'ordine Suo?
Kways-tahs-SAY-nyoh EH ahl-LOHR-dee-nay soo-oh?

Please endorse it (sign here).
Favorisca girarlo (apporre qui la Sua firma).
Fah-voh-REES-kah jee-RAHR-loh (ahp-POHR-ray KWEE lah soo-ah FEER-mah).

What time does the bank open?
A che ora si aprono gli sportelli?
Ah KAY OH-rah see AH-proh-noh lyee spohr-TEHL-lee?

It opens at 10 and stays open until 3.
Si aprono alle dieci e restano aperti fino alle tre.
See AH-proh-noh AHL-lay DYEH-chee ay REHS-tah-noh ah-PEHR-tee FEE-noh AHL-lay TRAY.

I should like to cash this check (make out a draft).
Vorrei riscuotere quest'assegno (fare una tratta).
Vohr-REH-ee rees-KWAW-tay-ray kways-tahs-SAY-nyoh (FAH-ray oo-nah TRAHT-tah).

Are you the teller?
È Lei il cassiere?
EH LEH-ee eel kahs-SYEH-ray?

May I speak to the manager?
Potrei parlare col direttore?
Poh-TREH-ee pahr-LAH-ray kohl dee-rayt-TOH-ray?

He's busy right now; will you wait?
In questo momento è occupato; può attendere?
Een KWAYS-toh moh-MAYN-toh EH ohk-koo-PAH-toh; PWAW aht-TEHN-day-ray?

EXCHANGE

Italian lira = $0.0016 (approximate)
$1.00 = 620 to 650 Italian lire
lira (*plural,* lire)
LEE-rah (LEE-ray)

Swiss franc = $0.25 (approximate)
$1.00 = 4 Swiss francs
franco (*plural,* franchi)
FRAHN-koh (FRAHN-kee)

MEASURES

Meter = 39.37 inches, or 3.38 feet, or 1.09 yards
metro (*plural,* metri)
MEH-troh (MEH-tree)

Centimeter = 0.39 inches.
centimetro (*plural,* centimetri)
chen-TEE-may-troh (chen-TEE-may-tree)

Kilometer = 0.621 miles
chilometro (*plural,* chilometri)
kee-LAW-may-troh (kee-LAW-may-tree)

Liter = 1.75 pints
litro (*plural,* litri)
LEE-troh (LEE-tree)

Gram = 0.0352 ounces
grammo (*plural,* grammi)
GRAHM-moh (GRAHM-mee)

Hectogram = 3.52 ounces
etto (*plural,* etti)
EHT-toh (EHT-tee)

Kilogram = 2.20 pounds
chilogrammo, chilo (*plural,* chilogrammi, chili)
kee-loh-GRAHM-moh, KEE-loh (kee-loh-GRAHM-mee, KEE-lee)

12. WRITING AND POST OFFICE

I want a pen, (ink, a pencil, writing paper).
Vorrei una penna (dell'inchiostro, un lapis, della carta da scrivere).
Vohr-REH-ee OO-nah PAYN-nah (dayl-leen-KYAWS-troh, oon LAH-pees, DAYL-lah KAHR-tah dah SKREE-vay-ray).

I want to write a letter (send a post card).
Vorrei scrivere una lettera (spedire una cartolina).
Vohr-REH-ee SKREE-vay-ray OO-nah LAYT-tay-rah (spay-DEE-ray OO-nah kahr-toh-LEE-nah).

Please mail this letter for me.
Per favore, m'imposti questa lettera.
Payr fah-VOH-ray, meem-PAWS-tee KWAYS-tah LAYT-tay-rah.

Have you any letters for me?
Ha lettere per me?
Ah LAYT-tay-ray payr MAY?

54

Where is the mailbox?
Dov'è la buca delle lettere?
Doh-VEH lah BOO-kah DAYL-lay LAYT-tay-ray?

the stamp window
lo sportello francobolli
loh spohr-TEHL-loh frahn-koh-BOHL-lee

the parcel-post window
lo sportello pacchi postali
loh sporh-TEHL-loh PAHK-kee pohs-TAH-lee

the registry window
lo sportello raccomandate
loh spohr-TEHL-loh rahk-koh-mahn-DAH-tay

the money-order window
lo sportello vaglia
loh spohr-TEHL-loh VAH-lyah

the general-delivery window
lo sportello fermo in posta
loh spohr-TEHL-loh FAYR-moh een PAWS-tah

Where is the post office?
Dov'è l'ufficio postale?
Doh-VEH loof-FEE-choh pohs-TAH-lay?

When is it open?
Quando è aperto?
KWAHN-doh EH ah-PEHR-toh?

What is the regular (air-mail) postage to the United States?
Qual'è la francatura per posta ordinaria (per via aerea) per gli
Stati Uniti?
Kwah-LEH lah frahn-kah-TOO-rah payr PAWS-tah ohr-dee-NAH-
ryah (payr VEE-ah ah-EH-ray-ah) payr lyee STAH-tee OO-NEE-
tee?

Give me five 10 lira stamps (ten post cards, eight envelopes).
Mi dia cinque francobolli da dieci lire (dieci cartoline, otto
buste).
Mee DEE-ah CHEEN-kway frahn-koh-BOHL-lee dah DYEH-chee
LEE-ray (DYEH-chee kahr-toh-LEE-nay, AWT-toh BOOS-tay).

**How much is an insured (registered, special-delivery) letter
to New York?**

Quanto costa una lettera assicurata (raccomandata, espresso)
per New York?

KWAHN-toh KAWS-tah OO-nah LAYT-tay-rah ahs-see-koo-RAH-tah
(rahk-koh-mahn-DAH-tah, ays-PREHS-soh) payr New York?

I want to send this parcel insured.

Vorrei assicurare questo pacco.

Vohr-REH-ee ahs-see-koo-RAH-ray KWAYS-toh PAHK-koh.

Sender.

Mittente.

Meet-TEHN-tay.

Receiver.

Destinatario.

Days-tee-nah-TAH-ryoh.

The regular (air mail) rate is 30 lire per gram.

La francatura per posta ordinaria (per via aerea) è di trenta
lire a grammo.

Lah frahn-kah-TOO-rah payr PAWS-tah ohr-dee-NAH-ryah (payr
VEE-ah ah-EH-ray-ah) EH dee TREHN-tah LEE-ray ah GRAHM-
moh.

13. CABLE AND TELEPHONE

Where is the telegraph (telephone) office?

Dov'è l'ufficio telegrafi (telefonico)?

Doh-VEH loof-FEE-choh tay-LEH-grah-fee (tay-lay-FAW-nee-
koh)?

What is the regular (night) rate per word to Paris?

Qual'è la tariffa ordinaria (notturna) per parola per Parigi?

Kwah-LEH lah tah-REEF-fah ohr-dee-NAH-ryah (noht-TOOR-nah)
payr pah-RAW-lah payr pah-REE-jee?

Send it collect.

La mandi contro assegno.

Lah MAHN-dee KOHN-troh ahs-SAY-nyoh.

When will it arrive?
Quando arriverà?
KWAHN-doh ahr-ree-vay-RAH?

Where are the forms?
Dove sono i moduli?
DOH-vay SOH-noh ee MAW-doo-lee?

Here is the address.
Ecco l'indirizzo.
EHK-koh leen-dee-REE-tsoh.

Where is the phone (booth)?
Dov'è il telefono (la cabina telefonica)?
Doh-VEH eel tay-LAY-foh-noh (lah kah-BEE-nah tay-lay-FAW-nee-kah)?

Do I need tokens for the phone?
C'è bisogno di gettoni per telefonare?
CHEH bee-SAW-nyoh dee jayt-TOH-nee payr tay-lay-foh-NAH-ray?

I want to make a local (long-distance) call to Parma.
Vorrei fare una telefonata urbana (interurbana) a Parma.
Vohr-REH-ee FAH-ray OO-nah tay-lay-foh-NAH-tah oor-BAH-nah (een-tayr-oor-BAH-nah) ah PAHR-mah.

How much is a call to Bari?
Quanto costa telefonare a Bari?
KWAHN-toh KAWS-tah tay-lay-foh-NAH-ray ah BAH-ree?

Will you accept double charge for double time?
Raddoppia?
Rahd-DOHP-pyah?

Operator, get me number Prati 254.
Telefonista, mi metta in comunicazione col numero Prati duecento cinquantaquattro.
Tay-lay-foh-NEES-tah, mee MAYT-tah een koh-moo-nee-kah-TSYOH-nay kohl NOO-may-roh PRAH-tee doo-ay-CHEHN-toh cheen-kwahn-tah-KWAHT-troh.

You are connected with Lucca.
Parli con Lucca.
PAHR-lee kohn LOOK-kah.

They don't answer.
Non rispondono.
Nohn rees-POHN-doh-noh.

The line is busy.
La linea è occupata.
Lah LEE-nay-ah EH ohk-koo-PAH-tah.

The operator will call you.
La telefonista La chiamerà.
Lah tay-lay-foh-NEES-tah lah kyah-may-RAH.

Whom do you want to speak to?
Con chi vuol parlare?
Kohn KEE VWAWL pahr-LAH-ray?

I should like to speak to Mr. Paoli.
Vorrei parlare col Signor Paoli.
Vohr-REH-ee pahr-LAH-ray kohl see-NYOHR PAH-oh-lee.

He is not here; may I take a message?
Non c'è; vuol lasciare un'ambasciata?
Nohn CHEH; VWAWL lah-SHAH-ray oo-nahm-bah-SHAH-tah?

Hold the wire.
Rimanga all'apparecchio.
Ree-MAHN-gah ahl-lahp-pah-RAYK-kyoh.

Hello! Who is speaking?
Pronto! Con chi parlo?
PROHN-toh! Kohn KEE PAHR-loh?

This is Mrs. Paoli.
Parla la Signora Paoli.
PAHR-lah lah see-NYOH-rah PAH-oh-lee.

At what time will he be back?
A che ora sarà di ritorno?
Ah KAY OH-rah sah-RAH dee ree-TOHR-noh?

He'll be back at seven.
Sarà di ritorno alle sette.
Sah-RAH dee ree-TOHR-noh AHL-lay SEHT-tay.

Tell him Mr. Rossi called.
Gli dica che ha telefonato il Signor Rossi.
Lyee DEE-kah kay AH tay-lay-foh-NAH-toh eel see-NYOHR ROHS-see.

Ask him to call me.
Gli chieda di telefonarmi.
Lyee KYEH-dah dee tay-lay-foh-NAHR-mee.

Mr. Rossi called; he left no message, but he'll call again at seven.
Ha telefonato il Signor Rossi; non ha lasciato ambasciata, ma ritelefonerà alle sette.
AH tay-lay-foh-NAH-toh eel see-NYOHR ROHS-see; nohn AH lah-SHAH-toh ahm-bah-SHAH-tah, mah ree-tay-lay-foh-nay-RAH AHL-lay SEHT-tay.

You can reach him at this number.
Può trovarlo a questo numero.
PWAW troh-VAHR-loh ah KWAYS-toh NOO-may-roh.

You have the wrong number *or* You gave me the wrong number.
Lei ha sbagliato numero.
LEH-ee ah zbah-LYAH-toh NOO-may-roh.

14. SHOPPING

I should like to go shopping today.
Oggi vorrei andare a far delle compere.
AW-jee vohr-REH-ee ahn-DAH-ray ah FAHR DAYL-lay KOHM-pay-ray.

There's a bargain sale.
C'è una vendita d'occasione.
CHEH OO-nah VAYN-dee-tah dohk-kah-SYOH-nay.

I should like to go to a ladies' (men's) clothing store.
Vorrei andare a un negozio di vestiario da signore (da uomini).
Vohr-REH-ee ahn-DAH-ray ah oon nay-GAW-tsyoh dee vays-TYAH-ryoh dah see-NYOH-ray (dah WAW-mee-nee).

59

to a department store
a un magazzino
ah oon mah-gah-DZEE-noh

to a hat shop
a una cappelleria
ah oo-nah kahp-payl-lay-REE-ah

to a shoe shop
a un negozio di scarpe
ah oon nay-GAW-tsyoh dee SKAHR-pay

to a tailor's
da un sarto
dah oon SAHR-toh

to a jeweler's
da un gioielliere
dah oon joh-yehl-LYAY-ray

to a bookstore
a una libreria
ah oo-nah lee-bray-REE-ah

to a perfume shop
a una profumeria
ah oo-nah proh-foo-may-REE-ah

to a cigar store
a una tabaccheria
ah oo-nah tah-bahk-kay-REE-ah

to a stationery store
da un cartolaio
dah oon kahr-toh-LAH-yoh

Where do they sell gloves?
Dove si vendono guanti?
DOH-vay see VAYN-doh-noh GWAHN-tee?

shoes   scarpe   (SKAHR-pay)
garters   giarrettiere   (jahr-rayt-TYEH-ray)
suspenders   bretelle   (bray-TEHL-lay)
panties   mutandine   (moo-tahn-DEE-nay)

60

socks   calzini   (kahl-TSEE-nee)
stockings   calze   (KAHL-tsay)
pins   spille   (SPEEL-lay)
needles   aghi   (AH-ghee)
diapers   pezze da bambini   (PEH-tsay dah bahm-BEE-nee)
slippers   pantofole   (pahn-TAW-foh-lay)
shorts   calzoncini corti   (kahl-tsohn-CHEE-nee KOHR-tee)
pajamas   pigiama   (pee-JAH-mah)

May I help you?
Posso servirla?
PAWS-soh sayr-VEER-lah?

What do you wish?
Cosa desidera?
KAW-sah day-SEE-day-rah?

I want a felt hat.
Vorrei un cappello di feltro.
Vohr-REH-ee oon kahp-PEHL-loh dee FAYL-troh.

a straw hat   un cappello di paglia   (oon kahp-PEHL-loh
   dee PAH-lyah)
a suit   un vestito   (oon vays-TEE-toh)
a tie   una cravatta   (oo-nah krah-VAHT-tah)
a dress   un abito da donna   (oon AH-bee-toh dah DAWN-
   nah)
a scarf   una sciarpa   (oo-nah SHAHR-pah)
a shawl   uno scialle   (oo-noh SHAHL-lay)
a skirt   una gonna   (oo-nah GAWN-nah)
a slip   una sottoveste   (oo-nah soht-toh-VEHS-tay)
a coat   una giacca   (oo-nah JAHK-kah)
a pair of pants   un paio di pantaloni   (oon PAH-yoh dee
   pahn-tah-LOH-nee)
a vest   un panciotto   (oon pahn-CHAWT-toh)
a bra   un reggiseno   (oon reh-jee-SAY-noh)
a girdle   una fascetta   (oo-nah fah-SHAYT-tah)
sandals   dei sandali   (day SAHN-dah-lee)
rubbers   delle soprascarpe   (DAYL-lay soh-prah-SKAHR-pay)
a belt   una cintura   (oo-nah cheen-TOO-rah)

61

a **blouse**   una camicetta   (oo-nah kah-mee-CHAYT-tah)

a **shirt**   una camicia   (oo-nah kah-MEE-chah)

a **sweater**   un maglione   (oon mah-LYOH-nay)

men's (women's) underwear   della biancheria da uomo (da donna)   (DAYL-lah byahn-kay-REE-ah dah WAW-moh (dah DAWN-nah))

a **handbag**   una borsetta (a mano)   (oo-nah bohr-SAYT-tah (ah MAH-noh))

thread   del filo   (dayl FEE-loh)

a **cap**   un berretto   (oon bayr-RAYT-toh)

darning cotton   del cotone da rammendo   (dayl koh-TOH-nay dah rahm-MAYN-doh)

a **nightgown**   una camicia da notte   (oo-nah kah-MEE-chah dah NAWT-tay)

an **overcoat**   un soprabito, pastrano, cappotto   (oon soh-PRAH-bee-toh, pah-STRAH-noh, kahp-PAWT-toh)

a **wallet**   un portafogli   (oon pawr-tah-FAW-lyee)

an **umbrella**   un ombrello   (oon ohm-BREHL-loh)

a **parasol**   un ombrellino   (oon ohm-brayl-LEE-noh)

a **raincoat**   un impermeabile   (oon eem-payr-may-AH-bee-lay)

a **bathing cap**   una cuffia da bagno   (oo-nah KOOF-fyah dah BAH-nyoh)

a **bathing suit**   un costume da bagno   (oon kohs-TOO-may dah BAH-nyoh)

a **handkerchief**   un fazzoletto   (oon fah-tsoh-LAYT-toh)

a **dressing gown**   una veste da camera   (oo-nah VEHS-tay dah KAH-may-rah)

a **bathrobe**   un accappatoio   (oon ahk-kahp-pah-TOH-yoh)

a **piece of cloth**   un pezzo di stoffa   (oon PEH-tsoh dee STAWF-fah)

What size (color)?

Di che misura (colore)?

Dee KAY mee-SOO-rah (koh-LOH-ray)?

This is cheap.

Questo è a buon mercato.

KWAYS-toh EH ah BWAWN mayr-KAH-toh.

I don't like this color (this size).
Non mi piace questo colore (questa misura).
Nohn mee PYAH-chay KWAYS-toh koh-LOH-ray (KWAYS-tah mee-soo-rah).

Do you have one that is larger?
Ce n'è uno più grande?
Chay NEH oo-noh PYOO GRAHN-day?

    smaller   più piccolo   (PYOO PEEK-koh-loh)
    shorter   più corto   (PYOO KOHR-toh)
    longer   più lungo   (PYOO LOON-goh)
    wider, looser   più largo   (PYOO LAHR-goh)
    tighter, narrower   più stretto   (PYOO STRAYT-toh)

Do you have it in black?
Ce l'ha nero?
Chay LAH NAY-roh?

    white   bianco   (BYAHN-koh)
    green   verde   (VAYR-day)
    blue   azzurro   (ah-DZOOR-roh)
    red   rosso   (ROHS-soh)
    brown   marrone   (mahr-ROH-nay)
    yellow   giallo   (JAHL-loh)
    pink   rosa   (RAW-sah)
    gray   grigio   (GREE-joh)
    purple   viola   (VYAW-lah)

Have you anything cheaper (better, more expensive)?
Ha niente di meno caro (di meglio, di più costoso)?
AH NYEHN-tay dee MAY-noh KAH-roh (dee MEH-lyoh, dee PYOO kohs-TOH-soh)?

I should like to see ——
Vorrei vedere ——
Vohr-REH-ee vay-DAY-ray ——

Show me ——
Mi faccia vedere ——
Mee FAH-chah vay-DAY-ray ——

Give me ——
Mi dia ——
Mee DEE-ah ——

How much is this (that)?
Quanto costa questo (quello)?
KWAHN-toh KAWS-tah KWAYS-toh (KWAYL-loh)?

Too much!
È troppo!
EH TRAWP-poh!

I'll pay five hundred lire for it.
Son disposto a pagarlo cinquecento lire.
SOHN dees-PAWS-toh ah pah-GAHR-loh cheen-kway-CHEHN-toh
LEE-ray.

Will you take it with you?
Lo vuol portare con sè?
Loh vwAWL pohr-TAH-ray kohn SAY?

Shall I send it?
Vuole che glielo mandi?
vwAW-lay kay LYAY-loh MAHN-dee?

Please wrap it up for me.
Per favore, me l'avvolga.
Payr fah-VOH-ray, may lahv-VAWL-gah.

Send it to the Hotel Excelsior.
Lo mandi all'Albergo Excelsior.
Loh MAHN-dee ahl-lahl-BEHR-goh ehk-CHEHL-see-ohr.

May I have a receipt?
Vuol favorirmi una ricevuta?
vwAWL fah-voh-REER-mee OO-nah ree-chay-voo-tah?

I shall pay on delivery.
Lo pagherò alla consegna.
Loh pah-gay-RAW AHL-lah kohn-SAY-nyah.

Could you send it to my ship (to the airport, to my U.S. address)?
Me lo potrebbe spedire al piroscafo (all'aeroporto, al mio recapito negli Stati Uniti)?
May loh poh-TRAYB-bay spay-DEE-ray ahl pee-RAW-skah-foh (ahl-lah-ay-roh-PAWR-toh, ahl MEE-oh ray-KAH-pee-toh NAY-lyee STAH-tee oo-NEE-tee)?

I want one made of cotton (wool, rayon, silk, leather, lace, rubber).
Ne vorrei uno di cotone (di lana, di rayon, di seta, di pelle, di merletto, di gomma).
Nay vohr-REH-ee oo-noh dee koh-TOH-nay (dee LAH-nah, dee rah-YAWN, dee SAY-tah, dee PEHL-lay, dee mayr-LAYT-toh, dee GOHM-mah).

Please take my measurements.
Mi vuol prendere la misura?
Mee VWAWL PREHN-day-ray lah mee-soo-rah?

Do you want to try it on?
Vuol provarselo?
VWAWL proh-VAHR-say-loh?

It does not fit.
Non va bene.
Nohn VAH BEH-nay.

The sleeves are too long (short, full, narrow).
Le maniche son troppo lunghe (corte, larghe, strette).
Lay MAH-nee-kay sohn TRAWP-poh LOON-gay (KOHR-tay, LAHR-gay, STRAYT-tay).

Could I have a zipper put in?
Mi ci potrebbe mettere la chiusura lampo?
Mee chee poh-TRAYB-bay MAYT-tay-ray lah kyoo-soo-rah LAHM-poh?

Could you put rubber heels on my shoes?
Potrebbe mettermi alle scarpe dei tacchi di gomma?
Poh-TRAYB-bay MAYT-tayr-mee AHL-lay SKAHR-pay day TAHK-kee dee GOHM-mah?

Is it handmade (imported, domestic)?
È fatto a mano (importato, nazionale)?
EH FAHT-toh ah MAH-noh (eem-pohr-TAH-toh, nah-tsyoh-NAH-lay)?

Can I return this article?
Potrei restituire quest'oggetto?
Poh-TREH-ee rays-tee-too-EE-ray kways-toh-JEHT-toh?

How much can you spend?
Quanto può spendere?
KWAHN-toh PWAW SPEHN-day-ray?

How much is it worth?
Quanto vale?
KWAHN-toh VAH-lay?

I should like to buy the watch in the showcase (window display).
Vorrei comprare l'orologio nella mostra (in vetrina).
Vohr-REH-ee kohm-PRAH-ray loh-roh-LAW-joh NAYL-lah MOHS-trah (een vay-TREE-nah).

the bracelet   il braccialetto   (eel brah-chah-LAYT-toh)
the ring   l'anello   (lah-NEHL-loh)
the earrings   gli orecchini   (lyee oh-rayk-KEE-nee)
the necklace   la collana   (lah kohl-LAH-nah)
the sunglasses   gli occhiali da sole   (lyee ohk-KYAH-lee dah SOH-lay)
the alarm clock   la sveglia   (lah ZVAY-lyah)
the pin   lo spillo   (loh SPEEL-loh)

Do you repair watches?
Fanno riparazioni agli orologi?
FAHN-noh ree-pah-rah-TSYOH-nee AH-lyee oh-roh-LAW-jee?

This watch is fast (slow).
Quest'orologio va avanti (addietro).
KWAYS-toh-roh-LAW-joh VAH ah-VAHN-tee (ahd-DYEH-troh).

66

The spring (crystal, strap) of my wrist watch is broken.
Si è rotta la molla (il cristallo, la cinghia) del mio orologio a polso.
See EH ROHT-tah lah MAWL-lah (eel krees-TAHL-loh, lah CHEEN-gyah) dayl MEE-oh oh-roh-LAW-joh ah POHL-soh.

I want some perfume.
Vorrei del profumo.
Vohr-REH-ee dayl proh-FOO-moh.

cold cream   del cold cream   (dayl kohl-KREHM)
lipstick   del rossetto per le labbra   (dayl rohs-SAYT-toh payr lay LAHB-brah)
rouge   del rossetto   (dayl rohs-SAYT-toh)
face powder   della cipria   (DAYL-lah CHEE-pryah)
cologne   dell'acqua di colonia   (DAYL-LAHK-kwah dee koh-LAW-nyah)
nail polish   della lacca per le unghie   (DAYL-lah LAHK-kah payr lay OON-gyay)
polish remover   dell'acetone   (dayl-lah-chay-TOH-nay)
a comb   un pettine   (oon PEHT-tee-nay)
a net   una rete   (oo-nah RAY-tay)
some soap   del sapone   (dayl sah-POH-nay)
a (safety) razor   un rasoio (di sicurezza)   (oon rah-SOH-yoh (dee see-koo-RAY-tsah))
razor blades   delle lamette da rasoio   (DAYL-lay lah-MAYT-tay dah rah-SOH-yoh)
a shaving brush   un pennello da barba   (oon payn-NEHL-loh dah BAHR-bah)
a toothbrush   uno spazzolino da denti   (OO-noh SPAH-tsoh-LEE-noh dah DEHN-tee)
toothpaste   della pasta dentifricia   (DAYL-lah PAHS-tah dehn-tee-FREE-chah)
a hairbrush   una spazzola da capelli   (oo-nah SPAH-tsoh-lah da kah-PAYL-lee)
hairpins   delle forcelle   (DAYL-lay fohr-CHEHL-lay)
shoelaces   dei lacci da scarpe   (day LAH-chee dah SKAHR-pay)

a flatiron un ferro da stiro (oon FEHR-roh dah STEE-roh)
a corkscrew un cavatappi (oon kah-vah-TAHP-pee)
a can opener un apriscatole (oon ah-pree-SKAH-toh-lay)
safety pins delle spille di sicurezza (DAYL-lay SPEEL-lay dee see-koo-RAY-tsah)
a clothesbrush una spazzola da vestiti (OO-nah SPAH-tsoh-lah dah vays-TEE-tee)
a suitcase una valigia (OO-nah vah-LEE-jah)
a deodorant un deodorante (oon day-oh-doh-RAHN-tay)
shaving cream della crema da barba (DAYL-lah KREH-mah dah BAHR-bah)
hand lotion una lozione per le mani (OO-nah loh-TSYOH-nay payr lay MAH-nee)
toilet paper della carta igienica (DAYL-lah KAHR-tah ee-JEH-nee-kah)

I should like a roll of camera film no. 5.
Vorrei un rotolo fotografico numero cinque.
Vohr-REH-ee oon RAW-toh-loh foh-toh-GRAH-fee-koh NOO-may-roh CHEEN-kway.

a roll of color film un rotolo di pellicola a colori (oon RAW-toh-loh dee payl-LEE-koh-lah ah koh-LOH-ree)
some movie film un rotolo cinematografico (oon RAW-toh-loh chee-nay-mah-toh-GRAH-fee-koh)
a camera una macchinetta fotografica (OO-nah mahk-kee-NAYT-tah foh-toh-GRAH-fee-kah)

How much does it cost to develop a roll?
Quanto costa sviluppare un rotolo?
KWAHN-toh KAWS-tah zVEE-loop-PAH-ray oon RAW-toh-loh?

I want one print of each.
Vorrei una copia di ogni pellicola.
Vohr-REH-ee OO-nah KAW-pyah dee OH-nyee payl-LEE-koh-lah

an enlargement un ingrandimento (oon een-grahn-dee-MAYN-toh)

When will it be ready?
Quando sarà pronto?
KWAHN-doh sah-RAH PROHN-toh?

Can you repair this camera?
Può riparare questa macchinetta?
PWAW ree-pah-RAH-ray KWAYS-tah mahk-kee-NAYT-tah?

Where is the liquor store?
Dov'è lo spaccio di bevande alcooliche?
Doh-VEH loh SPAH-choh dee bay-VAHN-day ahl-KAW-lee-kay?

I should like a package of cigarettes.
Vorrei un pacchetto di sigarette.
Vohr-REH-ee oon pahk-KAYT-toh dee see-gah-RAYT-tay.

> **a box of cigars** una scatola di sigari (OO-nah SKAH-toh-lah dee SEE-gah-ree)
>
> **a basket of fruit** una cesta di frutta (OO-nah CHAYS-tah dee FROOT-tah)
>
> **some pipe tobacco** del tabacco da pipa (dayl tah-BAHK-koh dah PEE-pah)
>
> **a silver cigarette case** un portasigarette d'argento (oon pawr-tah-see-gah-RAYT-tay dahr-JEHN-toh)
>
> **a lighter** un accendisigari (oon ah-chehn-dee-SEE-gah-ree)
>
> **some flints** delle pietrine (DAYL-lay pyay-TREE-nay)
>
> **some fluid** della benzina (DAYL-lah bayn-DZEE-nah)
>
> **some matches** dei fiammiferi (cerini) (day fyahm-MEE-fay-ree [chay-REE-nee])
>
> **a pipe** una pipa (OO-nah PEE-pah)
>
> **a tobacco pouch** una borsa da tabacco (OO-nah BOHR-sah dah tah-BAHK-koh)
>
> **a cigarette holder** un bocchino (oon bohk-KEE-noh)
>
> **a box of chocolates** una scatola di cioccolatini (OO-nah SKAH-toh-lah dee chohk-koh-lah-TEE-nee)

I want a novel
Vorrei un romanzo.
Vohr-REH-ee oon roh-MAHN-dzoh.

> **a magazine** una rivista (OO-nah ree-VEES-tah)
>
> **a newspaper** un giornale (oon johr-NAH-lay)
>
> **a pocket dictionary** un dizionario tascabile (oon dee-tsyoh-NAH-ryoh tahs-KAH-bee-lay)

a guidebook una guida (OO-nah GWEE-dah)

a city map una pianta della città (OO-nah PYAHN-tah DAYL-lah cheet-TAH)

an automobile map una carta automobilistica (OO-nah KAHR-tah ow-toh-moh-bee-LEES-tee-kah)

playing cards della carte da giuoco (DAYL-lay KAHR-tay dah JWAW-koh)

a fountain pen una penna stilografica (OO-nah PAYN-nah stee-loh-GRAH-fee-kah)

some string dello spago (DAYL-loh SPAH-goh)

some wrapping paper della carta da imballo (DAYL-lah KAHR-tah dah eem-BAHL-loh)

some carbon paper della carta copiativa (DAYL-lah KAHR-tah koh-pyah-TEE-vah)

some picture post cards with views of the city delle cartoline illustrate con vedute della città (DAYL-lay kahr-toh-LEE-nay eel-loos-TRAH-tay kohn vay-DOO-tay DAYL-lah cheet-TAH)

We have none.
Non ne abbiamo.
Nohn nay ah-BYAH-moh.

Anything else?
Altro?
AHL-troh?

Nothing else.
Nient'altro.
Nyehn-TAHL-troh.

That is all.
È tutto.
EH TOOT-toh.

Here is your change (receipt).
Ecco il resto (la ricevuta).
EHK-koh eel REHS-toh (lah ree-chay-voo-tah).

Thank you very much.
Grazie mille.
GRAH-tsyay MEEL-lay.

70

At your service.
Ai Suoi ordini.
AH-ee SWOY OHR-dee-nee.

Call again.
Passi di nuovo.
PAHS-see dee NWAW-voh.

15. PLACES OF INTEREST (CHURCH, THEATER, SIGHT-SEEING, NIGHT LIFE)

What are the places of interest here?
Che luoghi d'interesse ci sono qui?
KAY LWAW-ghee deen-tay-REHS-say chee SOH-noh KWEE?

Where is the cathedral?
Dov'è la cattedrale?
Doh-VEH lah kaht-tay-DRAH-lay?

the church la chiesa (lah KYEH-sah)
the synagogue la sinagoga (lah see-nah-GAW-gah)
the monastery il monastero (eel moh-nahs-TEH-roh)
the university l'università (loo-nee-vayr-see-TAH)
the royal palace il palazzo reale (eel pah-LAH-tsoh ray-AH-lay)
the opera house l'opera (LAW-pay-rah)
the museum il museo (eel moo-SEH-oh)
the picture gallery la pinacoteca (lah pee-nah-koh-TEH-kah)
the gallery la galleria (lah gahl-lay-REE-ah)
the monument il monumento (eel moh-noo-MAYN-toh)
the harbor il porto (eel PAWR-toh)
the river il fiume (eel FYOO-may)
the fountain la fontana (lah fohn-TAH-nah)
the garden il giardino (eel jahr-DEE-noh)
the park il parco (eel PAHR-koh)
the square la piazza (lah PYAH-tsah)
the bridge il ponte (eel POHN-tay)
the tower la torre (lah TOHR-ray)
the castle il castello (eel kahs-TEHL-loh)
the cemetery il cimitero (eel chee-mee-TEH-roh)

71

the gulf il golfo (eel GOHL-foh)
the main street il corso (eel KOHR-soh)
the basilica la basilica (lah bah-SEE-lee-kah)
the view la veduta (lah vay-DOO-tah)
the city wall le mura di cinta (lay MOO-rah dee CHEEN-tah)
the portico il portico (eel PAWR-tee-koh)
the lighthouse il faro (eel FAH-roh)
the cliff la rupe (lah ROO-pay)
the rock lo scoglio (loh SKAW-lyoh)
the boardwalk il lungomare (eel loon-goh-MAH-ray)
the canal il canale (eel kah-NAH-lay)
the island l'isola (LEE-soh-lah)
the fresco l'affresco (lahf-FRAYS-koh)
the mosaic il mosaico (eel moh-SAH-ee-koh)
the dome la cupola (lah KOO-poh-lah)
the temple il tempio (eel TAYM-pyoh)
the catacomb la catacomba (lah kah-tah-KOHM-bah)

What time is (High) Mass (service in English)?
A che ora è la Messa (cantata) (la funzione in inglese)?
AH KAY OH-rah EH lah MAYS-sah (kahn-TAH-tah) (lah foon-TSYOH-nay een een-GLAY-say)?

I want a priest (minister, rabbi).
Vorrei un prete (un ministro protestante, un rabbino).
Vohr-REH-ee oon PREH-tay (oon mee-NEES-troh proh-tays-TAHN-tay, oon rahb-BEE-noh).

Do you need a guide?
Ha bisogno d'una guida?
AH bee-SAW-nyoh DOO-nah GWEE-dah?

Is the museum open now (on Sunday)?
Il museo è aperto ora (di domenica)?
Eel moo-SEH-oh EH ah-PEHR-toh OH-rah (dee doh-MAY-nee-kah)?

It is closed on Mondays.
È chiuso di lunedì.
EH KYOO-soh dee loo-nay-DEE.

72

Is admission free?
L'entrata è gratuita?
Layn-TRAH-tah EH grah-TOO-ee-tah?

Admission is fifty lire.
L'entrata costa cinquanta lire.
Layn-TRAH-tah KAWS-tah cheen-KWAHN-tah LEE-ray.

Is it permitted to take photographs?
È permesso fare fotografie?
EH payr-MAYS-soh FAH-ray foh-toh-grah-FEE-ay?

It is forbidden; but we sell souvenir post cards.
È proibito; però qui si vendono cartoline ricordo.
EH proh-ee-BEE-toh; pay-RAW KWEE see VAYN-doh-noh kahr-toh-
   LEE-nay ree-KAWR-doh.

Where is the entrance (exit)?
Dov'è l'entrata (l'uscita)?
Doh-VEH layn-TRAH-tah (loo-SHEE-tah)?

Where are the theaters?
Dove sono i teatri?
DOH-vay SOH-noh ee tay-AH-tree?

**At what time does the performance start? At what time is it
   over?**
A che ora ha inizio la rappresentazione? A che ora finisce?
Ah KAY OH-rah ah ee-NEE-tsyoh lah rahp-pray-sayn-tah-TSYOH-
   nay? Ah KAY OH-rah fee-NEE-shay?

May I see your ticket?
Mi fa vedere il biglietto?
Mee FAH vay-DAY-ray eel bee-LYAYT-toh?

Are you the usher?
Lei è la maschera?
LEH-ee EH lah MAHS-kay-rah?

What opera (play, comedy, film) is playing tonight?
Che opera (dramma, commedia, pellicola) si esibisce stasera?
KAY AW-pay-rah (DRAHM-mah, kohm-MEH-dyah, payl-LEE-koh-
   lah) see ay-see-BEE-shay stah-SAY-rah?

Please give me an orchestra seat (a balcony seat, a box) for
   Wednesday afternoon.
Mi favorisce una poltrona in platea (un posto in galleria, un
   palco) per mercoledì dopopranzo?
Mee fah-voh-REE-shay oo-nah pohl-TROH-nah een plah-TEH-ah
   (oon PAWS-toh een gahl-lay-REE-ah, oon PAHL-koh) payr
   mayr-koh-lay-DEE doh-poh-PRAHN-dzoh?

Here is a seat in the third row.
Eccole una poltrona in terza fila.
EHK-koh-lay oo-nah pohl-TROH-nah een TEHR-tsah FEE-lah.

There is a concert tonight at eight thirty.
Stasera alle otto e mezza c'è un concerto.
Stah-SAY-rah AHL-lay AWT-oh ay MEH-dzah CHEH oon kohn-
   CHEHR-toh.

   festival una festa (oo-nah FEHS-tah)
   soccer game una partita di calcio (oo-nah pahr-TEE-tah
      dee KAHL-choh)
   ball un ballo (oon BAHL-loh)
   performance una rappresentazione (oo-nah rahp-pray-
      sayn-tah-TSYOH-nay)
   motion picture cinema (CHEE-nay-mah)
   vaudeville varietà (vah-ryay-TAH)

Do we have to stand in line?
C'è da far la coda?
CHEH dah FAHR lah KOH-dah?

Where is the check room?
Dov'è il guardaroba?
Doh-VEH eel gwahr-dah-RAW-bah?

May I buy a program?
Si può comprare un programma?
See PWAW kohm-PRAH-ray oon proh-GRAHM-mah?

Where can we go to dance?
Dove potremmo andare a ballare?
DOH-vay poh-TRAYM-moh ahn-DAH-ray ah bahl-LAH-ray?

I should like to visit a night club (cabaret).
Vorrei visitare un night club (tabarin).
Vohr-REH-ee vee-see-TAH-ray oon night club (tah-bah-REHN).

A table for two, please.
Tavola per due, per favore.
TAH-voh-lah payr DOO-ay, payr fah-VOH-ray.

The cover charge is 200 lire.
Il coperto è di duecento lire.
Eel koh-PEHR-toh EH dee doo-ay-CHEHN-toh LEE-ray.

Are evening clothes necessary?
È d'obbligo l'abito da sera?
EH DAWB-blee-goh LAH-bee-toh dah SAY-rah?

The menu (wine list, check), please.
Mi favorisca la lista delle vivande (la lista dei vini, il conto).
Mee fah-voh-REES-kah lah LEES-tah DAYL-lay vee-VAHN-day
(lah LEES-tah day VEE-nee, eel KOHN-toh).

Ask the orchestra to play "Santa Lucia Lontana."
Chieda all'orchestra di suonare "Santa Lucia Lontana."
KYEH-dah ahl-lohr-KEHS-trah dee swoh-NAH-ray SAHN-tah loo-
CHEE-ah lohn-TAH-nah.

16. MEDICAL, DENTAL, DRUGSTORE, PARTS OF BODY

Where can I find a good doctor (surgeon, dentist, oculist)?
Dove potrei trovare un buon medico (chirurgo, dentista, oculista)?
DOH-vay poh-TREH-ee troh-VAH-ray oon BWAWN MEH-dee-koh
(kee-ROOR-goh, dayn-TEES-tah, oh-koo-LEES-tah)?

I am ill (indisposed).
Sono malato (indisposto).
SOH-noh mah-LAH-toh (een-dees-PAWS-toh).

Here is Dr. Bianchi's address.
Ecco l'indirizzo del dottor Bianchi.
EHK-koh leen-dee-REE-tsoh dayl doht-TOHR BYAHN-kee.

I have a cold.
Ho un raffreddore.
AW oon rahf-frayd-DOH-ray.

> **cough** tosse (TOHS-say)
> **headache** mal di capo (MAHL dee KAH-poh)
> **stomach ache** mal di stomaco (MAHL dee STAW-mah-koh)
> **toothache** mal di denti (MAHL dee DEHN-tee)
> **indigestion** indigestione (een-dee-jay-STYOH-nay)
> **abscess** un ascesso (oon ah-SHEHS-soh)
> **sore throat** mal di gola (MAHL dee GOH-lah)

My arm hurts.
Mi fa male il braccio.
Mee FAH MAH-lay eel BRAH-choh.

> **leg** la gamba (lah GAHM-bah)
> **back** la schiena (lah SKYEH-nah)
> **neck** il collo (eel KAWL-loh)
> **ear** l'orecchio (loh-RAYK-kyoh)
> **eye** l'occhio (LAWK-kyoh)
> **nose** il naso (eel NAH-soh)
> **face** la faccia (lah FAH-chah)
> **lip** il labbro (eel LAHB-broh)
> **cheek** la guancia (lah GWAHN-chah)
> **head** la testa (lah TEHS-tah)

Where does it hurt?
Dove Le fa male?
DOH-vay lay FAH MAH-lay?

Here.
Qui.
KWEE.

I think I may have dysentery (seasickness).
Credo di soffrire di dissenteria (mal di mare).
KRAY-doh dee sohf-FREE-ray dee dees-sayn-tay-REE-ah (MAHL dee MAH-ray).

I have a pain in my chest.
Ho un dolore al petto.
AW oon doh-LOH-ray ahl PEHT-toh.

in my hand alla mano (AHL-lah MAH-noh)
in my foot al piede (ahl PYEH-day)
in my shoulder alla spalla (AHL-lah SPAHL-lah)
in my ankle alla caviglia (AHL-lah kah-VEE-lyah)
in my finger al dito (ahl DEE-toh)
in my thumb al pollice (ahl PAWL-lee-chay)
in my knee al ginocchio (ahl jee-NAWK-kyoh)
in my elbow al gomito (ahl GOH-mee-toh)
in the back of my head alla nuca (AHL-lah NOO-kah)
in my eyelid alla palpebra (AHL-lah PAHL-pay-brah)
in my right nostril alla narice destra (AHL-lah nah-REE-
  chay DEHS-trah)
in my tongue alla lingua (AHL-lah LEEN-gwah)
in my thigh alla coscia (AHL-lah KAW-shah)
in my calf al polpaccio (ahl pohl-PAH-choh)
in my abdomen all'addome (ahl-lahd-DAW-may)
in my groin all'inguine (ahl-LEEN-gwee-nay)

Are you nauseated?
Soffre di nausea?
SAWF-fray dee NOW-say-ah?

**No, but my forehead is hot, I am dizzy, and I have chills (a
  fever).**
No, ma mi scotta la fronte, ho vertigini, e ho brividi (febbre).
NAW, mah mee SKAWT-tah lah FROHN-tay, AW vayr-TEE-jee-nee,
  ay AW BREE-vee-dee (FEHB-bray).

Please call a doctor (nurse).
Per favore, mi chiami un medico (un'infermiera).
Payr fah-VOH-ray, mee KYAH-mee oon MEH-dee-koh (oo-neen-
  fayr-MYEH-rah).

Take your clothes off (to the waist).
Si spogli (fino alla cintola).
See SPAW-lyee (FEE-noh AHL-lah CHEEN-toh-lah).

Lie down.
Si corichi.
See KOH-ree-kee.

77

Open your mouth.
Apra la bocca.
AH-prah lah BOHK-kah.

Let me see your tongue.
Mi faccia veder la lingua.
Mee FAH-chah vay-DAYR lah LEEN-gwah.

Breathe hard.
Respiri forte.
Ray-SPEE-ree FAWR-tay.

The skin is broken.
È rotta la pelle.
EH ROHT-tah lah PEHL-lay.

Have you lost much blood?
Ha perduto molto sangue?
AH payr-DOO-toh MOHL-toh SAHN-gway?

The bone (rib) is broken.
È rotto l'osso (È rotta la costola).
EH ROHT-toh LAWS-soh (EH ROHT-tah lah KAWS-toh-lah).

The wrist is sprained.
È slogato il polso.
EH sloh-GAH-toh eel POHL-soh.

I broke a finger (toe) nail.
Mi son rotto un'unghia del dito (del dito del piede).
Mee SOHN ROHT-toh oo-NOON-gyah dayl DEE-toh (dayl DEE-toh dayl PYEH-day).

You have a fracture (bruise, cut, burn).
Lei ha una frattura (una contusione, un taglio, una scottatura).
LEH-ee AH OO-nah fraht-TOO-rah (oo-nah kohn-too-SYOH-nay, oon TAH-lyoh, oo-nah skoht-tah-TOO-rah).

How long have you had this pain?
Da quanto tempo soffre di questo dolore?
Dah KWAHN-toh TEHM-poh SAWF-fray dee KWAYS-toh doh-LOH-ray?

78

Since yesterday.
Da ieri.
Dah YEH-ree.

Let me examine your right (left) eye.
Mi lasci esaminare il Suo occhio destro (sinistro).
Mee LAH-shee ay-sah-mee-NAH-ray eel soo-oh AWK-kyoh DEHS-troh (see-NEES-troh).

Your heart and lungs are O.K.
Il cuore e i polmoni sono in regola.
Eel KWAW-ray ay ee pohl-MOH-nee SOH-noh een RAY-goh-lah.

You smoke too much.
Lei fuma troppo.
LEH-ee FOO-mah TRAWP-poh.

Stop smoking for a few days.
Tralasci di fumare per qualche giorno.
Trah-LAH-shee dee foo-MAH-ray payr KWAHL-kay JOHR-noh.

I cannot move my elbow (knee).
Non posso muovere il gomito (il ginocchio).
Nohn PAWS-soh MWAW-vay-ray eel GOH-mee-toh (eel jee-NAWK-kyoh).

Your hand is swollen.
La Sua mano è gonfia.
Lah soo-ah MAH-noh EH GOHN-fyah.

Do I have to go to the hospital?
Devo andare all'ospedale?
DAY-voh ahn-DAH-ray ahl-lohs-pay-DAH-lay?

No, but you must stay in bed.
No, ma deve rimanere a letto.
NAW, mah DAY-vay ree-mah-NAY-ray ah LEHT-toh.

Do you feel better today?
Si sente meglio oggi?
See SEHN-tay MEH-lyoh AW-jee?

No, I feel worse.
No, mi sento peggio.
NAW, mee SEHN-toh PEH-joh.

How often must I take this medicine?
Quante volte al giorno devo prendere questa medicina?
KWAHN-tay VAWL-tay ahl JOHR-noh DAY-voh PREHN-day-ray
KWAYS-tah may-dee-CHEE-nah?

One spoonful (teaspoonful) every two hours.
Una cucchiaiata (un cucchiaino) ogni due ore.
oo-nah kook-kyah-YAH-tah (oon kook-kyah-EE-noh) OH-nyee
DOO-ay OH-ray.

Take one pill with a glass of water three times a day before (after) meals.
Prenda una pillola con un bicchier d'acqua tre volte al giorno prima dei (dopo i) pasti.
PREHN-dah oo-nah PEEL-loh-lah kohn oon beek-KYEHR DAHK-kwah tray VAWL-tay ahl JOHR-noh PREE-mah day (DOH-poh ee) PAHS-tee.

Where is a drugstore?
Dove si trova una farmacia?
DOH-vay see TRAW-vah oo-nah fahr-mah-CHEE-ah?

Have you a prescription?
Ha una ricetta?
AH oo-nah ree-CHEHT-tah?

I want aspirin.
Vorrei dell'aspirina.
Vohr-REH-ee dayl-lahs-pee-REE-nah.

   iodine della tintura di iodio (DAYL-lah teen-TOO-rah dee
   YAW-dyoh)
   bicarbonate del bicarbonato (dayl bee-kahr-boh-NAH-
   toh)
   quinine tablets delle pastiglie di chinino (DAYL-lay pahs-
   TEE-lyay dee kee-NEE-noh)
   cough syrup dello sciroppo per la tosse (DAYL-loh shee-
   RAWP-poh payr lah TOHS-say)
   boric acid acido borico (AH-chee-doh BAW-ree-koh)
   castor oil olio di ricino (AW-lyoh dee REE-chee-noh)
   a mild laxative un purgante leggero (oon poor-GAHN-tay
   lay-JEH-roh)

gauze della garza (DAYL-lah GAHR-dzah)

talcum powder della polvere di talco (DAYL-lah POHL-vay-ray dee TAHL-koh)

a bandage una fasciatura (oo-nah fah-shah-TOO-rah)

adhesive tape del nastro adesivo (dayl NAHS-troh ah-day-SEE-voh)

absorbent cotton del cotone idrofilo (dayl koh-TOH-nay ee-DRAW-fee-loh)

a thermometer un termometro (oon tayr-MAW-may-troh)

a disinfectant un disinfettante (oon dee-seen-fayt-TAHN-tay)

a corn remedy un rimedio per i calli (oon ree-MEH-dyoh payr ee KAHL-lee)

When can I travel again?
Quando potrò rimettermi in viaggio?
KWAHN-doh poh-TRAW ree-MAYT-tayr-mee een VYA-joh?

Not before Monday.
Non prima di lunedì.
Nohn PREE-mah dee loo-nay-DEE.

My gums hurt me.
Mi fanno male le gengive.
Mee FAHN-noh MAH-lay lay jayn-JEE-vay.

This tooth should be extracted.
Questo dente andrebbe estratto.
KWAYS-toh DEHN-tay ahn-DRAYB-bay ays-TRAHT-toh.

The X-ray shows an abscess at the root.
La radioscopia rivela un ascesso alla radice.
Lah rah-dyoh-skoh-PEE-ah ree-VEH-lah oon ah-SHEHS-soh AHL-lah rah-DEE-chay.

I have lost a filling.
Ho perduto un'otturazione.
AW payr-DOO-toh oo-noht-too-rah-TSYOH-nay.

Can you fill it?
Me lo può otturare?
May loh PWAW oht-too-RAH-ray?

81

Can you repair this denture?
Può accomodare questa dentiera?
PWAW ahk-koh-moh-DAH-ray KWAYS-tah dayn-TYEH-rah?

How long will it take?
Quanto tempo ci vorrà?
KWAHN-toh TEHM-poh chee vohr-RAH?

I have broken my glasses. Can you put in a new lens?
Mi si son rotti gli occhiali. Può metterci una lente nuova?
Mee see SOHN ROHT-tee lyee ohk-KYAH-lee. PWAW MAYT-tayr-chee OO-nah LEHN-tay NWAW-vah?

Note: You may have to measure your temperature with a Centigrade thermometer. To change from Centigrade to Fahrenheit (the normal American thermometer), multiply by 9/5, then add 32. If you have taken your temperature with an American Fahrenheit thermometer, and wish to report it to an Italian doctor who is accustomed to Centigrade, subtract 32 from your Fahrenheit reading, then multiply the remainder by 5/9.

17. LAUNDRY, DRY CLEANING, BARBER SHOP, BEAUTY SALON

Please send the laundress (valet) up to my room.
Per favore, faccia salire alla mia stanza la lavandaia (il cameriere).
Payr fah-VOH-ray, FAH-chah sah-LEE-ray AHL-lah MEE-ah STAHN-tsah lah lah-vahn-DAH-yah (eel kah-may-RYEH-ray).

I have something to be washed (pressed, brushed, mended, dry-cleaned).
Ho della roba da far lavare (stirare, spazzolare, rammendare, pulire a secco).
AW DAYL-lah RAW-bah dah FAHR lah-VAH-ray (stee-RAH-ray, spah-tsoh-LAH-ray, rahm-mayn-DAH-ray, poo-LEE-ray ah SAYK-koh).

(Don't) starch the shirt collars.
(Non) inamidi i colli delle camicie.
(Nohn) ee-NAH-mee-dee ee KAWL-lee DAYL-lay kah-MEE-chay.

(Don't) use bleach.
(Non) usi candeggio.
(Nohn) oo-see kahn-DAY-joh.

When will you bring it back?
Quando me la riporta?
KWAHN-doh may lah ree-PAWR-tah?

I need it tonight.
Ne ho bisogno stasera.
Nay aw bee-SAW-nyoh stah-SAY-rah.

I'm leaving tomorrow.
Parto domani.
PAHR-toh doh-MAH-nee.

Here is the list:
Ecco la lista:
EHK-koh lah LEES-tah:

five shirts cinque camicie (CHEEN-kway kah-MEE-chay)
six handkerchiefs sei fazzoletti (SEH-ee fah-tsoh-LAYT-tee)
four pairs of socks quattro paia di calzini (KWAHT-troh PAH-yah dee kahl-TSEE-nee)
six shorts sei paia di mutande (SEH-ee PAH-yah dee moo-TAHN-day)
one blouse una camicetta (OO-nah kah-mee-CHAYT-tah)
two pajamas due pigiama (DOO-ay pee-JAH-mah)
one suit un vestito (oon vays-TEE-toh)
one overcoat un soprabito (oon soh-PRAH-bee-toh)
two neckties due cravatte (DOO-ay krah-VAHT-tay)
two cotton dresses due vestiti di cotone (DOO-ay vays-TEE-tee dee koh-TOH-nay)
one sweater un maglione (oon mah-LYOH-nay)
one pair of gloves un paio di guanti (oon PAH-yoh dee GWAHN-tee)

The belt (a button) is missing.
Manca la cintura (un bottone).
MAHN-kah lah cheen-TOO-rah (oon boht-TOH-nay).

Try to find it.
Cerchi di ritrovarlo.
CHAYR-kee dee ree-troh-VAHR-loh.

This suit is not properly cleaned.
Questo vestito non è pulito bene.
KWAYS-toh vays-TEE-toh nohn EH poo-LEE-toh BEH-nay.

Can't you get it cleaner?
Non lo può far venire più pulito?
Nohn loh PWAW FAHR vay-NEE-ray PYOO poo-LEE-toh?

Where is there a good barbershop (a good beauty parlor)?
Dove si trova una buona barberia (un buon salone di bellezza)?
DOH-vay see TRAW-vah oo-nah BWAW-nah bahr-bay-REE-ah
(oon BWAWN sah-LOH-nay dee bayl-LAY-tsah)?

Please give me a haircut (shave).
Mi vuol tagliare i capelli (far la barba)?
Mee VWAWL tah-LYAH-ray ee kah-PAYL-lee (FAHR lah BAHR-
bah)?

Don't cut it too short.
Non me li tagli troppo corti.
Nohn may lee TAH-lyee TRAWP-poh KOHR-tee.

Where do you part your hair?
Dove fa la divisa?
DOH-vay FAH lah dee-VEE-sah?

In the middle.
Nel mezzo.
Nayl MEH-dzoh.

More to the side.
Più di lato.
PYOO dee LAH-toh.

(Don't) use clippers.
(Non) usi la macchinetta.
(Nohn) oo-see lah mahk-kee-NAYT-tah.

Use the scissors.
Usi le forbici.
oo-see lay FAWR-bee-chee.

Here's a mirror.
Ecco uno specchio.
EHK-koh oo-noh SPEHK-kyoh.

Cut off more at the side (back).
Tagli un pò più di lato (di dietro).
TAH-lyee oon PAW PYOO dee LAH-toh (dee DYEH-troh).

Don't cut at the top.
Non tagli in cima alla testa.
Nohn TAH-lyee een CHEE-mah AHL-lah TEHS-tah.

Do you want hair tonic?
Desidera lozione per i capelli?
Day-SEE-day-rah loh-TSYOH-nay payr ee kah-PAYL-lee?

  pomade   pomata   (poh-MAH-tah)
  a scalp massage   un massaggio al cuoio capelluto   (oon
    mahs-SAH-joh ahl KWAW-yoh kah-payl-LOO-toh)
  a facial   un massaggio facciale   (oon mahs-SAH-joh fah-
    CHAH-lay)
  a shampoo   uno shampoo   (oo-noh shahm-POO)
  a permanent   un'ondulazione permanente   (oo-nohn-doo-
    lah-TSYOH-nay payr-mah-NEHN-tay)
  a finger wave   una messa in piega   (oo-nah MAYS-sah een
    PYEH-gah)

Is there a manicurist (chiropodist) here?
C'è qui una manicure (pedicure)?
CHEH KWEE oo-nah mah-nee-KYOOR (pay-dee-KYOOR)?

I want my hair washed, set and tinted.
Vorrei farmi lavare, mettere in piega e tingere i capelli.
Vohr-REH-ee FAHR-mee lah-VAH-ray, MAYT-tay-ray een PYEH-
gah ay TEEN-jay-ray ee kah-PAYL-lee.

The water is too hot (cold).
L'acqua è troppo calda (fredda).
LAHK-kwah EH TRAWP-poh KAHL-dah (FRAYD-dah).

Where can I get my shoes repaired?
Dove potrei farmi riparare le scarpe?
DOH-vay poh-TREH-ee FAHR-mee ree-pah-RAH-ray lay SKAHR-pay?

I want leather half-soles and rubber heels.
Vorrei farci mettere delle mezze suole di cuoio e tacchi di gomma.
Vohr-REH-ee FAHR-chee MAYT-tay-ray DAYL-lay MEH-dzay SWAW-lay dee KWAW-yoh ay TAHK-kee dee GOHM-mah.

18. FOOD, RESTAURANT, DISHES

I'm hungry and thirsty.
Ho fame e ho sete.
AW FAH-may ay AW SAY-tay.

What would you like to eat and drink?
Cosa vorrebbe da mangiare e da bere?
KAW-sah vohr-RAYB-bay dah mahn-JAH-ray ay dah BAY-ray?

Where can we find a good restaurant?
Dove possiamo trovare un buon ristorante?
DOH-vay pohs-SYAH-moh troh-VAH-ray oon BWAWN rees-toh-RAHN-tay?

Here's one.
Eccone uno.
EHK-koh-nay OO-noh.

How many?
In quanti sono?
Een KWAHN-tee SOH-noh?

A table for two, please, near the window.
Ci favorisca un tavolo per due, vicino alla finestra.
Chee fah-voh-REES-kah oon TAH-voh-loh payr DOO-ay, vee-CHEE-noh AHL-lah fee-NEHS-trah.

This table is reserved.
Questo tavolo è prenotato.
KWAYS-toh TAH-voh-loh EH pray-noh-TAH-toh.

This way, sir.
Di qua, signore.
Dee KWAH, see-NYOH-ray.

Do you want a cocktail?
Desidera un cocktail?
Day-SEE-day-rah oon kohk-TAYL?

Give us an apéritif (vermouth, whisky, gin, a liqueur).
Ci dia an aperitivo (un vermuth, un whiskey, un gin, un cordiale).
Chee DEE-ah oon ah-pay-ree-TEE-voh (oon VEHR-moot, oon WEESK-kee, oon JEEN, oon kohr-DYAH-lay).

Have you a table-d'hôte dinner (lunch, breakfast)?
C'è un pranzo (una colazione, una prima colazione) a prezzo fisso?
CHEH oon PRAHN-dzoh (oo-nah koh-lah-TSYOH-nay, oo-nah PREE-mah koh-lah-TSYOH-nay) ah PREH-tsoh FEES-soh?

Yes, sir; for 300 lire we give you appetizers, soup or spaghetti, a meat course with vegetables, salad and dessert.
Sissignore; per trecento lire Le diamo antipasto, minestra o pasta asciutta, un piatto di carne con contorno, insalata e dolce.
See-see-NYOH-ray; payr tray-CHEHN-toh LEE-ray lay DYAH-moh ahn-tee-PAHS-toh, mee-NEHS-trah oh PAHS-tah ah-SHOOT-tah, oon PYAHT-toh dee KAHR-nay kohn kohn-TOHR-noh, een-sah-LAH-tah ay DOHL-chay.

Let me have the menu (wine list).
Mi favorisca la lista delle vivande (dei vini).
Mee fah-voh-REES-kah lah LEES-tah DAYL-lay vee-VAHN-day (day VEE-nee).

What is today's special?
Qual'è il piatto del giorno?
Kwah-LEH eel PYAHT-toh dayl JOHR-noh?

What dish (wine) do you recommend?
Che piatto (vino) ci consiglia?
KAY PYAHT-toh (VEE-noh) chee kohn-SEE-lyah?

We should like to dine (have lunch) Italian style.
Vorremmo pranzare (far colazione) all'italiana.
Vohr-RAYM-moh prahn-DZAH-ray (FAHR koh-lah-TSYOH-nay)
ahl-lee-tah-LYAH-nah.

Bring us two orders of fish.
Ci porti due porzioni di pesce.
Chee PAWR-tee DOO-ay pohr-TSYOH-nee dee PAY-shay.

  oysters ostriche (AWS-tree-kay)
  soup minestra (mee-NEHS-trah)
  roast beef rosbif (rohs-BEEF)
  lamb agnello (ah-NYEHL-loh)
  duck anatra (AH-nah-trah)
  goose oca (AW-kah)
  chicken pollo (POHL-loh)
  ham prosciutto (proh-SHOOT-toh)
  eggs uova (WAW-vah)
  omelet frittata (freet-TAH-tah)
  liver fegato (FAY-gah-toh)
  sausage salsiccia (sahl-SEE-chah)
  shrimps gamberi (GAHM-bay-ree)
  lobster aragosta (ah-rah-GOHS-tah)
  kidneys rognoni (roh-NYOH-nee)
  tripe trippa (TREEP-pah)
  macaroni maccheroni (mahk-kay-ROH-nee)
  squid polipi (PAW-lee-pee)
  crabs granchi (GRAHN-kee)

What does the hors d'oeuvre consist of?
Di che consistono gli antipasti?
Dee KAY kohn-SEES-toh-noh lyee ahn-tee-PAHS-tee?

Cold cuts, salami, sardines, hard-boiled eggs, cucumbers, peppers.
Carni fredde, salame, sardine, uova sode, cetrioli, peperoni.
KAHR-nee FRAYD-day, sah-LAH-may, sahr-DEE-nay, WAW-vah
SAW-day, chay-tree-AW-lee, pay-pay-ROH-nee.

88

Do you prefer baked, broiled, boiled or stewed meat?
Preferisce la carne al forno, ai ferri, bollita, o in umido?
Pray-fay-REE-shay lah KAHR-nay ahl FOHR-noh, AH-ee FEHR-ree,
    bohl-LEE-tah, oh een OO-mee-doh?

I like the steak well done (medium, rare).
Mi piace la bistecca ben cotta (a mezza cottura, al sangue).
Mee PYAH-chay lah bees-TEHK-kah BEHN KAWT-tah (ah MEH-
    dzah koht-TOO-rah, ahl SAHN-gway).

Bring me another portion.
Me ne porti un'altra porzione.
May nay PAWR-tee oo-NAHL-trah pohr-TSYOH-nay.

What kind of chops do you have?
Che cotolette ci sono?
KAY koh-toh-LAYT-tay chee SOH-noh?

Lamb, pork and veal.
D'agnello, di maiale e di vitello.
Dah-NYEHL-loh, dee mah-YAH-lay ay dee vee-TEHL-loh.

Do you want fried, boiled or mashed potatoes?
Desidera patate fritte, bollite, o mascè?
Day-SEE-day-rah pah-TAH-tay FREET-tay, bohl-LEE-tay, oh mah-
    SHAY?

I'd rather have rice.
Preferirei del riso.
Pray-fay-ree-REH-ee dayl REE-soh.

What vegetables do you have?
Che verdure ci sono?
KAY vayr-DOO-ray chee SOH-noh?

We have beans.
Abbiamo fagioli.
Ahb-BYAH-moh fah-JAW-lee.

> **string beans** fagiolini (fah-joh-LEE-nee)
> **artichokes** carciofi (kahr-CHAW-fee)
> **peas** piselli (pee-SEHL-lee)
> **spinach** spinaci (spee-NAH-chee)

89

mushrooms funghi (FOON-ghee)
cabbage cavolo (KAH-voh-loh)
cauliflower cavolfiore (kah-vohl-FYOH-ray)
beets barbabietole (bahr-bah-BYEH-toh-lay)
asparagus asparagi (ahs-PAH-rah-jee)
carrots carote (kah-RAW-tay)

Shall I make you a salad with lettuce?
Vuole che Le faccia un'insalata di lattuga?
vwAW-lay kay lay FAH-chah oo-neen-sah-LAH-tah dee laht-TOO-gah?

celery sedano (SEH-dah-noh)
tomatoes pomidori (poh-mee-DAW-ree)
olives olive (oh-LEE-vay)
radishes ravanelli (rah-vah-NEHL-lee)
onions cipolle (chee-POHL-lay)

What have you for dessert?
Che c'è per finire?
KAY CHEH payr fee-NEE-ray?

cheese and fruit formaggio e frutta (fohr-MAH-joh ay
  FROOT-tah)
ice cream gelato (jay-LAH-toh)
pastry pasticceria (pahs-tee-chay-REE-ah)
pie pizza (PEE-tsah)
pudding budino (boo-DEE-noh)
cake torta (TOHR-tah)

Please bring me oil and vinegar.
Favorisca portarmi olio e aceto.
Fah-voh-REES-kah pohr-TAHR-mee AW-lyoh ay ah-CHAY-toh.

salt and pepper sale e pepe (SAH-lay ay PAY-pay)
bread and butter pane e burro (PAH-nay ay BOOR-roh)
some rolls dei panini (day pah-NEE-nee)
sugar and lemon zucchero e limone (TSOOK-kay-roh ay
  lee-MOH-nay)
milk and cream latte e panna (LAHT-tay ay PAHN-nah)
a knife and fork un coltello e una forchetta (oon kohl-
  TEHL-loh ay oo-nah fohr-KAYT-tah)

a spoon un cucchiaio (oon kook-KYAH-yoh)

a teaspoon un cucchiaino (oon kook-kyah-EE-noh)

a water glass un bicchiere da acqua (oon beek-KYEH-ray
dah AHK-kwah)

a wineglass un bicchiere da vino (oon beek-KYEH-ray
dah VEE-noh)

a cup una tazza (OO-nah TAH-tsah)

a saucer un piattino (oon pyaht-TEE-noh)

a napkin un tovagliolo (oon toh-vah-LYAW-loh)

another plate un altro piatto (oon AHL-troh PYAHT-toh)

a soup dish una scodella (OO-nah skoh-DEHL-lah)

ice water acqua ghiacciata (AHK-kwah gyah-CHAH-tah)

ice del ghiaccio (dayl GYAH-choh)

What would you like to drink?
Cosa vuole da bere?
KAW-sah vwAW-lay dah BAY-ray?

**Let me have a glass (bottle) of beer (red wine, white wine,
sparkling wine, mineral water).**
Mi favorisca un bicchiere (una bottiglia) di birra (di vino
rosso, di vino bianco, di spumante, di acqua minerale).
Mee fah-voh-REES-kah oon beek-KYEH-ray (OO-nah boht-TEE-
lyah) dee BEER-rah, (dee VEE-noh ROHS-soh, dee VEE-noh
BYAHN-koh, dee spoo-MAHN-tay, dee AHK-kwah mee-nay-RAH-
lay).

Let me have some more sauce.
Mi favorisca un po' più di salsa.
Mee fah-voh-REES-kah oon PAW PYOO dee SAHL-sah.

I should like a cup of tea (black coffee, coffee with milk).
Vorrei una tazza di tè (di caffè nero [espresso], di caffè e latte).
Vohr-REH-ee OO-nah TAH-tsah dee TEH (dee kahf-FEH NAY-roh
[ays-PREHS-soh], dee kahf-FEH ay LAHT-tay).

What fruit have you?
Che frutta c'è?
KAY FROOT-tah CHEH?

91

We have cherries.
Abbiamo ciliege.
Ahb-BYAH-moh chee-LYAY-jay.

grapes uva (OO-vah)
strawberries fragole (FRAH-goh-lay)
peaches pesche (PEHS-kay)
plums susine (SOO-SEE-nay)
apples mele (MAY-lay)
melon melone (may-LOH-nay)
watermelon cocomero (koh-KOH-may-roh)
pears pere (PAY-ray)
apricots albicocche (ahl-bee-KAWK-kay)
oranges aranci (ah-RAHN-chee)
tangerines mandarini (mahn-dah-REE-nee)
bananas banane (bah-NAH-nay)
figs fichi (FEE-kee)
pineapple ananasso (ah-nah-NAHS-soh)
walnuts noci (NOH-chee)
almonds mandorle (MAHN-dohr-lay)
hazelnuts nocciole (noh-CHAW-lay)
chestnuts castagne (kahs-TAH-nyay)

For breakfast I like orange juice.
Per la prima colazione vorrei succo d'arancio.
Payr lah PREE-mah koh-lah-TSYO-nay vohr-REH-ee SOOK-koh
dah-RAHN-choh.

grapefruit pompelmo (pohm-PAYL-moh)
prunes prugne cotte (PROO-nyay KAWT-tay)
bacon and eggs uova con pancetta (WAW-vah kohn pahn-
CHAYT-tah)
ham and eggs uova al prosciutto (WAW-vah ahl proh-
SHOOT-toh)
toast pan tostato (PAHN tohs-TAH-toh)
jam marmellata (mahr-mayl-LAH-tah)

Bring the coffee now.
Porti subito il caffè.
PAWR-tee soo-bee-toh eel kahf-FEH.

At once, sir.
Subito, signore.
soo-bee-toh, see-NYOH-ray.

More coffee (water), please.
Mi favorisca altro caffè (dell'acqua).
Mee fah-voh-REES-kah AHL-troh kahf-FEH (dayl-LAHK-kwah).

This meat is cold (tough, overdone, not cooked enough).
Questa carne è fredda (dura, troppo cotta, non è cotta abbastanza).
KWAYS-tah KAHR-nay EH FRAYD-dah (DOO-rah, TRAWP-poh KAWT-ah, nohn EH KAWT-tah ahb-bahs-TAHN-tsah).

Please call the waiter (waitress, headwaiter).
Favorisca chiamarmi il cameriere (la cameriera, il capo cameriere).
Fah-voh-REES-kah kyah-MAHR-mee eel kah-may-RYEH-ray (lah kah-may-RYEH-rah, eel KAH-poh kah-may-RYEH-ray).

This fork (tablecloth) is not clean.
Questa forchetta (tovaglia) non è pulita.
KWAYS-tah fohr-KAYT-tah (toh-VAH-lyah) nohn EH poo-LEE-tah.

Please change it.
Me la cambi.
May lah KAHM-bee.

I did not order this.
Questo non l'ho ordinato.
KWAYS-toh nohn LAW ohr-dee-NAH-toh.

May I change my order?
Potrei cambiare la mia ordinazione?
Poh-TREH-ee kahm-BYAH-ray lah MEE-ah ohr-dee-nah-TSYOH-nay?

The check, please.
Mi favorisca il conto.
Mee fah-voh-REES-kah eel KOHN-toh.

Is the service included?
Il servizio è compreso?
Eel sayr-VEE-tsyoh EH kohm-PRAY-soh?

This is for you.
Questo è per Lei.
KWAYS-toh EH payr LEH-ee.

Keep the change.
Tenga pure il resto.
TEHN-gah POO-ray eel REHS-toh.

There is a mistake in the bill.
C'è un errore nel conto.
CHEH oon ayr-ROH-ray nayl KOHN-toh.

Please pay the cashier.
Favorisca pagare alla cassa.
Fah-voh-REES-kah pah-GAH-ray AHL-lah KAHS-sah.

A PARTIAL LIST OF NATIVE ITALIAN DISHES AND COOKING TERMS

This list, which is not at all meant to be complete, is designed to familiarize the tourist with a few of the most common items to be encountered on menus in Italian restaurants. (For a more complete list of such terms, with full cooking directions, the reader is referred to *The Talisman Italian Cook-Book*, published by Crown Publishers, New York.)

ITALIAN DISHES AND RESTAURANT ITEMS

abbacchio al forno (ahb-BAHK-kyo AHL FOHR-noh) oven-baked young spring lamb, a specialty of Rome.

affumicato (ahf-foo-mee-KAH-toh) smoked.

agnolotti (ah-nyoh-LAWT-tee) dough dumplings stuffed with meat, similar to ravioli; a specialty of Turin.

ai ferri (AH-ee FEHR-ree) grilled, broiled; *bistecca ai ferri* broiled steak.

al burro e parmigiano (AHL BOOR-roh ay pahr-mee-JAH-noh) with butter and grated parmesan cheese, no sauce. Spaghetti is often eaten this way.

al dente (AHL DEHN-tay) chewy; not overcooked, in connection with spaghetti.

al doppio burro (AHL DOHP-pyoh BOOR-roh) with double

94

butter. *Fettuccine al doppio burro* (boiled noodles with plenty of butter and cream) are the specialty of a famous Roman restaurant.

al forno (AHL FOHR-noh)   in the oven; baked.

alla cacciatora (AHL-lah kah-chah-TOH-rah)   hunter style. There are two "hunter styles," one with tomato, the other with rosemary and vinegar.

alla casalinga (AHL-lah kah-sah-LEEN-gah)   home style.

alla marinara (AHL-lah mah-ree-NAH-rah)   seaman style. Sauce *alla marinara* for spaghetti contains no meat, but only tomatoes, oil, garlic and herbs.

alla matriciana (AHL-lah mah-tree-CHAH-nah)   Roman country style. *Spaghetti alla matriciana* has a sauce the chief components of which are tomatoes and chopped onions and bacon.

anguilla (ahn-GWEEL-lah)   eel.

animelle (ah-nee-MEHL-lay)   sweetbreads.

antipasto (ahn-tee-PAHS-toh)   hors d'oeuvre or appetizers.

arista (AH-rees-tah)   pork loin, oven-baked.

arreganato (ahr-ray-gah-NAH-toh)   fixed with oregano or origan.

arrosto (ahr-RAWS-toh)   roast.

baccalà (bahk-kah-LAH)   dried and salted codfish.

Bel Paese (BEHL pah-AY-say)   a semi-soft, mild cheese.

bistecca (bees-TEHK-kah)   steak. *Bistecca alla fiorentina* is a thick steak grilled over a charcoal fire.

brodetto (braw-DAYT-toh)   a meat or fish dish in which the main ingredient has a thick gravy based on flour, eggs and lemon juice.

brodo (BRAW-doh)   broth. *Pastina in brodo* is broth containing tiny macaroni.

cacciucco (kah-CHOOK-koh)   a fish soup, specialty of Leghorn, made with fish and shellfish, strongly spiced.

caciocavallo (kah-choh-kah-VAHL-loh)   a pungent cheese, similar to provolone.

caffè e latte (kahf-FEH ay LAHT-tay)   Italian breakfast coffee, half hot milk, half black-roast Italian coffee.

caffè espresso (see *espresso*).

cannelloni (kahn-nehl-LOH-nee) large round macaroni, stuffed with meat and other ingredients.

cannoli (kahn-NAW-lee) a Sicilian pastry.

capocollo (kah-poh-KAWL-loh) a pork product made from the pig's neck.

caponatina (kah-poh-nah-TEE-nah) a combination of pickled vegetables.

cappelletti (kahp-payl-LAYT-tee) dough stuffed with meat or other ingredients and served in soup.

capperi (kahp-PAY-ree) capers.

capretto al forno (kah-PRAYT-toh AHL FOHR-noh) oven-baked kid, a Roman specialty.

carciofini (kahr-choh-FEE-nee) small artichoke hearts, pickled and in oil.

cassata (kahs-SAH-tah) an ice cream similar to spumone.

cassata siciliana (kahs-SAH-tah see-chee-LYAH-nah) a Sicilian cake.

ceci (CHAY-chee) chick peas, or garbanzo beans.

cervello (chayr-VEHL-loh) calf's or pork brains, usually scrambled.

coppa (KAWP-pah) see *capocollo*.

coratella (koh-rah-TEHL-lah) lamb's lung, heart and liver, fried together with onion, peppers and other vegetables.

coscio d'agnello (KAW-shoh dah-NYEHL-loh) leg of lamb.

coteghino (koh-tay-GHEE-noh) a variety of salami to be eaten cooked with lentils or beans.

cotoletta (koh-toh-LAYT-tah) cutlet or chop. *Cotoletta alla milanese* is a thin, breaded veal chop.

cozza (KAW-tsah) mussel.

crostino (krohs-TEE-noh) bread spread with something and then toasted.

espresso (ays-PREHS-soh) *caffè espresso* is an Italian black-roast coffee made in a special machine which forces steam under pressure through the coffee powder.

fagiano (fah-JAH-noh) pheasant.

fave (FAH-vay) horse beans.

fegato (FAY-gah-toh) liver. *Fegatini* are sliced pork livers enclosed in a net of lamb's intestine lining with a bay leaf and fried or broiled.

fettuccine (fayt-too-CHEE-nay) long, thin, flat macaroni, usually fixed *al sugo* (with meat sauce), or *al burro e parmigiano* (butter and Parmesan).

filetto (fee-LAYT-toh) filet. *Filetto di manzo* is a thin steak.

finocchio (fee-NAWK-kyoh) fennel, used either as a vegetable or a fruit.

fondua (fohn-DOO-ah) a Piedmontese casserole dish of cheese and truffles.

Fra Diavolo (FRAH DYAH-voh-loh) a tomato-and-herb sauce frequently used on seafood, particularly lobster (*aragosta Fra Diavolo*).

fritto misto (FREET-toh MEES-toh) fried mixture, made with vegetables, brains, cheese, etc. *Fritto misto di pesce* is made with fish.

frittata (freet-TAH-tah) omelet.

gelato (jay-LAH-toh) ice cream.

gnocchi (NYAWK-kee) dumplings made of wheat or potato flour. Sometimes served with sauce (*gnocchi al sugo*), sometimes plain (*gnocchi alla romana*).

Gorgonzola (gohr-gohn-TSAW-lah) a cheese similar to Blue or Roquefort.

granita (grah-NEE-tah) sherbet or ice.

grappa (GRAHP-pah) a distilled alcoholic beverage produced from wine lees.

grissini (grees-SEE-nee) bread sticks.

in bianco (EEN BYAHN-koh) *pesce in bianco* is boiled fish served with oil, lemon juice and parsley.

in carrozza (EEN kahr-RAW-tsah) *mozzarella in carrozza* is a soft cheese, thinly sliced and baked between slices of bread.

lasagne (lah-SAH-nyay) giant noodles over an inch wide, usually boiled, then baked in the oven in layers, with sausage or meat balls, mozzarella and ricotta, and tomato sauce.

maccheroni (mahk-kay-ROH-nee) macaroni; applied in Italy only to the larger varieties.

manicotti (mah-nee-KAWT-tee) large hollow tubes of delicate dough, stuffed with ricotta and baked with sauce in a baking dish.

melanzane (may-lahn-TSAH-nay) eggplant. *Melanzane alla*

parmigiana is sliced eggplant baked with mozzarella and tomato sauce.

melone e prosciutto (may-LOH-nay ay proh-SHOOT-toh) melon and sliced Italian ham, used as hors d'oeuvre.

minestra (mee-NEHS-trah) soup. *Minestrone* (mee-nehs-TROH-nay) is a thick vegetable soup, usually with macaroni.

mortadella (mohr-tah-DEHL-lah) a large variety of salami, a specialty of Bologna.

mozzarella (moh-tsah-REHL-lah) a fresh cheese.

ossobuco (AWS-soh-BOO-koh) a knuckle of veal, stewed with rice in a saffron sauce, a specialty of Milan.

pane (PAH-nay) bread. The word appears in the names of many varieties of cake and pastry, such as *pan di Spagna*, *panettone* and *panforte*.

parmigiana (pahr-mee-JAH-nah) Parma style, which generally means with mozzarella and tomato sauce. *Parmigiano* is Parmesan cheese.

pasta (*asciutta*) (PAHS-tah (ah-SHOOT-tah)) generic name for all macaroni products. Combined with chick peas or beans to produce *pasta e ceci, pasta e fagioli*. The word *pasta* may also indicate a single piece of pastry.

pasticceria (pahs-tee-cheh-REE-ah) pastry.

pecorino (pay-koh-REE-noh) Roman cheese, made with sheep's milk, used for grating.

pesto (PAYS-toh) a green sauce for macaroni and potatoes, made with oil, garlic, herbs, anchovies, etc. A specialty of Genoa.

pizza (PEE-tsah) This is a generic name for any bakery product that is round and flat, like a pie. *Pizza di polenta* is a corn-meal pie. The Neapolitan pizza consists of a layer of dough with tomato sauce and mozzarella or anchovies, oven-baked.

polenta (poh-LEHN-tah) corn-meal mush, favored in the northeastern regions of Italy. Venice fancies a dish called *polenta cogli osei*, "corn-meal mush with little birds."

polipi (PAW-lee-pee) or *polpi* (POHL-pee) squid or cuttle-fish (also called *calamari* or *calamaretti*, according to size). They may be fried in oil, or served with a tomato sauce.

pollo (POHL-loh) chicken. Among favored chicken dishes
are *pollo alla cacciatora, pollo arrosto* or *ai ferri, fegatini di
pollo* (chicken livers).

polpetta (pohl-PAYT-tah) meat ball (the plural is *polpette*).
Spaghetti with meat balls is not too often consumed on
Italian soil. The *polpette* are more frequently fried in deep
fat or oil.

polpettone (pohl-payt-TOH-nay) meat loaf.

prosciutto (proh-SHOOT-toh) Italian-style ham; dried, salted,
spiced and pressed, but not sugar-cured or smoked. Prosciutto is at its best thinly sliced and eaten raw, with melon,
figs, or other antipasto meats, like salami, coppa and mortadella. It may also be fried with eggs in butter (*uova al
prosciutto*).

provola (PRAW-voh-lah) a soft, fresh cheese, similar to
mozzarella. It may also be salted or smoked (*provola affumi-
cata*).

provolone (proh-voh-LOH-nay) a hard, yellow cheese,
creamy and piquant.

ravioli (rah-VYAW-lee) chopped meat, spinach, cheese, etc.,
enclosed in a shell of dough, boiled, and eaten with a sauce.
Sweet ravioli are stuffed with ricotta, fried, and sprinkled
with sugar and cinnamon.

riccio (REE-choh) a shellfish, the sea urchin.

ricotta (ree-KAWT-tah) a fresh cheese obtained by the re-
peated skimming of boiled milk. Though rich in appearance
and delightful to the taste, it has very low caloric content.

rigatoni (ree-gah-TOH-nee) a large, grooved form of macaroni.

ripieno (ree-PYEH-noh) stuffing; used as an adjective, it
means "stuffed."

risotto (ree-SAWT-toh) boiled or steamed rice, with a sauce
and Parmesan cheese. The north of Italy, particularly Milan,
favors risotto with a sauce of saffron, chicken livers and
mushrooms or truffles. Other regions often use a tomato
sauce.

rognone (roh-NYOH-nay) kidney.

rotoli (RAW-toh-lee) meat that is thinly sliced and rolled up, with a stuffing of prosciutto and other ingredients, then baked or stewed in tomato sauce.

salame (sah-LAH-may) a salted and spiced pork product, eaten raw and sliced.

salsa (SAHL-sah) sauce. *Salsa piccante* is a piquant sauce.

salsiccia (sahl-SEE-chah) sausage. Subdivided into *salsiccia fresca* or *luganica* (fresh sausage) and *salsiccia forte,* in which pepper and spices predominate. Is often roasted (*salsiccia arrostita*) and eaten as a main course.

saltimbocca (sahl-teem-BOHK-kah) little rolls of thinly sliced veal stuffed with prosciutto, cheese and other ingredients. A Roman specialty.

scaloppine (skah-lohp-PEE-nay) thin slices of meat, usually veal, stewed or fried.

scampo (SKAHM-poh) a variety of shrimp or prawn found in the Adriatic. A specialty of Venice.

scarola (skah-RAW-lah) escarole. Generally eaten as a salad, but also in a soup (*scarola in brodo*).

scungilli (skoon-JEEL-lee) a conch, whose meat is extracted from the shell, boiled, and served with a hot sauce. A specialty of Naples.

sfogliatella (sfoh-lyah-TEHL-lah) a delicate pastry of the *Apfelstrudel* variety.

sogliola (SAW-lyoh-lah) sole or flounder. *Filetto di sogliola* is filet of sole.

spaghetti (spah-GAYT-tee) the thinner varieties of macaroni products, without a hole. *Spaghettini* is the extra-thin variety. There are infinite ways of serving spaghetti (*al burro e parmigiano,* with butter and cheese; *all'olio ed aglio,* with oil and garlic; *alle acciughe,* with anchovies; *al ragù,* with meat sauce; *al pomodoro* or *alla marinara,* with tomato sauce; *alle vongole,* with clams; the last has two varieties, *salsa bianca,* without tomato, and *salsa rossa,* with tomato).

spezzato or *spezzatino* (spay-TSAH-toh, spay-tsah-TEE-noh) stew. Made with veal (*di vitello*), lamb (*di agnello*), beef (*di manzo*), chicken (*di pollo*), etc.

spiedini (*di mozzarella*) (spyay-DEE-nee dee moh-tsah-REHL-lah) thin slices of bread, spread with mozzarella and anchovies and baked.

100

spumone (spoo-MOH-NAY) an Italian ice cream, combining several flavors.

stracchino (strahk-KEE-noh) a soft cheese of Milan.

stracciatella (strah-chah-TEHL-lah) a Roman egg-drop soup.

tonno (TOHN-noh) tuna fish.

torrone (tohr-ROH-nay) a nougat made with honey, almonds, nuts, etc.

tortellini (tohr-tayl-LEE-nee) a small shell of dough, filled with meat and other ingredients and served in broth. A specialty of Bologna.

triglia (TREE-lyah) the Mediterranean red mullet. *Triglie alla livornese* (Leghorn style) are fixed with a tomato sauce.

trippa (TREEP-pah) tripe. *Trippa al sugo* is a specialty of Rome.

uccelletti (oo-chehl-LAYT-tee) little strips of rolled and stuffed veal.

vitello (vee-TEHL-loh) veal.

vongole (VOHN-goh-lay) Mediterranean clams, quite small in size.

zabaione (dzah-bah-YOH-nay) Eggnog made of egg yolks, sugar and sweet wine, served hot or cold, in solid or liquid form, as a dessert.

zuppa (TSOOP-pah) thick soup. *Zuppa inglese* is not a soup, but a soft gooey Roman cake.

19. NUMERALS

Cardinal.

one uno, una (oo-noh, oo-nah)
two due (DOO-ay)
three tre (TRAY)
four quattro (KWAHT-troh)
five cinque (CHEEN-kway)
six sei (SEH-ee)
seven sette (SEHT-tay)
eight otto (AWT-toh)
nine nove (NAW-vay)
ten dieci (DYEH-chee)
eleven undici (OON-dee-chee)
twelve dodici (DOH-dee-chee)

101

thirteen tredici (TRAY-dee-chee)
fourteen quattordici (kwaht-TAWR-dee-chee)
fifteen quindici (KWEEN-dee-chee)
sixteen sedici (SAY-dee-chee)
seventeen diciassette (dee-chahs-SEHT-tay)
eighteen diciotto (dee-CHAWT-toh)
nineteen diciannove (dee-chahn-NAW-vay)
twenty venti (VAYN-tee)
twenty-one ventuno (vayn-TOO-noh)
twenty-two ventidue (vayn-tee-DOO-ay)
twenty-three ventitre (vayn-tee-TRAY)
twenty-eight ventotto (vayn-TAWT-toh)
thirty trenta (TREHN-tah)
forty quaranta (kwah-RAHN-tah)
fifty cinquanta (cheen-KWAHN-tah)
sixty sessanta (says-SAHN-tah)
seventy settanta (sayt-TAHN-tah)
eighty ottanta (oht-TAHN-tah)
ninety novanta (noh-VAHN-tah)
one hundred cento (CHEHN-toh)
two hundred duecento (doo-ay-CHEHN-toh)
five hundred cinquecento (cheen-kway-CHEHN-toh)
nine hundred novecento (noh-vay-CHEHN-toh)
one thousand mille (MEEL-lay)
five thousand cinquemila (cheen-kway-MEE-lah)
ten thousand diecimila (dyeh-chee-MEE-lah)
one million un milione (oon mee-LYOH-nay)
one billion un miliardo (oon mee-LYAHR-doh)

Ordinal.
first primo (PREE-moh)
second secondo (say-KOHN-doh)
third terzo (TEHR-tsoh)
fourth quarto (KWAHR-toh)
fifth quinto (KWEEN-toh)
sixth sesto (SEHS-toh)
seventh settimo (SEHT-tee-moh)
eighth ottavo (oht-TAH-voh)
ninth nono (NAW-noh)

102

tenth decimo (DEH-chee-moh)
eleventh undicesimo (oon-dee-CHAY-see-moh)
twelfth dodicesimo (doh-dee-CHAY-see-moh)
twentieth ventesimo (vayn-TAY-see-moh)
thirty-eighth trentottesimo (trayn-toht-TAY-see-moh)

Others.
one third un terzo (oon TEHR-tsoh)
two sevenths due settimi (DOO-ay SEHT-tee-mee)

half of the book
la metà del libro
lah may-TAH dayl LEE-broh

half a page
mezza pagina
MEH-dzah PAH-jee-nah

once
una volta
oo-nah VAWL-tah

twice
due volte
DOO-ay VAWL-tay

three times
tre volte
TRAY VAWL-tay

a hundred times
cento volte
CHEHN-toh VAWL-tay

the first time
la prima volta
lah PREE-mah VAWL-tah

the last time
l'ultima volta
LOOL-tee-mah VAWL-tah

this time
questa volta
KWAYS-tah VAWL-tah

103

a dozen eggs
una dozzina di uova
oo-nah doh-DZEE-nah dee WAW-vah

a pair of shoes
un paio di scarpe
oon PAH-yoh dee SKAHR-pay

20. TIME OF DAY, WEEK, MONTH, SEASONS, WEATHER, AGE

When were you here last?
Quando si è trovato qui l'ultima volta?
KWAHN-doh see EH troh-VAH-toh KWEE LOOL-tee-mah VAWL-tah?

I was here in the month of January (February, March, April, May, June).
Mi son trovato qui nel mese di gennaio (febbraio, marzo, aprile, maggio, giugno).
Mee SOHN troh-VAH-toh KWEE nayl MAY-say dee jayn-NAH-yoh (fayb-BRAH-yoh, MAHR-tsoh, ah-PREE-lay, MAH-joh, JOO-nyoh).

What is today's date?
Quanti ne abbiamo oggi?
KWAHN-tee nay ah-BYAH-moh AW-jee?

Today is the first (second, tenth) of July (August, September, October, November, December).
Oggi è il primo (il due, il dieci) luglio, agosto, settembre, ottobre, novembre, dicembre).
AW-jee EH eel PREE-moh (eel DOO-ay, eel DYEH-chee) LOO-lyoh (ah-GOHS-toh, sayt-TEHM-bray, oht-TOH-bray, noh-VEHM-bray, dee-CHEHM-bray).

The spring is beautiful in Italy.
È bella la primavera in Italia.
EH BEHL-lah lah pree-mah-VEH-rah een ee-TAH-lee-ah.

The summer, fall and winter are lovely, too.
Pure l'estate, l'autunno e l'inverno sono belli.
POO-ray lays-TAH-tay, low-TOON-noh ay leen-VEHR-noh SOH-noh BEHL-lee.

104

What day of the week is today?
Che giorno della settimana è oggi?
KAY JOHR-noh DAYL-lah sayt-tee-MAH-nah EH AW-jee?

Today is Sunday.
Oggi è domenica.
AW-jee EH doh-MAY-nee-kah.

Monday   lunedì   (loo-nay-DEE)
Tuesday   martedì   (mahr-tay-DEE)
Wednesday   mercoledì   (mayr-koh-lay-DEE)
Thursday   giovedì   (joh-vay-DEE)
Friday   venerdì   (vay-nayr-DEE)
Saturday   sabato   (SAH-bah-toh)

What time is it?
Che or'è or Che ore sono?
KAY oh-REH, KAY OH-ray SOH-noh?

It is noon.
È mezzogiorno.
EH meh-dzoh-JOHR-noh

midnight   mezzanotte   (meh-dzah-NAWT-tay)
one a.m.   l'una del mattino   (LOO-nah dayl maht-TEE-noh)
one p.m.   l'una pomeridiana   (LOO-nah poh-may-ree-
DYAH-nah)

It is two.
Sono le due.
SOH-noh lay DOO-ay.

two-thirty   le due e mezza   (lay DOO-ay ay MEH-dzah)
a quarter to three   le tre meno un quarto   (lay TRAY MAY-
noh oon KWAHR-toh)
ten minutes to three   le tre meno dieci   (lay TRAY MAY-noh
DYEH-chee)
ten minutes past three   le tre e dieci   (lay TRAY ay DYEH-
chee)
a quarter past three   le tre e un quarto   (lay TRAY ay oon
KWAHR-toh)

105

At what time do you wish to start?
A che ora vuol partire?
Ah KAY OH-rah VWAWL pahr-TEE-ray?

At (about) five in the morning (afternoon).
Alle (verso le) cinque del mattino (del pomeriggio).
AHL-lay (VEHR-soh lay) CHEEN-kway dayl maht-TEE-noh (dayl poh-may-REE-joh).

At eight in the evening.
Alle otto di sera.
AHL-lay AWT-toh dee SAY-rah.

At eleven at night.
Alle undici di notte.
AHL-lay OON-dee-chee dee NAWT-tay.

At noon.
A mezzogiorno.
Ah meh-dzoh-JOHR-noh.

At midnight.
A mezzanotte.
Ah meh-dzah-NAWT-tay.

At six at the latest.
Non più tardi delle sei.
Nohn PYOO TAHR-dee DAYL-lay SEH-ee.

It's early (late).
È presto (tardi).
EH PREHS-toh (TAHR-dee).

We must start on time.
Dobbiamo partire a tempo.
Dohb-BYAH-moh pahr-TEE-ray ah TEHM-poh.

We must not be late.
Non bisogna essere in ritardo.
Nohn bee-SAW-nyah EHS-say-ray een ree-TAHR-doh.

I saw him yesterday.
L'ho visto ieri.
LAW VEES-toh YEH-ree.

last night iersera (yehr-SAY-rah)
day before yesterday l'altro ieri (LAHL-troh YEH-ree)
last year l'anno scorso (LAHN-noh SKOHR-soh)
last month il mese scorso (eel MAY-say SKOHR-soh)
last week la settimana scorsa (lah sayt-tee-MAH-nah
  SKOHR-sah)
three days ago tre giorni fa (TRAY JOHR-nee FAH)
in the year 1954 nell'anno mille novecento cinquantaquattro (nayl-LAHN-noh MEEL-lay naw-vay-CHEHN-toh
  cheen-kwahn-tah-KWAHT-troh)

I shall see him today.
Lo vedrò oggi.
Loh vay-DRAW AW-jee.

tonight stasera (stah-SAY-rah)
this morning stamane (stah-MAH-nay)
this afternoon oggi dopopranzo (AW-jee doh-poh-PRAHN-
  dzoh)
tomorrow domani (doh-MAH-nee)
day after tomorrow dopodomani (daw-poh-doh-MAH-
  nee)
next year l'anno che viene (LAHN-noh kay VYEH-nay)
next month il mese entrante (eel MAY-say ayn-TRAHN-tay)
next week la settimana ventura (lah sayt-tee-MAH-nah
  vayn-TOO-rah)
in a few days tra pochi giorni (trah PAW-kee JOHR-nee)

I see him every day.
Lo vedo tutti i giorni
Loh VAY-doh TOOT-tee ee JOHR-nee.

every week tutte le settimane (TOOT-tay lay sayt-tee-MAH-
  nay)
every month tutti i mesi (TOOT-tee ee MAY-see)

I stayed here all day.
Son rimasto qui tutta la giornata.
Sohn ree-MAHS-toh KWEE TOOT-tah la johr-NAH-tah

107

all morning tutta la mattinata (TOOT-tah lah maht-tee-NAH-tah)

all evening tutta la serata (TOOT-tah lah say-RAH-tah)

all week tutta la settimana (TOOT-tah lah sayt-tee-MAH-nah)

all month tutto il mese (TOOT-toh eel MAY-say)

How is the weather?
Che tempo fa?
KAY TEHM-poh FAH?

It is fine weather.
Fa bel tempo.
FAH BEHL TEHM-poh.

bad weather cattivo tempo (kaht-TEE-voh TEHM-poh)

cold freddo (FRAYD-doh)

warm caldo (KAHL-doh)

sunny sole (SOH-lay)

cloudy nuvolo (NOO-voh-loh)

cool fresco (FRAYS-koh)

foggy nebbia (NAYB-byah)

It is windy.
Tira vento.
TEE-rah VEHN-toh.

It is starting to snow.
Comincia a nevicare.
Koh-MEEN-chah ah nay-vee-KAH-ray.

to rain a piovere (ah PYAW-vay-ray)

to clear up a rischiarare (ah rees-kyah-RAH-ray)

It is raining.
Piove.
PYAW-vay.

It is pouring.
Piove a dirotto.
PYAW-vay ah dee-ROHT-toh.

It is snowing.
Nevica.
NAY-vee-kah.

108

It is hailing.
Grandina.
GRAHN-dee-nah.

It is thundering.
Tuona.
TWAW-nah.

It is lightning.
Lampeggia.
Lahm-PAY-jah.

It is clearing up.
Rischiara.
Rees-KYAH-rah.

The sun (moon) is shining.
Splende il sole (la luna).
SPLEHN-day eel SOH-lay (lah LOO-nah).

The stars are out.
Brillano le stelle.
BREEL-lah-noh lay STAYL-lay.

Do you feel cold?
Sente freddo?
SEHN-tay FRAYD-doh?

I am warm and sleepy.
Ho caldo e ho sonno.
AW KAHL-doh ay AW SAWN-noh.

It's too hot (cold) to go there today.
Fa troppo caldo (freddo) per andarci oggi.
FAH TRAWP-poh KAHL-doh (FRAYD-doh) payr ahn-DAHR-chee
AW-jee.

**I don't like the cold (heat, sun, fog, rain, snow, hail, wind,
cloudy weather).**
Non mi piace il freddo (il caldo, il sole, la nebbia, la pioggia, la
neve, la grandine, il vento, il tempo nuvoloso).
Nohn mee PYAH-chay eel FRAYD-doh (eel KAHL-doh, eel SOH-
lay, lah NAYB-byah, lah PYAW-jah, lah NAY-vay, lah GRAHN-
dee-nay, eel VEHN-toh, eel TEHM-poh noo-voh-LOH-soh).

Note: European weather thermometers usually register in Centigrade. To get a Fahrenheit reading from a Centigrade thermometer, multiply your Centigrade reading by 9/5 and add 32. To change a Fahrenheit reading to Centigrade, subtract 32 and multiply by 5/9.

How old are you?
Quanti anni ha?
KWAHN-tee AHN-nee AH?

I am twenty-five years old.
Ho venticinque anni.
AW vayn-tee-CHEEN-kway AHN-nee.

21. EMERGENCIES AND LANGUAGE DIFFICULTIES

Help!
Soccorso!
Sohk-KOHR-soh!

Fire!
Al fuoco!
Ahl FWAW-koh!

Police!
Polizia!
Poh-lee-TSEE-ah!

Call the police!
Chiami la polizia!
KYAH-mee lah poh-lee-TSEE-ah!

I've been robbed!
Sono stato derubato!
SOH-noh STAH-toh day-roo-BAH-toh!

Where is the police station?
Dov'è la questura?
Doh-VEH lah kways-TOO-rah?

Stop!
Ferma!
FAYR-mah!

Stop that man!
Fermate quell'uomo!
Fayr-MAH-tay KWAYL-LWAW-moh!

Where did he go?
Dov'è andato?
Doh-VEH ahn-DAH-toh?

That way?
Di là?
Dee LAH?

What is he (it) like?
Com'è?
Koh-MEH?

What was he (it) like?
Com'era?
Koh-MEH-rah?

Is this the one?
È questo qui?
EH KWAYS-toh KWEE?

Go away!
Vada via!
VAH-dah VEE-ah!

Get out!
Fuori!
FWAW-ree!

Don't bother me!
Non mi secchi!
Nohn mee SAYK-kee!

Who are you?
Lei chi è?
LEH-ee KEE EH?

I don't know you!
Io non La conosco!
EE-oh nohn lah koh-NOHS-koh!

111

Look!
Guardi!
GWAHR-dee!

Listen!
Ascolti!
Ahs-KOHL-tee!

Will you help (direct) me?
Vuol aiutarmi (darmi delle indicazioni)?
VWAWL ah-yoo-TAHR-mee (DAHR-mee DAYL-lay een-dee-kah-TSYOH-nee)?

Come here!
Venga qua!
VEHN-gah KWAH!

Hurry!
Si sbrighi!
See ZBREE-ghee!

Look out!
Attento!
Aht-TEHN-toh!

One moment!
Un momento!
Oon moh-MAYN-toh!

Come with me!
Venga con me!
VEHN-gah kohn MAY!

I have lost ——
Ho perduto ——
AW payr-DOO-toh ——

I can't find ——
Non posso trovare ——
Nohn PAWS-soh troh-VAH-ray ——

Where did you leave it?
Dove l'ha lasciato?
DOH-vay LAH lah-SHAH-toh?

Where is the lost-and-found desk?
Dov'è l'ufficio oggetti smarriti?
Doh-VEH loof-FEE-choh oh-JEHT-tee zmahr-REE-tee?

What is happening?
Che succede?
KAY soo-CHEH-day?

What's the matter?
Che c'è?
KAY CHEH?

What's the matter with you?
Che ha?
KAY AH?

What do you want?
Che vuole?
KAY VWAW-lay?

Who did it?
Chi l'ha fatto?
KEE lah FAHT-toh?

Don't worry!
Non si preoccupi!
Nohn see pray-AWK-koo-peel

Take it easy!
Calma!
KAHL-mah!

I don't remember.
Non ricordo.
Nohn ree-KAWR-doh.

I forgot.
Ho dimenticato.
AW dee-mayn-tee-KAH-toh.

Can you ——?
Può ——?
PWAW ——?

I can't.
Non posso.
Nohn PAWS-soh.

I've lost my way.
Mi son smarrito.
Mee SOHN zmahr-REE-toh.

I missed my train.
Ho perduto il treno.
AW payr-DOO-toh eel TREH-noh.

Do you know ——?
Sa ——?
SAH ——?

I don't know.
Non so.
Nohn SAW.

Do you understand?
Capisce?
Kah-PEE-shay?

I don't understand.
Non capisco.
Nohn kah-PEES-koh.

I'm in trouble.
Mi trovo in guai.
Mee TRAW-voh een GWAH-ee.

Write it down for me.
Me lo scriva.
May loh SKREE-vah.

Do you speak English?
Parla inglese?
PAHR-lah een-GLAY-say?

A little.
Un po'.
Oon PAW.

114

I don't speak Italian.
Non parlo italiano.
Nohn PAHR-loh ee-tah-LYAH-noh.

Speak more slowly.
Parli più adagio.
PAHR-lee PYOO ah-DAH-joh.

Please repeat.
Ripeta, per favore.
Ree-PEH-tah, payr fah-VOH-ray.

What are you saying?
Che dice?
KAY DEE-chay?

What do you call this in Italian?
Come si chiama questo in italiano?
KOH-may see KYAH-mah KWAYS-toh een ee-tah-LYAH-noh?

How do you say —— in Italian?
Come si dice —— in italiano?
KOH-may see DEE-chay —— een ee-tah-LYAH-noh?

What does that mean?
Cosa vuol dire?
KAW-sah VWAWL DEE-ray?

What do you mean?
Cosa vuol dire?
KAW-sah VWAWL DEE-ray?

What are you talking about?
Di che parla?
Dee KAY PAHR-lah?

I am an American.
Sono americano (americana).
SOH-noh ah-may-ree-KAH-noh (-nah).

Take me to the American consul.
Mi conduca dal console americano.
Mee kohn-DOO-kah dahl KAWN-soh-lay ah-may-ree-KAH-noh.

Where is the lavatory?
Dov'è il gabinetto?
Doh-VEH eel gah-bee-NAYT-toh?

Upstairs and to the right.
In capo alle scale e a destra.
Een KAH-poh AHL-lay SKAH-lay ay ah DEHS-trah.

I have left my coat on the bus (plane, train, boat).
Ho lasciato il soprabito nell'autobus (nell'aeroplano, nel treno, nel piroscafo).
AW lah-SHAH-toh eel soh-PRAH-bee-toh nayl-LOW-toh-boos (nayl-lah-ay-roh-PLAH-noh, nayl TREH-noh, nayl pee-RAW-skah-foh).

How can I get it back?
Come potrò riaverlo?
KOH-may poh-TRAW ree-ah-VAYR-loh?

Please forward it to me in Rome.
Me lo spedisca a Roma.
May loh spay-DEES-kah ah ROH-mah.

I'm in a hurry!
Ho fretta (premura)!
AW FRAYT-tah (pray-MOO-rah)!

Why?
Perchè?
Payr-KAY?

What next?
E poi?
Ay POY?

22. EXCLAMATIONS, COLLOQUIALISMS, SLANG

What a pity!
Che peccato!
KAY payk-KAH-toh!

Too bad!
Peccato!
Payk-KAH-toh!

116

For Heaven's sake!
Per carità!
Payr kah-ree-TAH!

Darn it!
Accidenti!
Ah-chee-DEHN-tee!

Gangway!
Permesso?
Payr-MAYS-soh?

That's fine!
Va benissimo!
VAH bay-NEES-see-moh!

That's enough!
Basta così!
BAHS-tah koh-SEE!

Never mind!
Non importa!
Nohn eem-PAWR-tah!

You don't say so!
Possibile?
Pohs-SEE-bee-lay?

Honest?
Davvero?
Dahv-VAY-roh?

Nonsense!
Fandonie!
Fahn-DAW-nyay!

What a guy!
Che tipo!
KAY TEE-poh!

What nerve!
Che barbaro coraggio!
KAY BAHR-bah-roh koh-RAH-joh!

117

He's a louse (dumbbell, pest)!
È una canaglia (un imbecille, un seccatore)!
EH OO-nah kah-NAH-lyah (oon eem-bay-CHEEL-lay, oon sayk-kah-TOH-ray)!

What an awful dump!
Che postaccio!
KAY pohs-TAH-choh!

That's swell!
Benissimo!
Bay-NEES-see-moh!

Scram!
Mi si levi dai piedi!
Mee see LEH-vee DAH-ee PYEH-dee!

Cut it out!
La finisca!
Lah fee-NEES-kah!

What the devil!
Che diavolo!
KAY DYAH-voh-loh!

Hell!
Diavolo!
DYAH-voh-loh!

Go to the devil!
Vada al diavolo!
VAH-dah ahl DYAH-voh-loh!

And how!
E come!
Ay KOH-may!

You bet I did!
L'ho fatto, e come!
LAW FAHT-toh, ay KOH-may!

Good luck!
In bocca al lupo!
Een BOHK-kah ahl LOO-poh!

118

Ouch!
Ahi!
AH-ee!

23. GREETINGS, ETIQUETTE, SOCIAL AMENITIES

Good morning (afternoon, day).
Buon giorno.
BWAWN JOHR-noh.

Good evening (night).
Buona sera (notte).
BWAW-nah SAY-rah (NAWT-tay).

Good-by.
Arrivederci.
Ahr-ree-vay-DAYR-chee.

Farewell.
Addio.
Ahd-DEE-oh.

See you later (tonight, tomorrow).
A più tardi (a stasera, a domani).
Ah PYOO TAHR-dee (ah stah-SAY-rah, ah doh-MAH-nee).

Hello!
Ciao!
CHAH-oh!

How are you (How do you do)?
Come sta?
KOH-may STAH?

How's everything?
Come va?
KOH-may VAH?

Very well, thank you, and you?
Bene, grazie, e Lei?
BEH-nay, GRAH-tsyay, ay LEH-ee?

I'm much better.
Sto molto meglio.
STAW MOHL-toh MEH-lyoh.

Please.
Per piacere, *or* per favore, *or* favorisca (only if a verb follows).
Payr pyah-CHAY-ray, payr fah-VOH-ray, fah-voh-REES-kah.

Thank you (very much).
Grazie (mille, infinite), tante grazie.
GRAH-tsyay (MEEL-lay, een-fee-NEE-tay), TAHN-tay GRAH-tsyay.

Please come in.
Favorisca.
Fah-voh-REES-kah.

Don't mention it (you're welcome).
Prego, *or* non c'è di che, *or* niente.
PREH-goh, nohn CHEH dee KAY, NYEHN-tay.

Pardon (excuse) me.
Scusi.
SKOO-see.

It doesn't matter.
Non fa niente.
Nohn FAH NYEHN-tay.

I'm sorry.
Mi dispiace.
Mee dees-PYAH-chay.

It's nothing.
Non è niente.
Nohn EH NYEHN-tay.

Don't trouble yourself.
Non si scomodi.
Nohn see SKAW-moh-dee.

Sorry to trouble you.
Scusi il disturbo.
SKOO-see eel dees-TOOR-boh.

I'm glad.
Son contento.
Sohn kohn-TEHN-toh.

120

Is it not so?
Non è vero?
Nohn EH VAY-roh?

Yes.
Sì.
SEE.

No.
No.
NAW.

Perhaps.
Forse, *or* chissà.
FOHR-say, kees-SAH.

Certainly.
Certo, *or* certamente.
CHEHR-toh, chehr-tah-MAYN-tay.

Of course.
Naturalmente, *or* ben inteso.
Nah-too-rahl-MAYN-tay, BEHN een-TAY-soh.

Not at all.
Affatto, *or* nient'affatto.
Ahf-FAHT-toh, nyehn-tahf-FAHT-toh.

I agree.
Son d'accordo.
Sohn dahk-KAWR-doh.

I think so.
Credo di sì.
KRAY-doh dee SEE.

I don't think so.
Credo di no, *or* non credo.
KRAY-doh dee NAW, nohn KRAY-doh.

You're right (wrong).
Ha ragione (torto).
AH rah-JOH-nay (TAWR-toh).

121

It's all right.
Va (*or* sta) bene.
VAH (STAH) BEH-nay.

O.K.
Benissimo.
Bay-NEES-see-moh.

Do you like ——?
Le piace ——?
Lay PYAH-chay ——?

Would you like ——?
Le piacerebbe ——?
Lay pyah-chay-RAYB-bay ——?

Do you want ——?
Desidera (*or* vuole) ——?
Day-SEE-day-rah (VWAW-lay) ——?

Help yourself!
Faccia (*or* prenda) pure.
FAH-chah (PREHN-dah) POO-ray.

To your health!
Salute!
Sah-LOO-tay!

To yours!
Salute!
Sah-LOO-tay!

Congratulations!
Felicitazioni!
Fay-le-chee-tah-TSYOH-nee!

(Best) wishes!
(Tanti) auguri!
(TAHN-tee) ow-GOO-ree!

Merry Christmas!
Buon Natale!
BWAWN nah-TAH-lay!

122

Happy New Year!
Buon Capo d'Anno!
BWAWN KAH-poh DAHN-noh!

Please sit down.
Si accomodi.
See akh-KAW-moh-dee.

Make yourself at home.
Faccia come se fosse in casa Sua.
FAH-chah KOH-may say FOHS-say een KAH-sah SOO-ah.

Give my regards to your family.
Mi saluti tanto i Suoi.
Mee sah-LOO-tee TAHN-toh ee SWOY.

In any case, let me hear from you.
In ogni caso, mi faccia avere Sue notizie.
Een OH-nyee KAH-soh, mee FAH-chah ah-VAY-ray SOO-ay noh-TEE-tsyay.

Here's my card.
Ecco il mio biglietto (da visita).
EHK-koh eel MEE-oh bee-LYAYT-toh (dah VEE-see-tah).

Regards to your wife.
Ossequi alla Sua Signora!
Ohs-SEH-kwee AHL-lah SOO-ah see-NYOH-rah!

May I introduce my friend?
Permette che Le presenti il mio amico (la mia amica)?
Payr-MAYT-tay kay lay pray-SEHN-tee eel MEE-oh ah-MEE-koh (lah MEE-ah ah-MEE-kah)?

    my wife mia moglie (MEE-ah MOH-lyay)
    my husband mio marito (MEE-oh mah-REE-toh)
    my son mio figlio (MEE-oh FEE-lyoh)
    my daughter mia figlia (MEE-ah FEE-lyah)
    my sister mia sorella (MEE-ah soh-REHL-lah)
    my brother mio fratello (MEE-oh frah-TEHL-loh)
    my father mio padre (MEE-oh PAH-dray)
    my mother mia madre (MEE-ah MAH-dray)
    my uncle mio zio (MEE-oh TSEE-oh)

my aunt mia zia (MEE-ah TSEE-ah)

my cousin mio cugino, mia cugina (MEE-oh koo-JEE-noh, MEE-ah koo-JEE-nah)

my son-in-law mio genero (MEE-oh JEH-nay-roh)

my daughter-in-law mia nuora (MEE-ah NWAW-rah)

my father-in-law mio suocero (MEE-oh SWAW-chay-roh)

my mother-in-law mia suocera (MEE-ah SWAW-chay-rah)

my brother-in-aw mio cognato (MEE-oh koh-NYAH-toh)

my sister-in-law mia cognata (MEE-ah koh-NYAH-tah)

my nephew, grandson mio nipote (MEE-oh nee-POH-tay)

my niece, granddaughter mia nipote (MEE-ah nee-POH-tay)

my grandfather mio nonno (MEE-oh NAWN-noh)

my grandmother mia nonna (MEE-ah NAWN-nah)

my boss il mio principale (eel MEE-oh preen-chee-PAH-lay)

my partner il mio socio (eel MEE-oh SAW-choh)

my assistant il mio assistente (eel MEE-oh ahs-sees-TEHN-tay)

my professor il mio professore (eel MEE-oh proh-fays-SOH-ray)

Glad to meet you!
Fortunatissimo! *or* Tanto piacere!
Fohr-too-nah-TEES-see-moh! TAHN-toh pyah-CHAY-ray!

The pleasure is mine!
Il piacere è mio!
Eel pyah-CHAY-ray EH MEE-oh!

As you wish.
Come vuole.
KOH-may vwAW-lay.

Gladly.
Volentieri.
Voh-layn-TYEH-ree.

As quickly as possible.
Al più presto (possibile).
Ahl PYOO PREHS-toh (pohs-SEE-bee-lay).

How long have you been waiting?
Da quanto tempo aspetta?
Dah KWAHN-toh TEHM-poh ahs-PET-tah?

Sorry to keep you waiting.
Mi dispiace di averla fatta aspettare.
Mee dees-PYAH-chay dee ah-VAYR-lah FAHT-tah ahs-payt-TAH-ray.

You are very kind.
Lei è molto gentile.
LEH-ee EH MOHL-toh jayn-TEE-lay.

I am most grateful.
Le son molto riconoscente.
Lay SOHN MOHL-toh ree-koh-noh-SHEHN-tay.

A pleasant journey!
Buon viaggio!
BWAWN VYAH-joh!

A pleasant stay!
Buona permanenza!
BWAW-nah payr-mah-NEHN-tsah!

24. DIRECTIONS AND SIGNS

Where are you (we) going?
Dove va (andiamo)?
DOH-vay VAH (ahn-DYAH-moh)?

Where is?
Dov'è?
Doh-VEH?

Where are?
Dove sono?
DOH-vay SOH-noh?

Here is, here are.
Ecco.
EHK-koh.

Which way?
Da che parte?
Dah KAY PAHR-tay?

125

To the right (left).
A destra (sinistra).
Ah DEHS-trah (see-NEES-trah).

Straight ahead.
Dritto.
DREET-toh.

This way.
Di qua.
Dee KWAH.

That way.
Di là.
Dee LAH.

I'm looking for ——
Cerco ——
CHAYR-koh ——

Can you tell me ——?
Può dirmi ——?
PWAW DEER-mee ——?

Please show me ——
Vuol indicarmi ——?
VWAWL een-dee-KAHR-mee ——?

It is forbidden.
È vietato *or* proibito.
EH vyay-TAH-toh (proy-BEE-toh).

No smoking (spitting, admittance)
Vietato fumare (sputare, l'ingresso)
Vyay-TAH-toh foo-MAH-ray (spoo-TAH-ray, leen-GREHS-soh)

No parking (standing)
Divieto di sosta
Dee-VYEH-toh dee SAWS-tah

Notice!
Avviso!
Ahv-VEE-soh!

126

Danger!
Pericolo!
Pay-REE-koh-loh!

Keep right (left)
Tenere la destra (sinistra)
Tay-NAY-ray lah DEHS-trah (see-NEES-trah)

Entrance
Entrata
Ayn-TRAH-tah

Exit
Uscita
Oo-SHEE-tah

Danger of death!
Pericolo di morte!
Pay-REE-koh-loh dee MAWR-tay!

Do not touch!
Non toccare!
Nohn tohk-KAH-ray!

High tension wires!
Fili ad alta tensione!
FEE-lee ahd AHL-tah tayn-SYOH-nay!

Cross roads
Incrocio (stradale)
Een-KROH-choh (strah-DAH-lay)

Grade crossing
Passaggio a livello
Pahs-SAH-joh ah lee-VEHL-loh

Watch out for trains!
Attenti ai treni!
Aht-TEHN-tee AH-ee TREH-nee!

Detour
Deviazione
Day-vyah-TSYOH-nay

127

Caution
Attenzione
Aht-tayn-TSYOH-nay

Road closed
Strada interrotta
STRAH-dah een-tayr-ROHT-tah

Narrow bridge *or* **passage**
Strettoia
Strayt-TOH-yah

Dangerous curve
Voltata pericolosa
Vohl-TAH-tah pay-ree-koh-LOH-sah

Steep grade
Pendenza
Payn-DEHN-tsah

Halt *or* **Stop** *or* **Full Stop**
Ferma *or* Stop
FAYR-mah, STAWP

Road repairs
Lavori in corso
Lah-VOH-ree een KOHR-soh

Slow
Rallentare
Rahl-layn-TAH-ray

School
Scuola
SKWAW-lah

One way
Senso unico
SEHN-soh OO-nee-koh

No thoroughfare
Divieto di transito (*or* passaggio)
Dee-VYEH-toh dee TRAHN-see-toh (pahs-SAH-joh)

128

Wrong way, *or* **Do not enter**
Senso proibito
SEHN-soh proy-BEE-toh

No trespassing
Vietato l'ingresso
Vyay-TAH-toh leen-GREHS-soh

Speed limit fifty kilometers an hour
Velocità massima cinquanta chilometri all'ora
Vay-loh-chee-TAH MAHS-see-mah cheen-KWAHN-tah kee-LAW-may-tree ahl-LOH-rah

No right (left) turn
Vietato girare a destra (sinistra)
Vyay-TAH-toh jee-RAH-ray ah DEHS-trah (see-NEES-trah)

Pedestrians
Pedoni
Pay-DOH-nee

Do not lean out of windows
Vietato sporgersi dai finestrini
Vyay-TAH-toh SPOHR-jayr-see DAH-ee fee-nays-TREE-nee

Regular (signal) stop
Fermata obbligatoria (facoltativa)
Fayr-MAH-tah ohb-blee-gah-TAW-ryah (fah-kohl-tah-TEE-vah)

Full bus or streetcar (no more passengers)
Completo
Kohm-PLEH-toh

Push
Spingere
SPEEN-jay-ray

Knock
Bussare
Boos-SAH-ray

Ring the bell
Suonare il campanello
Swoh-NAH-ray eel kahm-pah-NEHL-loh

Wet paint
Verniciato di fresco
Vayr-nee-CHAH-toh dee FRAYS-koh

Keep off the grass
Vietato passeggiare sui prati
Vyay-TAH-toh pahs-say-JAH-ray SOO-ee PRAH-tee

Quiet
Silenzio
See-LEHN-tsyoh

Closed Sundays
Chiuso la domenica
KYOO-soh lah doh-MAY-nee-kah

Cashier
Cassa
KAHS-sah

Ladies
Signore
See-NYOH-ray

Gentlemen
Signori
See-NYOH-ree

Free
Libero
LEE-bay-roh

Occupied
Occupato
Ohk-koo-PAH-toh

Water not drinkable
Acqua non potabile
AHK-kwah nohn poh-TAH-bee-lay

Do not cross the tracks
Vietato attraversare i binari
Vyay-TAH-toh aht-trah-vayr-SAH-ray ee bee-NAH-ree

Poison!
Veleno!
Vay-LAY-noh!

Tourist Information Office
Ufficio Informazioni Turistiche
Oof-FEE-choh een-fohr-mah-TSYOH-nee too-REES-tee-kay

Youth Hostel
Ostello della Gioventù
Ohs-TEHL-loh DAYL-lah joh-vayn-TOO

Closed for repairs
Chiuso per riparazioni
KYOO-soh payr ree-pah-rah-TSYOH-nee

Closed (theaters).
Riposo.
Ree-PAW-soh

Smokers
Fumatori
Foo-mah-TOH-ree

Very slow
Veicoli a passo d'uomo
Vay-EE-koh-lee ah PAHS-soh DWAW-moh

For rent
Affittasi
Ahf-FEET-tah-see

III GRAMMATICAL OUTLINE

ITALIAN

SPEAKERS AND LOCATION

(All population figures are approximate)

Europe—Italy (50,000,000); Switzerland (southern section: about 300,000); also spoken in Corsica and in extreme south-eastern section of France, up to, but not including, Nice; widely spoken and understood, as a secondary and cultural language, along the eastern Adriatic coast (Yugoslavia, Albania, Greece), in Malta, and in the Dodecanese Islands.

Africa—former colonial language of Libya (1,000,000); of Eritrea, Italian Somaliland, and, to a more limited extent, of Ethiopia (total native populations about 12,000,000); widely spoken and understood, as a secondary and cultural language, in Tunisia, Egypt, and, generally, along the European, African and Asiatic Mediterranean coast.

Western Hemisphere—spoken by large Italian immigrant groups in United States, Argentina, Brazil and Chile, amounting, with their descendants, to a total of perhaps 10,000,000.

ALPHABET AND SOUNDS

a, b, c, d, e, f, g, h, i, l, m, n, o, p, q, r, s, t, u, v, z. (The symbol j is very occasionally used with the value of y, and is generally replaced by i; the symbols k, w, x, y occur only in foreign words.)

Vowel sounds: Italian vowels have, whether stressed or unstressed, equal length.

a: = f*a*ther (p*a*dre, donn*a*)

e: = m*e*t (f*e*rro, b*e*ne); or = initial part of *a* in Eng. g*a*te (fr*e*ddo, ben*e*)[1]

i: = mach*i*ne (b*i*rra)

132

o: = d*aw*n (but with *aw* cut short: f*o*rte, d*o*nna); or = initial part of *o* in Eng. g*o* (m*o*ndo)[1]

u: = f*oo*d (l*u*na)

Consonant sounds: b, d, f, l, m, n, p, q, s, t, v, approximately as in English; but Italian *t* and *d* are pronounced with the tip of the tongue touching the back of the teeth, not the upper gums, as in English. The tongue is curled downward, not upward. This downward curl of the tongue is generally characteristic of Italian speech, while the upward curl is characteristic of English.

c: before a, o, u or consonant, and ch before e, i = *c*at (*c*aro, *c*redo, *ch*i)

c: before e, i = *ch*urch (in the groups cia, cie, cio, ciu, the i is almost silent: *c*iascuno, pronuonced chas-KOO-noh).

g: before a, o, u or consonant, and gh before e, i = *g*o (*g*usto, la*g*rima, lar*gh*i).

g: before e, i = *g*in (in the groups gia, gie, gio, giu, the i is almost silent: *g*ià, pronounced JAH).

gn: = o*ni*on (a*gn*ello, pronounced ah-NYEHL-loh).

gl: = mi*lli*on (me*gl*io, pronounced MEH-lyoh).

h: is completely silent (*h*anno, pronounced AHN-noh); but note its uses in the ch and gh combinations above.

r: is trilled as in British ve*r*y; rr is trilled over a longer period.

sc: before e, i = *s*ure (in the groups scia, scio, sciu, the i is almost silent: *sc*iacallo, pronounced shah-KAHL-loh). Before a, o, u or consonant, sc = Eng. *sc*one.

z: = dz or ts (me*zz*o, pronounced MEH-dzoh; pe*zz*o, pronounced PEH-tsoh). Learn by observation; the ts pronunciation generally prevails in groups of zi followed by a vowel (giusti*zi*a, pronounced joos-TEE-tsyah).

Double consonants are not merely more strongly uttered than single consonants; they are also pronounced over a longer

[1] The closed pronunciation (initial part of g*a*te and g*o*) is always used for e and o, respectively, when unstressed. Either the open (m*e*t, d*aw*n) or the closed pronunciation may appear when the vowel is stressed. Learn by observation, and from transcriptions in phrases and English-Italian vocabulary.

period of time (in the case of f, l, m, n, r, s, v, it is the period of utterance that is prolonged; in the case of b, c, d, g, p, t, what is prolonged is the silent pause between the preceding vowel and the release of the consonant sound). Take the case of *fato* (fate, destiny) and *fatto* (done, made). In pronouncing *fato*, you pass immediately from the *a* to the *t*; in pronouncing *fatto*, you pause for a fraction of a second after the *a*, then release your breath for the *t*. This pause causes the *t* to come out more vigorously when it is finally released.

The English sounds of *y* and *w* appear in Italian, but they are represented in writing by *i* and *u*, respectively. An unstressed *i* before or after another vowel normally has the sound of *y*, and an unstressed *u* before or after another vowel has the sound of *w*: *buoi*, (oxen) is pronounced BWOY.

English sounds not appearing in Italian: all vowel sounds save the ones described above; h; plea*s*ure; *th*in; *th*is; American r.

Italian sounds not appearing in English: closed sounds of e and o; Italian r; all double consonants.

CAPITALIZATION, SYLLABIFICATION, ACCENTUATION

Do not capitalize *io* ("I"); capitalize *Lei, Ella, Loro,* when they mean "you" (polite), *Suo* and *Loro* when they mean "your" (polite). Do not capitalize adjectives of nationality (*inglese,* "English") even when used as the name of a language (*parlo inglese,* "I speak English"); to indicate people, use your own choice (*gli americani* or *gli Americani,* "the Americans").

In dividing words into syllables, a single consonant between two vowels goes with the *following,* not with the preceding vowel: *generale* is to be divided and pronounced *ge ne ra le*.

The only written accent is the grave (`); this appears whenever a word of more than one syllable ending in a vowel is stressed on the final vowel: *città, perchè, tornerò*. The accent mark is also occasionally used on words of a single syllable to distinguish them from similar words having different meaning: *e,* "and"; *è,* "is"; *da,* "from"; *dà,* "gives." Otherwise, no written accent appears, and words are generally stressed on the next to the last or third from the last syllable; in these cases, the place of the accent is to be determined by observation, or from the transcription in the phrases and the English-Italian vocabulary. In this grammatical survey, for the convenience of the student, the place of the stress will be indicated by a grave accent whenever the stress falls elsewhere than on the second syllable from the last. We shall therefore write *uòmini,* but with the understanding that in ordinary written Italian this word appears as *uomini.*

The apostrophe is used to indicate the elimination of a vowel before another vowel: *l'uomo* (for *lo uomo*); *t'amo* (for *ti amo*).

GRAMMATICAL SURVEY

1. *Nouns and Articles.*

Italian has only two genders, masculine and feminine. Nouns denoting males are usually masculine, those denoting females feminine. For nouns which in English are neuter, the ending often helps to determine the gender. Nouns ending in *-o* (plural changes *-o* to *-i*) are usually masculine; [2] those ending in *-a* (plural changes *-a* to *-e*) normally feminine; the gender of nouns ending in *-e* (plural changes *-e* to *-i*) must be determined by observation.

The indefinite article is *un* (*uno* before *s* followed by consonant, and before *z*) for the masculine; *una* (*un'* before vowels) for the feminine:

un fratello, a brother; *un uomo,* a man; *un padre,* a father; *uno specchio,* a mirror; *uno zio,* an uncle;

[2] A considerable number of nouns which in the singular are masculine and end in *-o* become feminine in the plural, with change from *-o* to *-a:* *il labbro,* "the lip," pl. *le labbra; il dito,* "the finger," pl. *le dita;* such nouns are indicated in the vocabulary thus: "**arm,** *il braccio* (pl., *le braccia*)."

una donna, a woman; *una madre*, a mother; *un'idea*, an idea.

The definite article takes the following forms: [3]

Masculine singular:

l' before vowels: *l'uomo*, the man;

lo before *s* plus consonant, or *z*: *lo specchio*, the mirror; *lo zio*, the uncle;

il in all other cases: *il fratello*, the brother; *il padre*, the father.

Feminine singular:

l' before vowels: *l'idea*, the idea.

[3] This system applies also to *quello*, "that," "those," and to *bello*, "beautiful," "fine," when used as adjectives before nouns: *quel padre*, that father; *quei padri*, those fathers; *quello specchio*, that mirror; *quegli specchi*, those mirrors; *quell'idea*, that idea; *quell'uomo*, that man; *un bel ragazzo*, a fine boy; *bei ragazzi*, fine boys; *begli uòmini*, fine men; *un bello specchio*, a fine mirror; *bell'idea*, fine idea; *bell'uomo*, fine man.

It applies also to the article when combined with the prepositions *di*, "of"; *a*, "to"; *da*, "from," "by," "at the house of"; *in* (changed to *ne-* in combination), "in"; *su*, "on"; *con* (changed to *co-* in combination), "with"; *per* (changed to *pe-* in combination), "for," "by." This combination is compulsory with the first five prepositions mentioned, optional with the last two:

del padre, of the father; *dell'uomo*, of the man; *dello zio*, of the uncle; *della donna*, of the woman; *dell'idea*, of the idea; *dei padri*, of the fathers; *degli uòmini*, of the men; *delle donne*, of the women;

al fratello, to the brother; *allo specchio*, to the mirror; *agli specchi*, to the mirrors; *allo zio*, to the uncle;

dal figlio, from the son; *dalla figlia*, from the daughter; *dai figli*, from the sons; *dagli uòmini*, from the men;

nel muro, in the wall; *nell'ànima*, in the soul; *negli àlberi*, in the trees; *sull'àlbero*, on the tree; *sugli àlberi*, on the trees; *sulle mura*, on the walls;

coi parenti, or *con i parenti*, with the relatives; *pei figli*, or *per i figli*, for the children.

Del, *della*, *dei*, etc., also translate "some" or "any," save in negative sentences: *ho del pane*, I have some bread; *non ho pane*, I have no bread.

la before consonants: *la donna,* the woman; *la madre,* the mother;

Masculine plural:

gli before vowels, *s* plus consonant, or *z: gli uòmini,* the men; *gli specchi,* the mirrors; *gli zii,* the uncles;

i in all other cases: *i fratelli,* the brothers; *i padri,* the fathers.

Feminine plural:

le: le madri, the mothers; *le donne,* the women; *le idee,* the ideas.

2. *Adjectives and Adverbs.*

Adjectives agree with the nouns they modify. Like nouns, they have the endings -*o* (feminine -*a,* masc. pl. -*i,* fem. pl. -*e*); or -*e* (no difference between masculine and feminine; plural -*i*). Agreement with the noun does not necessarily mean identical endings; the noun may be of the -*a* (pl. -*e*) variety, while the adjective may be of the -*e* (pl. -*i*) type: *la donna forte,* the strong woman; *le donne forti,* the strong women. Adjectives usually follow the noun, though a few common ones precede:

il libro rosso, the red book	*i libri rossi,* the red books
la casa rossa, the red house	*le case rosse,* the red houses
l'àlbero verde, the green tree	*gli àlberi verdi,* the green trees
la casa verde, the green house	*le case verdi,* the green houses

The comparative degree is formed by prefixing *più,* "more," to the adjective; for the superlative, the definite article is placed before *più* or the noun: *un libro fàcile,* an easy book; *un libro più fàcile,* an easier book; *il libro più fàcile,* the easiest book; *il più grande generale,* the greatest general. "Than" is usually translated by *di: un libro più fàcile di questo,* an easier book than this.

The adverb is generally formed by adding -*mente* to the feminine singular of the adjective: *chiaro,* clear; *chiaramente,* clearly; *forte,* strong; *fortemente,* strongly.

137

3. Numerals. (see also pp. 101–103)

a. Cardinal.[4]

1—*uno, una*	20—*venti*
2—*due*	21—*ventuno* [5]
3—*tre*	22—*ventidue*
4—*quattro*	23—*ventitrè*
5—*cinque*	28—*ventotto* [5]
6—*sei*	29—*ventinove*
7—*sette*	30—*trenta*
8—*otto*	40—*quaranta*
9—*nove*	50—*cinquanta*
10—*dieci*	60—*sessanta*
11—*ùndici*	70—*settanta*
12—*dòdici*	80—*ottanta*
13—*trèdici*	90—*novanta*
14—*quattòrdici*	100—*cento*
15—*quìndici*	200—*duecento*
16—*sèdici*	300—*trecento*
17—*diciassette*	1000—*mille*
18—*diciotto*	2000—*duemila*
19—*diciannove*	1,000,000—*un milione* (*di*)

b. Ordinal.

1st—*primo*	7th—*sèttimo*
2nd—*secondo*	8th—*ottavo*
3rd—*terzo*	9th—*nono*
4th—*quarto*	10th—*dècimo*
5th—*quinto*	11th—*undècimo* or **undicèsimo**
6th—*sesto*	20th—*ventèsimo*

[4] Use these in dates, save for "the first": *il primo maggio,* May first; *il dieci maggio,* May 10th. Note also the following expressions: *lo vedrò lunedì,* I shall see him on Monday; *lunedì scorso,* last Monday; *lunedì prossimo,* next Monday; *tutti i lunedì,* every Monday (nouns ending in stressed vowels usually do not change in the plural: *la città,* the city; *le città,* the cities); *il cinque maggio mille novecento quarantatrè,* May 5, 1943. Note also that no capitals are used for seasons, months, days of week.

[5] Note the fall of the final vowel of *venti, trenta,* etc., in *ventuno, ventotto, trentuno, trentotto.*

Beyond 11th, ordinals are formed by dropping the final vowel of the cardinal and adding *-èsimo*: *trentaquattrèsimo*, 34th.

4. Pronouns.

a. Personal (Subject).[6]

I, *io*	we, *noi, noialtri*
you (familiar), *tu*	you (fam. pl.), *voi, voialtri*
he, *egli* or *lui*	they (masc.), *essi, loro*
she, *ella* or *essa* or *lei*	they (fem.), *esse, loro*
you (polite), *Ella* or *Lei*[7]	you (pol. pl.), *Loro*[7]

b. Personal (Direct Object).

me, *mi*	us, *ci*
you (fam.), *ti*	you (fam. pl.), *vi*
him, it (standing for an It. masc. noun), *lo, l'*	them (It. masc.), *li*
her, it (It. fem. noun), *la, l'*	them (It. fem.), *le*
you (pol. sing.), *La*	you (pol. pl.), *Li, Le*

c. Personal (Indirect Object).

to me, *mi* (*me*)[8]	to us, *ci* (*ce*)
to you, *ti* (*te*)	to you, *vi* (*ve*)
to him, *gli* (*glie*)[9]	to them, *loro*[10]
to her, *le* (*glie*)[9]	
to you (pol.), *Le* (*glie*)[9]	to you (pol. pl.) *Loro*[10]

[6] Generally used only for emphasis or clarification: *non sai farlo*, you don't know how to do it; *tu non sai farlo*, *you* don't know how to do it.

[7] In polite address, use *Ella* or *Lei* with the *third* person singular of the verb for a single person, *Loro* with the third plural of the verb for more than one person: *tu sei forte*, you (fam. sing.) are strong; *Lei è forte*, you (pol. sing.) are strong; *voi siete forti*, you (fam. pl.) are strong; *Loro sono forti*, you (pol. pl.) are strong.

[8] If two object pronouns appear together, the indirect pronoun precedes the direct, and the form in parentheses ending in *-e* is used for the indirect instead of the form ending in *-i*: *mi dà il libro*, he gives me the book; *me lo dà*, he gives it to me; *dagli il libro*, give him the book; *dàglielo*, give it to him.

139

Direct and indirect object pronouns *precede* the verb (*mi vede*, he sees me; *gli do il libro*, I give him the book), save with the *familiar affirmative* forms of the imperative (*prèndilo!* take it!), the infinitive (*voglio vederlo*, or *lo voglio vedere*, I want to see him), and the gerund (*sto parlàndogli*, or *gli sto parlando*, I am speaking to him), to all of which forms they are appended (but note the double possibility when the infinitive or gerund depends on another verb; in such cases, one has the choice of appending the object pronoun to the infinitive or gerund, or placing it separately before the governing verb). With the imperative *polite* or *negative*, the pronoun precedes: *lo prenda!* take it! (polite); *non lo prèndere!* don't take it! (familiar); *non lo prenda!* don't take it! (polite).

"Of it," "of them," "some," or "any," as a pronoun is expressed by *ne*, which follows other object pronouns and conforms to all the above rules: *me ne dà due*, he gives me two (of them); *gliene ho parlato*, I spoke to him of it.

d. Personal (after a preposition).

me, *me*	us, *noi*
you, *te*	you, *voi*
him, *lui*	them, *loro, essi, esse*
her, *lei*	
it, *esso, essa*	
you (polite), *Lei*	you (polite plural), *Loro*

Con me, with me; *per lui*, for him; *prima di loro*, before them.

e. Possessive.

my, mine, *il mio; la mia; i miei; le mie*
your, yours (fam. sing.), *il tuo; la tua; i tuoi; le tue*
his, her, hers, its, *il suo; la sua; i suoi; le sue*

---

[9] *Glie*, in writing, is always joined to a following direct-object pronoun: *glielo do*, I give it to him.

[10] *Loro* is an exception to all rules of position; it always follows the verb, and is never joined to anything else: *do loro il libro*, I give them the book; *lo do loro*, I give it to them.

our, ours, *il nostro; la nostra; i nostri; le nostre*
your, yours, *il vostro; la vostra; i vostri; le vostre*
their, theirs, *il loro; la loro; i loro; le loro*
your, yours (pol. sing.), *il Suo; la Sua; i Suoi; le Sue*
your, yours (pol. pl.), *il Loro; la Loro; i Loro; le Loro*

These agree with the noun they modify or replace, and regularly appear with the article, whether used as adjectives or pronouns: *il mio libro,* my book; *voglio il mio,* I want mine. The article is, however, generally omitted after the verb "to be" (*questo libro è mio,* this book is mine), and before nouns of family relationship in the singular, but not in the plural (*mia sorella,* my sister; *le mie sorelle,* my sisters); also in direct address (*amico mio!* my friend!).

f. Demonstrative.

this, these, *questo* (*-a, -i, -e*): *questa donna,* this woman; *ecco i Suoi libri; voglio questi,* here are your books, I want these.
that, those, the one, the ones, *quello;* see footnote 3 for its forms when used as an adjective (*quel libro,* that book; *quei libri,* those books; *quegli specchi,* those mirrors); when used as a pronoun, the scheme is regular (*quello-a-i-e*): *i miei libri e quelli sulla tàvola,* my books and the ones on the table.

g. Relative and Interrogative.

who, whom, which, that, *che: l'uomo che ho visto,* the man I saw (note that the relative, often omitted in English, cannot be omitted in Italian); *la donna che è venuta,* the woman who came.

Il quale (*la quale, i quali, le quali*), and *cui* are generally used after prepositions: *il signore con cui* (or *col quale*) *ho pranzato,* the gentleman with whom I dined.

whose, *di cui; il* (*la, i, le*) *cui; del* (*della*) *quale* (pl. *dei* or *delle quali*): *l'uomo di cui ho visto ieri la sorella; l'uomo la cui sorella ho visto ieri, l'uomo del quale ho visto ieri la sorella; l'uomo la sorella del quale ho visto ieri,* the man

141

whose sister I saw yesterday (note the different word order used with each expression).

who? whom? *chi?*: *chi è venuto?* who came?; *chi ha visto?* whom did you see?

what, *che? cosa? che cosa?*: *che* (or *cosa*, or *che cosa*) *è successo?* what happened?; *che (cosa, che cosa) ha fatto?* what did you do?

which? which one? which ones? *quale?* (pl. *quali?*): *quali libri vuole?* which books do you want?; *quali desìdera?* which ones do you wish?

whose? *di chi?*: *di chi è quella casa?* whose house is that?

5. Verbs.

Italian verbs fall into three main classes, with the infinitive ending respectively in *-are, -ere,*[11] and *-ire.*[11]

1. Present Indicative.

to speak *parl-are*

I speak (am speaking, do speak)[12] *parl-o*	we speak *parl-iamo*
you speak *parl-i*	you speak *parl-ate*
he, she speaks *parl-a*	they speak *pàrl-ano*

[11] *-are* and *-ire* verbs have the stress on the *-a* and *-i*, respectively; some *-ere* verbs have the stress on the first *e* of the ending (*godere*), others have it on the preceding vowel of the stem (*ricèvere*), but no difference appears outside of the infinitive. A considerable number of *-ire* verbs have the following scheme of present indicative endings: *fin-isco, -isci, -isce, -iamo, -ite, -ìscono*. The inserted *-isc-* reappears in the subjunctive and imperative singular and third plural. They are otherwise regular, and appear in the vocabulary thus: "finire (-isc-)."

[12] A progressive conjugation, formed with *stare*, "to stand," "to be," followed by the gerund, corresponds in use to the English "I am speaking," "I was speaking," etc. The gerund is formed by adding *-ando* to the stem of *-are* verbs, *-endo* to the stem of other verbs, and is invariable; used by itself, it carries the meaning of "by," or "while" (*parlando, s'impara*, by speaking, one learns; *parlando, siamo usciti dalla casa*, while speaking, we left the house). The present of *stare* is: *sto, stai, sta, stiamo, state, stanno*; imperfect, future and conditional are regular

to receive *ricèv-ere*

I receive *ricev-o*	we receive *ricev-iamo*
you receive *ricev-i*	you receive *ricev-ete*
he, she receives *ricev-e*	they receive *ricèv-ono*

to sleep *dorm-ire*

I sleep *dorm-o*	we sleep *dorm-iamo*
you sleep *dorm-i*	you sleep *dorm-ite*
he, she sleeps *dorm-e*	they sleep *dòrm-ono*

to be, *èssere: sono, sei, è, siamo, siete, sono.*
to have, *avere: ho, hai, ha, abbiamo, avete, hanno.*
to know (a fact), to know how, *sapere: so, sai, sa, sappiamo, sapete, sanno.*
to go, *andare: vado, vai, va, andiamo, andate, vanno.*
to give, *dare: do, dai, dà, diamo, date, dànno.*
to do, to make, *fare: faccio, fai, fa, facciamo, fate, fanno.*
to come, *venire: vengo, vieni, viene, veniamo, venite, vèngono.*
to want, *volere: voglio, vuoi, vuole, vogliamo, volete, vògliono.*

2. Imperfect Indicative (meaning: I was speaking, used to speak).

parl-avo, -avi, -ava, -avamo, -avate, -àvano, I was speaking, used to speak.
ricev-evo, -evi, -eva, -evamo, -evate, -èvano, I was receiving, used to receive.
dorm-ivo, -ivi, -iva, -ivamo, -ivate, -ìvano, I was sleeping, used to sleep.
to be, *èssere: ero, eri, era, eravamo, eravate, èrano,* I was, etc.
to have, *avere,* is regular: *av-evo,* etc.; so are other verbs with an irregular present: *sapevo, andavo, davo, venivo, volevo;* but *fare* has *fac-evo.*

3. Past Indicative (meaning: I spoke).

parl-ai, parl-asti, parl-ò, parl-ammo, parl-aste, parl-àrono, I spoke, etc.

(*stavo; starò; starei*). *Parlo* and *sto parlando* are interchangeable in the sense of "I am speaking"; *parlavo* and *stavo parlando* in the sense of "I was speaking."

ricev-ei, ricev-esti, ricev-è (or *ricev-ette*), *ricev-emmo, ricev-este, ricev-èrono* (or *ricev-èttero*), I received, etc.

dorm-ii, dorm-isti, dorm-ì, dorm-immo, dorm-iste, dorm-ìrono, I slept, etc.

èssere: *fui, fosti, fu, fummo, foste, fùrono,* I was, etc.

avere: *ebbi, avesti, ebbe, avemmo, aveste, èbbero,* I had, etc.[13]

4. Future and Conditional (I shall write; I should write).

parl-erò, -erai, -erà, -eremo, -erete, -eranno, I shall speak, etc.

ricev-erò, -erai, -erà, -eremo, -erete, -eranno, I shall receive, etc.

dorm-irò, -irai, -irà, -iremo, -irete, -iranno, I shall sleep, etc.

èssere: *sarò, sarai, sarà, saremo, sarete, saranno,* I shall be, etc.

avere: *avrò, avrai, avrà, avremo, avrete, avranno,* I shall have, etc.

For the conditional of *any* verb, retain the form of the future down to the -*r*- and add: -*ei, -esti, -ebbe, -emmo, -este, -èbbero;* thus:

I should speak, *parler-ei,* he would speak, *parler-ebbe;* we would sleep, *dormir-emmo;* they would be, *sar-èbbero.* It being understood that the conditional invariably follows the future in any irregularity the latter may have, the first person of the future alone in the vocabulary indicates that both tenses are irregular; thus: to come, *venire* (Fut. *verrò*); this indicates that the conditional is *verrei.*

5. Compound Tenses.

These are formed as in English, by using the auxiliary "to have" (*avere*) with the past participle.[14] Many intransitive

[13] Note carefully the irregular scheme of the past of *avere;* most verbs with an irregular past follow the same scheme; the irregular forms are the first singular, third singular and third plural, while the remaining three forms are quite regular; thus: to write, *scrìv-ere;* I wrote, *scrissi;* he wrote, *scrisse;* they wrote, *scrìssero;* but you wrote (sing.) *scriv-esti,* (pl.) *scriv-este;* we wrote, *scriv-emmo.* Whenever a past is irregular according to this scheme, only the first singular appears in the vocabulary ("**write**, scrivere; Past, scrissi").

[14] The past participle ends in -*ato* for -*are* verbs, -*uto* for -*ere* verbs, -*ito* for -*ire* verbs (*parl-ato,* spoken; *ricev-uto,* received; *dorm-ito,* slept).

verbs of motion (*andare,* to go; *venire,* to come), change of state (*divenire,* to become; *morire,* to die) and *èssere* itself use *èssere* as an auxiliary instead of *avere;* in this case, the past participle changes its ending to agree with the subject, just as though it were an adjective: *è andato,* he went; *è andata,* she went; *siamo andati,* we went; *le signore sono andate,* the ladies went. Verbs used with *èssere* are indicated thus in the vocabulary: "(essere)."

Present Perfect:

ho parlato, hai parlato, etc., I have spoken, I spoke;
sono andato (-a), I went; *siamo andati (-e),* we went;

Past Perfect:

avevo ricevuto, I had received; *avevi dormito,* you had slept;
ero stato, I had been; *eravamo tornati,* we had come back;

Future Perfect:

avrò scritto, I shall have written; *sarà partito,* he will have left;

Past Conditional:

avrei perduto, I would have lost; *sarebbe andato,* he would have gone.

Many past participles are irregular, and individually given in the vocabulary. The past participle is normally invariable (*abbiamo parlato,* we have spoken), but changes its endings like an adjective in the following cases:

1. When used as an adjective: *la lingua parlata,* the spoken tongue;

2. When used with the auxiliary "to be," in which case it must agree with the subject; this occurs (a) with intransitive verbs of motion, etc., as described above: *gli uòmini sono venuti,* the men have come; (b) in the passive: *noi siamo amati dai nostri genitori,* we are loved by our parents; (c) in the reflexive: *si sono alzati,* they got up;

3. When used with "to have," to agree with the *direct* object; this agreement is compulsory if the object is a *personal direct* object *pronoun: li ho visti,* I have seen them; optional in all other cases: *le donne che abbiamo viste* (or *visto*), the women we saw; *abbiamo visto* (or *viste*) *quelle donne,* we saw those women.

145

6. Imperative. (meaning: speak! let us speak).

	-are	-ere	-ire	èssere	avere
Fam. Sing.[15]	parl-a	ricev-i	dorm-i	sii	abbi
Fam. Pl.	parl-ate	ricev-ete	dorm-ite	siate	abbiate
Pol. Sing.	parl-i	ricev-a	dorm-a	sia	abbia
Pol. Pl.	pàrl-ino	ricèv-ano	dòrm-ano	sìano	àbbiano
"let us"	parl-iamo	ricev-iamo	dorm-iamo	siamo	abbiamo

7. Reflexive Verbs.

The reflexive is more extensively used in Italian than in English. Reflexive pronouns are: *mi, ti, si, ci, vi, si.*[16] The auxiliary used in compound tenses is *èssere*, and the past participle agrees with the subject: they saw each other, *si sono visti.*[17]

mi lavo, I wash myself   *ci laviamo,* we wash ourselves
ti lavi, you wash yourself   *vi lavate,* you wash yourselves
si lava, he washes himself *si làvano,* they wash themselves

mi sono lavato (-a), I washed myself; *ci siamo lavati (-e),* we washed ourselves

ti sei lavato (-a), you washed yourself; *vi siete lavati (-e),* you washed yourselves

si è lavato, he washed himself; *si è lavata,* she washed herself; *si sono lavati (-e),* they washed themselves

8. Passive.

This is formed as in English, by using "to be" with the past participle; the latter agrees with the subject: *noi siamo amati*

[15] The familiar singular form is never used in the negative, being replaced by the infinitive: *non parlare!* don't speak! *non dormire!* don't sleep! Object pronouns are attached to the *familiar* imperatives in the *affirmative* (*pàrlagli! parlàtegli!* speak to him! *parliàmogli!* let us speak to him!); but precede the *polite* forms (*gli parli! gli pàrlino!* speak to him!) and all *negative* forms, familiar or polite (*non gli parlare! non gli parlate! non gli parli! non gli pàrlino!* don't speak to him! *non gli parliamo!* let us not speak to him!)

[16] Note that the *-i* of all these forms changes to *-e* if another object pronoun follows: *se lo mette,* he puts it on (himself).

[17] Note that in the plural the reflexive may mean not only "ourselves," "yourselves," "themselves," but also "each other," "one another."

146

dai nostri genitori, we are loved by our parents; *fu punita,* she was punished.

A second passive form with *venire* instead of *èssere* indicates more intensive and immediate action: *il treno venne sùbito fermato,* the train was stopped at once.

The reflexive often replaces the passive, especially when the subject is a thing: *qui si parla italiano,* Italian is spoken here; *questi libri si vèndono a due dòllari l'uno,* these books are sold for two dollars apiece.

9. Subjunctive.

The Italian subjunctive has four tenses, and is frequently used in subordinate clauses. The endings of the present subjunctive are:

-are verbs: *parl-i, -i, -i, -iamo, -iate, '-ino*

-ere and *-ire* verbs: *ricev-* or *dorm-a, -a, -a, -iamo, iate, '-ano.*

The imperfect subjunctive ends in *-ssi, -ssi, -sse, '-ssimo, -ste, '-ssero,* with a preceding *-a-* for *-are* verbs (*parl-assi*), *-e-* for *-ere* verbs (*ricev-essi*), *-i-* for *-ire* verbs (*dorm-issi*).

The present perfect subjunctive uses the present subjunctive of "to have" (*abbia, abbia, abbia, abbiamo, abbiate, àbbiano*) or "to be" (*sia, sia, sia, siamo, siate, sìano*), with the past participle (*abbia parlato, sia venuto*); while the past perfect subjunctive uses the imperfect subjunctive of *avere* (*avessi*) or *èssere* (*fossi*), with the past participle (*avessi parlato, fossi venuto*).

Three important uses of the subjunctive are:

1. In subordinate clauses following verbs of mental action or emotion, such as belief, fear, joy, sorrow, doubt. If the verb of mental action indicates complete or even reasonable certainty in the mind of the speaker, the indicative is often used instead of the subjunctive: *crede che venga* (or *verrà*) *oggi?* do you think he will come today? *non credo che venga* (or *verrà*), I don't think he will come; *sono sicuro che verrà,* I am sure he will come; *ho paura che lo faccia,* I'm afraid he will do it; *dùbito che voglia farlo oggi,* I doubt that he wants to do it today.

147

2. After verbs indicating an action of the will exerted by one individual upon another, such as wanting, wishing, allowing, forbidding, ordering: *non voglio che Lei lo faccia,* I don't want you to do it (compare this with *non voglio farlo,* I don't want to do it); *permette che entri?* will you allow me to come in? *proibisce che io ci vada,* he forbids me to go there. With allow, forbid, order, etc., one may optionally use the infinitive: *mi permette di entrare?* will you allow me to come in? *mi proibisce di andarci,* he forbids me to go there. The substitution of the infinitive for the subjunctive is not possible with *volere* or *desiderare* because, with these verbs, the infinitive indicates that the subject wants or wishes to do something himself.

3. After certain conjunctions, especially *prima che* (before), *benchè, quantunque* (although), *a meno che* (unless; this also demands the use of *non* before the subjunctive, even though the clause is affirmative); *purchè* (provided that), *affinchè* (so that), *perchè, acciocchè* (in order that), *senza che* (without): *facciàmolo prima che venga,* let's do it before he comes; *benchè gli abbia scritto, non mi ha risposto,* although I have written him, he hasn't answered me; *a meno che Lei non venga, noi non ci andremo,* unless you come along, we won't go there.

10. Gerund and Infinitive.

Where English normally uses the gerund of the verb as the subject of a sentence, Italian normally uses the infinitive preceded by the article: *il parlare è il miglior modo di farsi comprèndere,* speaking is the best way of making oneself understood.

Where English normally uses the gerund of the verb after a preposition, Italian normally uses the infinitive: *senza parlare,* without speaking; *prima di entrare,* before going in. But English "by" or "while" with the gerund is translated by the Italian gerund without any preposition (see page 142): *parlando, s'impara,* one learns by speaking; *chiacchierando, siamo usciti insieme dalla casa,* while chatting, we left the house together.

148

6. A Few Points of Syntax.

a. Word Order.

Italian word order is more elastic than English. The subject may, and frequently does, come after the verb, even in a declarative sentence: *è arrivato ieri mio fratello,* my brother arrived yesterday; *questo libro non l'ho ancora letto,* I haven't read this book yet. This placing of the subject after the verb is particularly frequent in relative clauses: *la casa che ha visto ieri mio fratello è molto più grande di questa,* the house my brother saw yesterday is much larger than this one.

Interrogation is more often expressed by the intonation of the voice than by the inversion regularly used in English. The verb "to do" is never used in Italian as an interrogative or negative auxiliary, as it is in English: *li ha visti,* you have seen them; *li ha visti?* have you seen them? *le scrive sempre,* he still writes to her; *le scrive sempre?* does he still write to her?

The Italian adjective more usually (but by no means always) follows its noun, and the Italian adverb its verb. This is particularly true of adjectives of color, nationality, religion and party affiliation: *un libro rosso,* a red book; *il consolato americano,* the American Consulate; *una chiesa protestante,* a Protestant church. A few adjectives, like *bello,* normally come before the noun; others, like *pòvero* and *bravo,* take on different shades of meaning according to their position: *una pòvera donna,* a poor (unfortunate) woman; *una donna pòvera,* a poor (penniless) woman; *un bravo ragazzo,* a good boy; *un ragazzo bravo,* a brave boy.

b. Some uses of the Definite Article.

Abstract nouns (like "freedom," "beauty," "kindness") and concrete nouns used in a general sense regularly take the definite article: *la libertà è preziosa,* freedom is precious; *l'oro è un metallo prezioso,* gold is a precious metal; *l'acqua è necessaria,* water is necessary.

When referring to parts of the body and articles of clothing, Italian generally uses the definite article where English

149

uses a possessive adjective; but the verb in the Italian sentence is generally put into the reflexive, thus clearly indicating the possessor of the part of the body or article of clothing in question: *mi son tagliato il dito* (I cut the finger to myself), I cut my finger; *si è messa i guanti* (she put on the gloves to herself), she put on her gloves.

The definite article combined with the preposition *di* generally expresses "some" or "any" before a noun (see p. 136; if the noun is understood, *ne* is used to indicate "some" or "any"; see p. 140): *vorrei del pane*, I should like to have some bread; *ha delle sigarette?* have you any cigarettes? *non ne ho*, I haven't any. However, while *ne* is required if the noun does not appear, the use of *di* with the article before the noun is not altogether compulsory in Italian (as it is in French), and in the negative both *di* and the article are regularly omitted: *vorrei pane e formaggio*, I should like to have bread and cheese; *ha sigarette?* have you cigarettes? *non ho danaro*, I have no money; *non voglio seccature*, I don't want any trouble.

Names of countries and provinces are capitalized and regularly used with the definite article: *l'Italia*, Italy; *il Belgio*, Belgium; *la Gran Brettagna*, Great Britain; *la Lombardìa*, Lombardy. While most such names are feminine, there is a liberal sprinkling of masculines: *il Giappone*, Japan; *il Brasile*, Brazil; *il Piemonte*, Piedmont. "To" or "in" with names of countries and provinces is usually translated by *in* without the article with feminine names, by *in* with the article with masculine names: *in Italia*, in or to Italy; *nel Belgio*, in or to Belgium. *In* with the article is generally used if the name of the country is modified: *nell'Italia meridionale*, to or in southern Italy; *nell'Amèrica del Sud*, to or in South America.

Adjectives of nationality, religion and party affiliation are normally not capitalized, save when used as nouns, in which case the use of the capital is optional: *una città francese*, a French city; *una chiesa cattòlica*, a Catholic church; *il partito comunista*, the Communist party; *i francesi* or *i Francesi*, the French; *i comunisti* or *i Comunisti*, the Communists.

Names of languages are not capitalized. They are used with the article, save where they *immediately* follow the verb *par-*

lare or the preposition *in: l'inglese è una lingua difficile,* English is a hard language; *parla inglese?* do you speak English? *Lei parla molto bene l'inglese,* you speak English very well; *mi ha risposto in inglese,* he answered me in English.

Nouns of profession and titles followed by the person's name take the article, save when used in direct address: *è arrivato il dottor Bianchi,* Dr. Bianchi has arrived; *Capitano Castelli, vuol favorire?* Captain Castelli, won't you come in? Italian, however, seldom uses a name after a title, preferring the use of *signor, signora: favorisca, Signor Capitano,* come in, Captain; *Signora Contessa, potrei parlarle?* may I speak to you, Countess?

151

IV ENGLISH-ITALIAN VOCABULARY

The gender of nouns is indicated by the article. The definite article is given except when the noun begins with a vowel, in which case the indefinite article appears (*un* for masculine nouns, *un'* for feminines).

Irregularities in the plural of nouns are indicated thus: *il braccio* (pl. *le braccia*); this means that the plural is feminine and takes an *-a* ending instead of the normal *-i* ending. Spelling changes are also noted: *fuoco* (pl. *fuochi*).

Verbs of the *-ire* type that take *-isc-* between the root and the ending are indicated thus: **finish,** finire (-isc-). Other important irregularities are also noted in parentheses. An irregular first singular in the past tense normally implies the same irregularity in the third singular and third plural, with the other three persons regular; thus, "scrivere, Past, scrissi," indicates the scheme: *scrissi, scrivesti, scrisse, scrivemmo, scriveste, scrissero* (cf. Footnote 13). Verbs requiring *essere* as an active auxiliary appear thus: "**become** ... divenire ... (essere)." This indication is not given in the case of reflexive verbs, which are *all* conjugated with *essere*. An irregular first person singular future implies the same irregularity running throughout the future and conditional.

The English transcription is given only for the singular form for nouns, masculine singular form for adjectives. In the case of verbs, it is given for the infinitive and any other forms where it seems necessary.

a, an un, uno (m.) (OON, OO-noh); una, un' (f.) (oo-nah, OON)

able (to be) potere (poh-TAY-ray)

Present: posso, puoi, può, possiamo, potete, possono (PAWS-soh, PWAW-ee, PWAW, pohs-SYAH-moh, poh-TAY-tay, PAWS-soh-noh); Fut: potrò (poh-TRAW).

about circa (CHEER-kah), verso (VEHR-soh)

above sopra (SOH-prah), su (SOO)

abscess un ascesso (ah-SHEHS-soh)

absorbent cotton il cotone idrofilo (koh-TOH-nay ee-DRAW-fee-loh)

accelerator un acceleratore (ah-chay-lay-rah-TOH-ray)

accept accettare (ah-chayt-TAH-ray).

accident un incidente (een-chee-DEHN-tay)

ache il dolore, il male (doh-LOH-ray, MAH-lay)

  head- . . . mal di capo (KAH-poh)

  stomach . . . mal di stomaco (STAW-mah-koh)

  tooth- . . . mal di denti (DEHN-tee)

across attraverso (aht-trah-VEHR-soh)

address un indirizzo (een-dee-REE-tsoh)

adhesive tape il nastro adesivo (NAHS-troh ah-day-SEE-voh)

adjust aggiustare, regolare, accomodare (ah-joos-TAH-ray, ray-goh-LAH-ray, ahk-koh-moh-DAH-ray)

admittance (no) vietato l'ingresso (vyay-TAH-toh leen-GREHS-soh)

afraid (to be) aver paura (pah-oo-rah) (see *to have* for conjugation of aver)

after dopo, appresso (DAW-poh, ahp-PREHS-soh)

afternoon il dopopranzo, il pomeriggio (doh-poh-PRAHN-dzoh, poh-may-REE-joh)

afterward dopo, poi, più tardi, in seguito (DAW-poh, PAW-ee, PYOO TAHR-dee, een SAY-gwee-toh)

again ancora, di nuovo, nuovamente (ahn-KOH-rah, dee NWAW-voh, nwoh-vah-MAYN-tay)

against contro (KOHN-troh)

ago fa (FAH)

agree convenire, esser d'accordo (kohn-vay-NEE-ray, EHS-sayr dahk-KAWR-doh) (see *to come* and *to be* for conjugation)

ahead avanti (ah-VAHN-tee)

air un'aria (AH-ryah)

air mail la posta aerea (PAWS-tah ah-EH-ray-ah)

airfield un aeroporto (ah-ay-roh-PAWR-toh)

airline la linea aerea (LEE-nay-ah ah-EH-ray-ah)

airplane un aeroplano (ah-ay-roh-PLAH-noh)

airport un aeroporto (ah-ay-roh-PAWR-toh)

alarm clock la sveglia (ZVAY-lyah)

all tutto (TOOT-toh)

all aboard! Tutti in carrozza! (TOOT-tee een kahr-RAW-tsah)

allow permettere (payr-MAYT-tay-ray); Past, permisi; P. P., permesso.

almond la mandorla (MAHN-dohr-lah)

almost quasi (KWAH-see)

alone solo (SOH-loh)

already già (JAH)

always sempre (SEHM-pray)

a.m. antimeridiane, del mattino (ahn-tee-may-ree-DYAH-nay, dayl maht-TEE-noh)

am sono (SOH-noh)

American americano (ah-may-ree-KAH-noh)

American plan la pensione completa (payn-SYOH-nay kohm-PLEH-tah)

among tra, fra (TRAH, FRAH)

and e (AY)

ankle la caviglia (kah-VEE-lyah)

annoy seccare (sayk-KAH-ray)

another un altro (OO-NAHL-troh)

answer (noun) la risposta (rees-PAWS-tah)

answer (verb) rispondere (rees-POHN-day-ray); Past, risposi (rees-POH-see); P. P., risposto (rees-PAWS-toh)

any qualunque, qualsiasi, ne (kwah-LOON-kway, kwahl-SEE-ah-see, NAY)

anybody, anyone chiunque, nessuno (kee-OON-kway, nays-SOO-noh)

anything qualche cosa, niente (KWAHL-kay KAW-sah, NYEHN-tay)

anything else? altro? (AHL-troh)

apartment un appartamento (ahp-pahr-tah-MAYN-toh)

apéritif un aperitivo (ah-pay-ree-TEE-voh)

appetizer un antipasto (ahn-tee-PAHS-toh)

apple la mela (MAY-lah)

apricot un'albicocca (ahl-bee-KAWK-kah) (pl., -che)

April aprile (ah-PREE-lay)

Arab (Arabic, Arabian) arabo (AH-rah-boh)

are siamo, siete, sono (SYAH-moh, SYAY-tay, SOH-noh)

Argentinian argentino (ahr-jayn-TEE-noh)

arm il braccio (BRAH-choh) (pl., le braccia, BRAH-chah)

armchair la poltrona (pohl-TROH-nah)

around attorno (aht-TOHR-noh)

arrival un arrivo (ahr-REE-voh)

arrive arrivare, giungere (ahr-ree-VAH-ray, JOON-jay-ray) Past, giunsi (JOON-see); P. P., giunto (JOOH-toh) (essere)

artichoke il carciofo (kahr-CHAW-foh)

article un articolo (ahr-TEE-koh-loh)

as come (KOH-may)

ash tray il portacenere (pohr-tah-CHAY-nay-ray)

ask, ask for domandare, chiedere (doh-mahn-DAH-ray, KYEH-day-ray) Past, chiesi (KYEH-see); P. P., chiesto (KYEHS-toh)

asparagus gli asparagi (pl.) (ahs-PAH-rah-jee)

aspirin un'aspirina (ahs-pee-REE-nah)

at a (AH)

at all affatto (ahf-FAHT-toh)

at least almeno (ahl-MAY-noh)

at once subito (SOO-bee-toh)

attention! attenzione! attento! (aht-tayn-TSYOH-nay, aht-TEHN-toh)

August agosto (ah-GOHS-toh)

aunt la zia (TSEE-ah)

Austrian austriaco (ows-TREE-ah-koh)

automobile un'automobile, la macchina (ow-toh-MAW-bee-lay, MAHK-kee-nah)

automobile map la carta automobilistica (stradale) (KAHR-tah ow-toh-moh-bee-LEES-tee-kah (strah-DAH-lay))

autumn un autunno (ow-TOON-noh)

avoid evitare (ay-vee-TAH-ray)

awful terribile, brutto (tayr-REE-bee-lay, BROOT-toh)

baby il bambino (bahm-BEE-noh)

back (noun) la schiena, il dorso (SKYEH-nah, DAWR-soh)

back (preposition, adverb) dietro, indietro, di ritorno (DYEH-troh, een-DYEH-troh, dee ree-TOHR-noh)

bacon la pancetta (pahn-CHAYT-tah)

bad cattivo (kaht-TEE-voh)

bad (too . . . !) peccato! (payk-KAH-toh)

badly male (MAH-lay)

bag (hand-) la borsa, la borsetta (BOHR-sah, bohr-SAYT-tah)

bag (valise) la valigia (vah-LEE-jah)

baggage i bagagli (pl.) (bah-GAH-lyee)

baggage car il bagagliaio, il vagone bagagli (bah-gah-LYAH-yoh, vah-GOH-nay bah-GAH-lyee)

baggage room il deposito bagagli (day-PAW-see-toh bah-GAH-lyee)

baked al forno (ahl FOHR-noh)

balcony (theater) la galleria (gahl-lay-REE-ah)

ball (dance) il ballo (BAH-loh

ball (sphere) la palla (PAHL-lah)

banana la banana (bah-NAH-nah)

bandage (noun) la fasciatura (fah-shah-TOO-rah)

bandage (verb) fasciare (fah-SHAH-ray)

bank la banca, il banco (BAHN-kah, BAHN-koh)

barber il barbiere, il parrucchiere (bahr-BYEH-ray, pahr-rook-KYEH-ray)

barbershop la barberia (bahr-bay-REE-ah)

bargain sale la vendita d'occasione (VAYN-dee-tah dohk-kah-SYOH-nay)

basket la cesta, il canestro (CHAYS-tah, kah-NEHS-troh)
lunch basket (sold in R.R. stations) il cestino di viaggio (chays-TEE-noh dee VYAH-joh)

bath il bagno (BAH-nyoh)

bath mat lo scendibagno (shayn-dee-BAH-nyoh)

bathe fare un bagno (FAH-ray oon BAH-nyoh)

bathing cap la cuffia da bagno (KOOF-fyah dah BAH-nyoh)

bathing suit il costume da bagno (kohs-TOO-may dah BAH-nyoh)

bathrobe un accappatoio (ahk-kahp-pah-TOH-yoh)

bathroom la stanza da bagno, il bagno (STAHN-tsah dah BAH-nyoh)

battery (car) la batteria (baht-teh-REE-ah)

be essere (EHS-say-ray); Pres.: sono, sei, è, siamo, siete, sono; Imp., ero; Fut., sarò; Past:

155

fui, fosti, fu, fummo, foste, furono (essere).

be back essere di ritorno (EHS-say-ray dee ree-TOHR-noh)

beach la spiaggia (SPYAH-jah)

bean il fagiuolo (fah-JWAW-loh)

bearing (car) il cuscinetto (koo-shee-NAYT-toh)

beautiful bello (BEHL-loh)

beauty salon il salone di bellezza (sah-LOH-nay dee bayl-LAY-tsah)

because perchè (payr-KAY)

become diventare, divenire (dee-vayn-TAH-ray, dee-vay-NEE-ray) (see *to come*, venire, for conjugation of divenire) (essere)

bed il letto (LEHT-toh)

bedroom la camera (stanza) da letto (KAH-may-rah, STAHN-tsah dah LEHT-toh)

beef il manzo, il bue (MAHN-tsoh, BOO-ay)

beef (roast) il rosbif (rohs-BEEF)

beer la birra (BEER-rah)

beet la barbabietola (bahr-bah-BYEH-toh-lah)

before prima (di), avanti (di) davanti (a) (PREE-mah, ah-VAHN-tee, dah-VAHN-tee)

begin cominciare, aver inizio (koh-meen-CHAH-ray, ah-VAYR ee-NEE-tsyoh) (see *to have*, avere)

behind dietro (a) (DYEH-troh)

Belgian belga (BEHL-gah)

believe credere (KRAY-day-ray)

bell (door) il campanello (kahm-pah-NEHL-loh)

bellboy il cameriere (kah-may-RYEH-ray)

belong appartenere (a) (ahp-payr-tay-NAY-ray) (see *to hold*, tenere, for conjugation)

belongings gli effetti (pl.) (ayf-FEHT-tee)

belt la cintura (cheen-TOO-rah)

berth la cuccetta (koo-CHAYT-tah)

best migliore (adj.); meglio (adv.) (mee-LYOH-ray, MEH-lyoh)

bet scommettere (skoh-MAYT-tay-ray) (see *to put*, mettere, for conjugation): **you bet!** e come! (ay KOH-may)

better migliore (adj.), meglio (adv.) (mee-LYOH-ray, MEH-lyoh)

between tra, fra (TRAH, FRAH)

bicarbonate of soda il bicarbonato (di soda) (bee-kahr-boh-NAH-toh (dee SAW-dah))

big grande, grosso (GRAHN-day, GRAWS-soh)

bill (bank note) il biglietto (bee-LYAYT-toh)

bill (to be paid) il conto (KOHN-toh)

billion il miliardo (mee-LYAHR-doh)

bird un uccello (oo-CHEHL-loh)

bite il boccone (bohk-KOH-nay) **to get a bite** mangiare un boccone

bitter amaro (ah-MAH-roh)

black nero (NAY-roh)

blade la lama (LAH-mah); **razor blade,** la lametta da rasoio (lah-MAYT-tah dah rah-SOH-yoh)

blank il modulo (MAW-doo-loh)
blanket la coperta (koh-PEHR-tah)
bleach (laundry) il candeggio (kahn-DAY-joh)
bleach (hair) tingere (TEEN-jay-ray); Past, tinsi; P. P., tinto
block (city) un isolato (ee-soh-LAH-toh)
blood il sangue (SAHN-gway)
blouse la camicetta (kah-mee-CHAYT-tah)
blue blu, azzurro, celeste (BLOO, ah-DZOOR-roh, chay-LEHS-tay)
board (on) a bordo (ah BOHR-doh)
boardinghouse la pensione (payn-SYOH-nay)
boat il piroscafo (pee-RAWS-kah-foh)
body il corpo (KAWR-poh)
boiled bollito (bohl-LEE-toh)
bolt (car) il bullone (bool-LOH-nay)
bone l'osso; pl., le ossa (AWS-soh)
book il libro (LEE-broh)
book (guide) la guida (GWEE-dah)
bookstore la libreria (lee-bray-REE-ah)
booth (phone) la cabina telefonica (kah-BEE-nah tay-lay-FAW-nee-kah)
boric acid l'acido borico (m.) (AH-chee-doh BAW-ree-koh)
born (to be) nascere (NAH-shay-ray); Past, nacqui (NAH-kwee); P. P., nato (NAH-toh); (essere)
borrow prendere in prestito (PREHN-day-ray een PREHS-tee-toh); Past, presi (PRAY-see); P. P. preso
both ambedue, entrambi, tutti e due (ahm-bay-DOO-ay, ayn-TRAHM-bee, TOOT-tee ay DOO-ay)
bother (noun) il disturbo (dees-TOOR-boh)
bother seccare, annoiare (sayk-KAH-ray, ahn-noh-YAH-ray); **don't bother** non si scomodi (nohn see SKAW-moh-dee)
bottle la bottiglia (boht-TEE-lyah)
box la scatola (SKAH-toh-lah); **(theater)** il palco (PAHL-koh), (pl., i palchi)
box office il botteghino (boht-tay-GHEE-noh)
boy il ragazzo (rah-GAH-tsoh)
bra, brassière il reggipetto (ray-jee-PEHT-toh)
bracelet il braccialetto (brah-chah-LAYT-toh)
brakes i freni (FRAY-nee)
Brazilian brasiliano (brah-see-LYAH-noh)
bread il pane (PAH-nay)
break rompere (ROHM-pay-ray); Past, ruppi (ROOP-pee); P. P., rotto (ROHT-toh)
breakdown (auto) il guasto (al motore) (GWAHS-toh ahl moh-TOH-ray)
breakfast la (prima) colazione (PREE-mah koh-lah-TSYOH-nay)
breathe respirare (rays-pee-RAH-ray)
bridge il ponte (POHN-tay)
bring portare (pohr-TAH-ray)
broiled ai ferri (AH-ee FEHR-ree)

157

broken rotto (ROHT-toh)

brother il fratello (frah-TEHL-loh)

brown marrone (mahr-ROH-nay)

bruise la contusione (kohn-too-SYOH-nay)

brush (noun) la spazzola (SPAH-tsoh-lah); shaving brush il pennello da barba (payn-NEHL-loh dah BAHR-bah)

brush (verb) spazzolare (spah-tsoh-LAH-ray)

building un edificio (ay-dee-FEE-choh)

bulb (electric) la lampadina (lahm-pah-DEE-nah)

bumper (car) il paraurti (pl., i paraurti) (pah-rah-OOR-tee)

burn (noun) la bruciatura (broo-chah-TOO-rah)

burn (verb) bruciare (broo-CHAH-ray)

bus un autobus (ow-toh-boos) (pl., gli autobus)

busy occupato (ohk-koo-PAH-toh)

but ma, però (MAH, pay-RAW)

butter il burro (BOOR-roh)

button il bottone (boht-TOH-nay)

buy comprare (kohm-PRAH-ray)

by per, da (PAYR, DAH); by the day al giorno, alla giornata (ahl JOHR-noh, AHL-lah johr-NAH-tah)

cab il tassì, la vettura da nolo (tahs-SEE, vayt-TOO-rah dah NAW-loh)

cabaret il tabarin (tah-bah-REHN)

cabbage il cavolo (KAH-voh-loh)

cable (noun) il cablogramma (kah-bloh-GRAHM-mah)

cable (verb) cablografare (kah-bloh-grah-FAH-ray)

cake la torta (TOHR-tah)

call (noun) la chiamata, la telefonata (kyah-MAH-tah, tay-lay-foh-NAH-tah)

call (verb) chiamare, telefonare (kyah-MAH-ray, tay-lay-foh-NAH-ray)

camera la macchinetta fotografica (mahk-kee-NAYT-tah foh-toh-GRAH-fee-kah)

can (noun) il barattolo, la scatola (bah-RAHT-toh-loh, SKAH-toh-lah)

can (verb) potere (poh-TAY-ray); Pres.: posso, puoi, può, possiamo, potete, possono (PAWS-soh, PWAW-ee, PWAW, poh-SYAH-moh, poh-TAY-tay, PAWS-soh-noh); Fut., potrò (poh-TRAW)

can opener un apriscatole (ah-pree-SKAH-toh-lay); pl. gli apriscatole

Canadian canadese (kah-nah-DAY-say)

cancel cancellare (kahn-chayl-LAH-ray)

candle la candela (kahn-DAY-lah)

candy i dolci, i cioccolatini (DOHL-chee, chohk-koh-lah-TEE-nee)

cap il berretto (bay-RAYT-toh)

captain il capitano (kah-pee-TAH-noh)

car (auto) un'automobile, la

macchina (ow-toh-MAW-bee-lay, MAHK-kee-nah)

car (R.R.) il vagone (vah-GOH-nay)

car (street) il tram, il tranvai (TRAHM, trahn-VAH-ee); pl., i tram, i tranvai

carbon paper la carta copiativa (KAHR-tah koh-pyah-TEE-vah)

carburetor il carburatore (kahr-boo-rah-TOH-ray)

card (playing) la carta da giuoco (KAHR-tah dah JWAW-koh)

card (visiting) la carta, il biglietto, da visita (KAHR-tah, bee-LYAYT-toh dah VEE-see-tah)

care (noun) la cura, l'attenzione (f.) (KOO-rah, aht-tayn-TSYOH-nay)

careful attento (aht-TEHN-toh)

carefully con cura, con attenzione (kohn KOO-rah, kohn aht-tayn-TSYOH-nay)

carriage (horse) la carrozza (kahr-RAW-tsah)

carrot la carota (kah-RAW-tah)

carry portare (pohr-TAH-ray)

case (cigarette) il portasigarette (pohr-tah-see-gah-RAYT-tay) (pl., i portasigarette)

case (in any . . .) in ogni caso (een OH-nyee KAH-soh)

cash (noun) i contanti, il danaro (kohn-TAHN-tee, dah-NAH-roh)

cash (verb) incassare, riscuotere (een-kahs-SAH-ray, rees-KWAW-tay-ray); Past, riscossi (rees-KAWS-see); P. P., riscosso

cashier il cassiere, la cassa (kahs-SYEH-ray, KAHS-sah)

castle il castello (kahs-TEHL-loh)

castor oil l'olio di ricino (m.) (AW-lyoh dee REE-chee-noh)

cat il gatto (GAHT-toh)

catch prendere (PREHN-day-ray); Past, presi (PRAY-see); P. P., preso

cathedral la basilica, la cattedrale (bah-SEE-lee-kah, kaht-tay-DRAH-lay)

Catholic cattolico (kaht-TAW-lee-koh)

cauliflower il cavolfiore (kah-vohl-FYOH-ray)

caution la cautela, la prudenza (kow-TEH-lah, proo-DEHN-tsah)

ceiling il soffitto (sohf-FEET-toh)

celery il sedano (SEH-dah-noh)

center il centro (CHAYN-troh)

certainly certo, certamente (CHEHR-toh, chehr-tah-MAYN-tay)

certificate il certificato (chayr-tee-fee-KAH-toh)

chain la catena (kah-TAY-nah)

chair la sedia (SEH-dyah)

change (noun) il resto (REHS-toh); small change gli spiccioli (pl.) (SPEE-choh-lee)

change (verb) cambiare (kahm-BYAH-ray)

charge (cover) il coperto (koh-PEHR-toh)

charge (verb) far pagare (FAHR pah-GAH-ray) (see to do, to make, fare, for conjugation) cheap a buon mercato (ah BWAWN mayr-KAH-toh)

check (baggage, noun) lo scontrino (skohn-TREE-noh)

check (baggage, verb) lasciare in deposito (lah-SHAH-ray een day-PAW-see-toh)

check (traveler's) un assegno di viaggio (ahs-SAY-nyoh dee VYA-joh)

check room il guardaroba (gwahr-dah-RAW-bah); pl., i guardaroba

cheek la guancia (GWAHN-chah)

cheese il formaggio, il cacio (forh-MAH-joh, KAH-choh)

cherry la ciliegia (chee-LYAY-jah)

chest (breast) il petto (PEHT-toh)

chestnut la castagna (kahs-TAH-nyah)

chicken il pollo (POHL-loh)

child il bambino, il fanciullo (bahm-BEE-noh, fahn-CHOOL-loh)

Chilean cileno (chee-LEH-noh)

chill il brivido (BREE-vee-doh)

chin il mento (MAYN-toh)

Chinese cinese (chee-NAY-say)

chiropodist il pedicure (pay-dee-KYOOR)

chocolate il cioccolato (chohk-koh-LAH-toh)

chocolates i cioccolatini (chohk-koh-lah-TEE-nee)

choose scegliere (SHAY-lyay-ray); Pres.: scelgo, scegli . . . scelgono; Past, scelsi (SHAYL-see), P. P. scelto (SHAYL-toh)

chop (noun) la cotoletta (koh-toh-LAYT-tah)

Christmas il Natale (nah-TAH-lay)

church la chiesa (KYEH-sah)

cigar il sigaro (SEE-gah-roh)

cigar store la tabaccheria (tah-bahk-kay-REE-ah)

cigarette la sigaretta (see-gah-RAYT-tah)

cigarette case il portasigarette (pohr-tah-see-gah-RAYT-tay); pl., i portasigarette

cigarette holder il bocchino (bohk-KEE-noh)

city la città (cheet-TAH)

city hall il municipio (moo-nee-CHEE-pyoh)

class la classe (KLAHS-say)

clean (adj.) pulito (poo-LEE-toh)

clean (verb) pulire (poo-LEE-ray) (-isc-)

cleaner's la tintoria (teen-toh-REE-ah)

clear chiaro (KYAH-roh)

clear up rischiarare (rees-kyah-RAH-ray)

climb salire (sah-LEE-ray); Pres., salgo, sali . . . salgono or salisco

clippers (barber's) la macchinetta (mahk-kee-NAYT-tah)

clock un orologio (oh-roh-LAW-joh)

close (adj., near) vicino (vee-CHEE-noh)

close (verb) chiudere (KYOO-day-ray); Past, chiusi (KYOO-see); P. P., chiuso (KYOO-soh) closed chiuso (KYOO-soh)

closet un armadio (ahr-MAH-dyoh)

cloth la tela, la pezza, la stoffa, il panno (TAY-lah, PEH-tsah, STAWF-fah, PAHN-noh)

clothes i vestiti, il vestiario, gli indumenti (vays-TEE-tee, vays-TYAH-ryoh, een-doo-MAYN-tee)

clothes (evening) abito da sera (AH-bee-toh dah SAY-rah)

clothesbrush la spazzola da vestiti (SPAH-tsoh-lah dah vays-TEE-tee)

clothing see *clothes*

cloud la nuvola (NOO-voh-lah)

cloudy nuvoloso (noo-voh-LOH-soh)

club (night) il night club

clutch (car) la frizione (free-TSYOH-nay)

coach (horse) la carrozza, la vettura (kahr-RAW-tsah, vayt-TOO-rah)

coach (R.R.) il vagone (vah-GOH-nay)

coachman il cocchiere, il vetturino (kohk-KYEH-ray, vayt-too-REE-noh)

coat hanger un attaccapanni (aht-tahk-kah-PAHN-nee); pl., gli attaccapanni

cocktail il cocktail (kohk-TEHL)

coffee il caffè (kahf-FEH)

coin la moneta (moh-NAY-tah)

cold (weather) il freddo (FRAYD-doh)

cold (respiratory) il raffreddore (rahf-frayd-DOH-ray)

cold (adjective) freddo (FRAYD-doh)

cold cream il cold cream (kohl-KREHM)

cold cuts affettato (m.), carni fredde (ahf-fayt-TAH-toh, KAHR-nee FRAYD-day)

collar il colletto, il collo (kohl-LAYT-toh, KAWL-loh)

collect riscuotere (rees-KWAW-tay-ray); Past, riscossi, P. P., riscosso

cologne water acqua di Colonia (f.) (AHK-kwah dee koh-LAW-nyah)

color il colore (koh-LOH-ray)

color film la pellicola a colori (payl-LEE-koh-lah ah koh-LOH-ree)

comb (noun) il pettine (PEHT-tee-nay)

come venire (vay-NEE-ray); Present: vengo, vieni, viene, veniamo, venite, vengono (VEHN-goh, VYEH-nee, VYEH-nay, vay-NYAH-moh, vay-NEE-tay, VEHN-goh-noh); Past, venni (VAYN-nee); Fut., verrò (vayr-RAW); P. P., venuto (vay-NOO-toh) (essere)

come for venire a prendere, venire a cercare (vay-NEE-ray ah PREHN-day-ray, vay-NEE-ray ah chayr-KAH-ray)

come in entrare (ayn-TRAH-ray) (essere)

come in! avanti! (ah-VAHN-tee)

comedy la commedia (kohm-MEH-dyah)

comfortable comodo (KAW-moh-doh)

company la compagnia (kohm-pah-NYEE-ah)

161

compartment il compartimento (kohm-pahr-tee-MAYN-toh)

complain lagnarsi (lah-NYAHR-see), fare un reclamo (FAH-ray oon ray-KLAH-moh)

complaint il reclamo (ray-KLAH-moh)

concert il concerto (kohn-CHEHR-toh)

conductor (train) il controllore (kohn-trohl-LOH-ray)

congratulations le felicitazioni (fay-lee-chee-tah-TSYOH-nee)

connected (to be, phone) essere in comunicazione (EHS-say-ray een koh-moo-nee-kah-TSYOH-nay)

consist consistere (kohn-SEES-tay-ray); P. P., consistito

consul il console (KAWN-soh-lay)

consulate il consolato (kohn-soh-LAH-toh)

continue continuare a + infinitive (kohn-tee-noo-AH-ray ah)

convent il convento (kohn-VEHN-toh)

cooked cotto (KAWT-toh)

cool fresco (FRAYS-koh)

corkscrew il cavatappi (kah-vah-TAHP-pee); pl., i cavatappi

corn (Indian) il granturco (grahn-TOOR-koh)

corner un angolo, il cantone (AHN-goh-loh, kahn-TOH-nay)

cost (noun) il costo (KAWS-toh)

cost (verb) costare (kohs-TAH-ray)

cotton il cotone (koh-TOH-nay); **absorbent cotton** cotone idro-

filo (ee-DRAW-fee-loh); **darning cotton** cotone da rammendo (dah rahm-MAYN-doh)

cough la tosse (TOHS-say)

cough syrup lo sciroppo per la tosse (shee-RAWP-poh payr lah TOHS-say)

count (verb) contare (kohn-TAH-ray)

country (nation) il paese (pah-AY-say)

country (outside city) la campagna (kahm-PAH-nyah)

course (in meal) la portata (pohr-TAH-tah)

course, of ben inteso, naturalmente (BEHN een-TAY-soh, nah-too-rahl-MAYN-tay)

courtyard il cortile (kohr-TEE-lay)

cover charge il coperto (koh-PEHR-toh)

crazy matto, pazzo (MAHT-toh, PAH-tsoh)

cream la crema, la panna (KREH-mah, PAHN-nah); **ice cream** il gelato (jay-LAH-toh); **shaving cream** la crema da barba (KREH-mah dah BAHR-bah)

crossroad un incrocio (stradale) (een-KROH-choh strah-DAH-lay)

crossing (R.R.) il passaggio a livello (pahs-SAH-joh ah lee-VEHL-loh)

crystal il cristallo (krees-TAHL-loh)

Cuban cubano (koo-BAH-noh)

cucumber il cetriolo (chay-tree-AW-loh)

cuff links i bottoni da polso, i

gemelli (boht-TOH-NEE dah POHL-soh, jay-MEHL-lee)

cup la tazza (TAH-tsah)

currency la valuta (vah-LOO-tah)

curtain la cortina, la tendina (kohr-TEE-nah, tayn-DEE-nah)

curve la curva, la voltata (KOOR-vah, vohl-TAH-tah)

customs la dogana, il dazio (doh-GAH-nah, DAH-tsyoh)

cut (verb) tagliare (tah-LYAH-ray)

cut it out! la finisca! la faccia finita! (LAH fee-NEES-kah, lah FAH-chah fee-NEE-tah)

cutlet la cotoletta (koh-toh-LAYT-tah)

Czech cecoslovacco (cheh-koh-sloh-VAHK-koh)

daily (by the day) al giorno, alla giornata (ahl JOHR-noh, AHL-lah johr-NAH-tah)

damp umido (OO-mee-doh)

dance (noun) il ballo (BAHL-loh)

dance (verb) ballare (bahl-LAH-ray)

danger il pericolo (pay-REE-koh-loh)

dangerous pericoloso (pay-ree-koh-LOH-soh)

Danish danese (dah-NAY-say)

dark scuro, oscuro (SKOO-roh, oh-SKOO-roh)

darn rammendare (rahm-mayn-DAH-ray)

darn it! accidenti! (ah-chee-DEHN-tee)

darning cotton il cotone da rammendo, il refe (koh-TOH-nay dah rahm-MAYN-doh, REH-fay)

date la data (lah DAH-tah); **what is today's date?** quanti ne abbiamo oggi? (KWAN-tee nay ahb-BYAH-moh AW-jee)

daughter la figlia (FEE-lyah)

day il giorno, la giornata (JOHR-noh, johr-NAH-tah)

dead morto (MAWR-toh); **dead battery** batteria scarica (baht-tay-REE-ah SKAH-ree-kah)

death la morte (MAWR-tay)

December il dicembre (dee-CHEHM-bray)

deck la coperta (koh-PEHR-tah); **on deck** sopra (SOH-prah) coperta

deck chair la sedia a sdraio (SEH-dyah ah ZDRAH-yoh)

deck steward il cameriere di coperta (kah-may-RYEH-ray dee koh-PEHR-tah)

declaration la dichiarazione (dee-kyah-rah-TSYOH-nay)

declare dichiarare (dee-kyah-RAH-ray)

deep profondo (proh-FOHN-doh)

deliver consegnare, recapitare (kohn-say-NYAH-ray, ray-kah-pee-TAH-ray)

delivery la consegna (kohn-SAY-nyah); **special delivery** (per) espresso (ays-PREHS-soh)

dental dentale (dayn-TAH-lay)

dentist il dentista (dayn-TEES-tah); pl., i dentisti

denture la dentiera (dayn-TYEH-rah)

deodorant il deodorante (day-oh-doh-RAHN-tay)

department store il magazzino (mah-gah-DZEE-noh)

desk (information) un ufficio informazioni (oof-FEE-choh een-fohr-mah-TSYOH-nee)

dessert il dessert, il (piatto) dolce (days-SEHR, PYAHT-toh DOHL-chay)

detour la deviazione (stradale) (day-vyah-TSYOH-nay strah-DAH-lay)

develop (film) sviluppare (zvee-loop-PAH-ray)

devil il diavolo (DYAH-voh-loh)

diaper la pezza da bambini (PEH-tsah dah bahm-BEE-nee)

dictionary il dizionario (dee-tsyoh-NAH-ryoh)

different differente, diverso (deef-fay-REHN-tay, dee-VEHR-soh)

difficult difficile (deef-FEE-chee-lay)

difficulty la difficoltà, il guaio (deef-fee-kohl-TAH, GWAH-yoh)

dining car il vagone ristorante (vah-GOH-nay rees-toh-RAHN-tay)

dining room la sala da pranzo (SAH-lah dah PRAHN-dzoh)

dining salon il salone da pranzo (sah-LOH-nay dah PRAHN-dzoh)

dinner il pranzo (PRAHN-dzoh)

direct (verb) indicare (een-dee-KAH-ray)

direction la direzione (dee-ray-TSYOH-nay)

dirty sporco (pl., -chi), sudicio (SPAWR-koh, soo-dee-choh)

discount lo sconto (SKOHN-toh)

dish il piatto (PYAHT-toh)

display window la vetrina (vay-TREE-nah)

district il distretto, il rione (dees-TRAYT-toh, ree-OH-nay)

disturb disturbare (dees-toor-BAH-ray)

dizzy (to feel) aver le vertigini (a-VAYR lay vayr-TEE-jee-nee)

do fare (FAH-ray); Pres.: faccio, fai, fa, facciamo, fate, fanno (FAH-choh, FAH-ee, FAH, fah-CHAH-moh, FAH-tay, FAHN-noh); Impf., facevo (fah-CHAY-voh); Fut., farò (fah-RAW); Past, feci (FAY-chee); P. P., fatto (FAHT-toh)

dock il molo, la banchina (MAW-loh, bahn-KEE-nah)

doctor il medico, il dottore (MAY-dee-kho, doht-TOH-ray)

document il documento (doh-koo-MAYN-toh)

dog il cane (KAH-nay)

dollar il dollaro (DAWL-lah-roh)

domestic (not imported) nazionale (nah-tsyoh-NAH-lay)

done (well) ben cotto (BEHN KAWT-toh)

door la porta (PAWR-tah)

door handle la maniglia (mah-NEE-lyah)

doorman il portiere (pohr-TYEH-ray)

double (phone charges) raddoppiare (rahd-dohp-PYAH-ray)

double room la stanza a due letti (STAHN-tsah ah DOO-ay LEHT-tee)

164

down giù, sotto, in basso (JOO, SOHT-toh, een BAHS-soh)

dozen la dozzina (doh-DZEE-nah)

draft (bank) la tratta (TRAHT-tah)

draft (current of air) la corrente (kohr-REHN-tay)

draw tirare (tee-RAH-ray)

drawer il tiretto (tee-RAYT-toh)

dress (noun) il vestito, un abito (vays-TEE-toh, AH-bee-toh)

dress (verb) vestire, vestirsi (vays-TEE-ray, vays-TEER-see)

dressing gown la veste da camera (VEHS-tay dah KAH-may-rah)

drink (noun) la bibita, la bevanda (BEE-bee-tah, bay-VAHN-dah)

drink (verb) bere (BAY-ray); Pres., bevo; Impf., bevevo; Fut., berrò; Past, bevvi; P. P., bevuto

drive (noun) la gita (JEE-tah)

drive (verb) guidare, condurre (gwee-DAH-ray, kohn-DOOR-ray); Pres., conduco; Impf., conducevo; Fut., condurrò; Past, condussi; P. P., condotto

driver un autista (ow-TEES-tah); pl., gli autisti

dropper il contagoccie (kohn-tah-GOH-chay); pl., i contagoccie

drugstore la farmacia (fahr-mah-CHEE-ah)

drunk ubbriaco (oob-bree-AH-koh)

dry secco (pl., -chi), asciutto (SAYK-koh, ah-SHOOT-toh)

dry-clean pulire a secco (poo-LEE-ray ah SAYK-koh) (-isc-)

duck un'anatra (AH-nah-trah)

dumbbell (slang) un imbecille (eem-bay-CHEEL-lay)

dump (slang) il postaccio (pohs-TAH-choh)

Dutch olandese (oh-lahn-DAY-say)

dutiable soggetto a dogana (soh-JEHT-toh ah doh-GAH-nah)

duty (customs) la dogana, il dazio (doh-GAH-nah, DAH-tsyoh)

dysentery la dissenteria (dees-sayn-tay-REE-ah)

each, each one ciascuno (chahs-KOO-noh)

ear un orecchio (oh-RAYK-kyoh); pl., gli orecchi or le orecchie

earache mal d'orecchi (MAHL doh-RAYK-kee)

early presto, di buon'ora (PREHS-toh, dee bwaw-NOH-rah)

earring un orecchino (oh-rayk-KEE-noh)

east est, levante, oriente (EHST, lay-VAHN-tay, oh-RYEHN-tay)

easy facile (FAH-chee-lay); take it easy! calma! (KAHL-mah)

eat mangiare (mahn-JAH-ray)

egg un uovo (WAW-voh); pl., le uova

eight otto (AWT-toh)

eighteen diciotto (dee-CHAWT-toh)

eighth ottavo (oht-TAH-voh)

eighty ottanta (oht-TAHN-tah)

elbow il gomito (GOH-mee-toh)

electric elettrico (ay-LEHT-tree-koh)

elevator un ascensore (ah-shayn-SOH-ray)

eleven undici (OON-dee-chee)

else (nothing) nient'altro (nyehn-TAHL-troh); **what else?** che altro? (KAY AHL-troh)

empty (adj.) vuoto (VWAW-toh)

end (noun) la fine (FEE-nay)

end (verb) finire (fee-NEE-ray) (-isc-)

engine il motore (moh-TOH-ray)

English inglese (een-GLAY-say)

enlargement un ingrandimento (een-grahn-dee-MAYN-toh)

enough abbastanza (ahb-bahs-TAHN-tsah)

entrance un'entrata (ayn-TRAH-tah)

envelope la busta (BOOS-tah)

evening la sera (SAY-rah)

evening clothes abito da sera (AH-bee-toh dah SAY-rah)

every ogni (OH-nyee)

everybody, everyone ognuno, tutti (oh-NYOO-noh, TOOT-tee)

everything tutto (TOOT-toh)

examine esaminare (ay-sah-mee-NAH-ray)

excess weight il peso in eccesso (PAY-soh een ay-CHEHS-soh)

exchange il cambio (KAHM-byoh)

exchange office un ufficio di cambio (oof-FEE-choh dee KAHM-byoh)

excursion un'escursione, una gita (ays-koor-SYOH-nay, JEE-tah)

excuse (verb) scusare (skoo-SAH-ray)

exhaust (car) lo scappamento (skahp-pah-MAYN-toh)

exit un'uscita (OO-SHEE-tah)

expect aspettare (ahs-payt-TAH-ray)

expensive caro, costoso (KAH-roh, kohs-TOH-soh)

express (train) il diretto (dee-REHT-toh)

extra in eccesso, in più (een ay-CHEHS-soh, een PYOO)

extract estrarre (ays-TRAHR-ray); Pres.: estraggo, estrai, estrae, estraiamo, estraete, estraggono; Impf., estraevo; Fut., estrarrò; Past, estrassi, estraesti, etc.; P. P., estratto

eye un occhio (AWK-kyoh)

eyebrow il sopracciglio (soh-prah-CHEE-lyoh); pl., le sopracciglia

eyeglasses gli occhiali (ohk-KYAH-lee)

eyelash il ciglio (CHEE-lyoh); pl., le ciglia

eyelid la palpebra (PAHL-pay-brah)

face (noun) la faccia, il viso, il volto (FAH-chah, VEE-soh, VOHL-toh)

face (verb) dare su (DAH-ray soo) (see *to give*, dare, for conjugation)

face powder la cipria (CHEE-pryah)

facecloth la pezzuola da bagno (pay-TSWAW-lah dah BAH-nyoh)

facial facciale (fah-CHAH-lay)

fall (autumn) un autunno (ow-TOON-noh)

166

fall (noun) la caduta (kah-
DOO-tah)

fall (verb) cadere (kah-
DAY-ray); Fut., cadrò; Past,
caddi (KAHD-dee)

false falso (FAHL-soh)

family la famiglia (fah-MEE-
lyah)

fan (car or electric) il ventilatore (vayn-tee-lah-TOH-ray)

fan (hand) il ventaglio (vayn-
TAH-lyoh)

fan belt la cinghia del ventilatore (CHEEN-gyah dayl vayn-
tee-lah-TOH-ray)

far lontano, distante (lohn-TAH-
noh, dees-TAHN-tay)

fare (noun) la corsa (KOHR-sah)

fast presto (PREHS-toh); **the
watch is fast**, l'orologio va
avanti (loh-roh-LAW-joh VAH
ah-VAHN-tee)

faster più presto (PYOO PREHS-
toh)

father il padre (PAH-dray)

faucet il rubinetto (roo-bee-
NAYT-toh)

fear (noun) la paura (pah-OO-
rah), il timore (tee-MOH-ray)

fear (verb) aver paura (ah-
VAYR pah-OO-rah)

February il febbraio (fayb-
BRAH-yoh)

feel (health) sentirsi (sayn-
TEER-see)

feel like aver voglia di (+ infinitive) (ah-VAYR VAW-lyah
dee)

felt (noun) il feltro (FAYL-troh)

fender il parafango (pah-rah-
FAHN-goh); pl., i parafanghi

festival la festa (FEHS-tah)

fever la febbre (FEHB-bray)

few, a few pochi (PAW-kee)

field glasses il binoccolo, il
canocchiale (bee-NAWK-koh-
loh, kah-nohk-KYAH-lay)

fifteen quindici (KWEEN-dee-
chee)

fifth quinto (KWEEN-toh)

fifty cinquanta (cheen-KWAHN-
tah)

fig il fico (FEE-koh)

fill, fill out riempire (ree-aym-
PEE-ray); **fill a tooth** otturare
un dente (oht-too-RAH-ray
oon DEHN-tay); **fill her up!**
faccia il pieno (FAH-chah eel
PYEH-noh)

filling un'otturazione (oht-too-
rah-TSYOH-nay)

film la pellicola (payl-LEE-koh-
lah)

find trovare (troh-VAH-ray)

fine (noun) la multa, la contravvenzione (MOOL-tah,
kohn-trahv-vayn-TSYOH-nay)

fine (adj.) fino, bello (FEE-noh,
BEHL-loh)

finger il dito (DEE-toh); pl., le
dita

finger wave la messa in piega
(MAYS-sah een PYEH-gah)

finish finire (fee-NEE-ray)
(-isc-)

fire (noun) il fuoco (pl., -chi)
(FWAW-koh)

first primo (PREE-moh)

first aid il pronto soccorso
(PROHN-toh sohk-KOHR-soh)

fish il pesce (PAY-shay)

fit (verb) andare, stare (ahn-
DAH-ray, STAH-ray) (see *to go*
and *to stand* for conjugation)

167

five cinque (CHEEN-kway)

fix (verb) accomodare, aggiustare, riparare (ahk-koh-moh-DAH-ray, ah-joos-TAH-ray, ree-pah-RAH-ray)

flashlight la lampadina tascabile (lahm-pah-DEE-nah tahs-KAH-bee-lay)

flat tire la gomma a terra (GOHM-mah ah TEHR-rah)

flatiron il ferro da stiro (FEHR-roh dah STEE-roh)

flight (plane) il volo (VOH-loh)

flint (lighter) la pietrina (pyay-TREE-nah)

floor il piano (in sense of "story"), il pavimento (PYAH-noh, pah-vee-MAYN-toh)

flower il fiore (FYOH-ray)

fluid (lighter) la benzina (bayn-DZEE-nah)

fog la nebbia (NAYB-byah)

foggy nebbioso (nayb-BYOH-soh)

follow seguire (say-GWEE-ray)

foot il piede (PYEH-day)

for per (PAYR)

forbidden vietato, proibito (vyay-TAH-toh, proh-ee-BEE-toh)

forehead la fronte (FROHN-tay)

foreign straniero (strah-NYEH-roh)

forget dimenticare (dee-mayn-tee-KAH-ray)

fork la forchetta (fohr-KAYT-tah)

form (document) il modulo (MAW-doo-loh)

forty quaranta (kwah-RAHN-tah)

forward (adv.) avanti (ah-VAHN-tee)

forward (verb) spedire (-isc-), inoltrare, far recapitare (spay-DEE-ray, ee-nohl-TRAH-ray, FAHR ray-kah-pee-TAH-ray)

fountain la fontana (fohn-TAH-nah)

fountain pen la penna stilografica (PAYN-nah stee-loh-GRAH-fee-kah)

four quattro (KWAHT-troh)

fourteen quattordici (kwaht-TAWR-dee-chee)

fourth quarto (KWAHR-toh)

fracture (noun) la frattura (fraht-TOO-rah)

free libero (LEE-bay-roh); (of charge) gratuito (grah-TOO-ee-toh)

French francese (frahn-CHAY-say)

Friday il venerdì (vay-nayr-DEE)

fried fritto (FREET-toh)

friend un amico, un'amica (ah-MEE-koh, ah-MEE-kah)

from da (DAH)

front (adj.) davanti (dah-VAHN-tee)

fruit il frutto, la frutta (FROOT-toh, FROOT-tah)

fuel pump la pompa di alimentazione (POHM-pah dee ah-lee-mayn-tah-TSYOH-nay)

full pieno (PYEH-noh); (referring to bus or street-car) completo (kohm-PLEH-toh)

furnished mobiliato, ammobiliato (ahm-moh-bee-LYAH-toh)

gallery (theater) la galleria, il loggione (gahl-lay-REE-ah, loh-JOH-nay)

game il giuoco, la partita (JWAW-koh, pahr-TEE-tah)

gangway! permesso? (payr-MAYS-soh)

garage un'autorimessa (ow-toh-ree-MAYS-sah)

garden il giardino (jahr-DEE-noh)

garlic l'aglio (m.) (AH-lyoh)

garter la giarrettiera (jahr-rayt-TYEH-rah)

gas station il distributore di benzina, la pompa (dees-tree-boo-TOH-ray dee bayn-DZEE-nah, POHM-pah)

gasoline la benzina (bayn-DZEE-nah)

gate la porta, il cancello (PAWR-tah, kahn-CHEHL-loh)

gauze la garza (GAHR-dzah)

gears (car) la marcia (MAHR-chah)

general delivery fermo (in) posta (FAYR-moh een PAWS-tah)

gentleman il signore (see-NYOH-ray)

German tedesco (pl., -schi) (tay-DAYS-koh)

get (obtain) avere, ottenere (ah-VAY-ray, oht-tay-NAY-ray (see *to have* and *to hold* for conjugation)

get back (have given back) riavere (ree-ah-VAY-ray)

get back (be back) ritornare, essere di ritorno (ree-tohr-NAH-ray, EHS-say-ray dee ree-TOHR-noh)

get dressed vestirsi (vays-TEER-see)

get off scendere (SHAYN-day-ray); Past, scesi; P. P., sceso (SHAY-soh) (essere)

get out andar via, andarsene ahn-DAHR VEE-ah, ahn-DAHR-say-nay); see *to go* for conjugation (essere)

get up alzarsi, levarsi (ahl-TSAHR-see, lay-VAHR-see)

gift il dono, il regalo (DOH-noh, ray-GAH-loh)

gin il gin (JEEN)

girdle la fascetta, il busto (fah-SHAYT-tah, BOOS-toh)

girl la ragazza, la fanciulla (rah-GAH-tsah, fahn-CHOOL-lah)

give dare (DAH-ray); Pres.: do, dai, dà, diamo, date, danno (DAW, DAH-ee, DAH, DYAH-moh, DAH-tay, DAHN-noh); Past, diedi, desti, etc. (DYAY-dee, DAYS-tee)

give back ridare, restituire (ree-DAH-ray, rays-tee-too-EE-ray) (-isc-)

glad contento (kohn-TEHN-toh)

gladly volentieri (voh-layn-TYEH-ree)

glass (drinking) il bicchiere (beek-KYEH-ray)

glass (material) il vetro (VAY-troh)

glasses (eye) gli occhiali (ohk-KYAH-lee)

glove il guanto (GWAHN-toh)

go andare (ahn-DAH-ray); Present: vado, vai, va, andiamo, andate, vanno (VAH-doh, VAH-ee, VAH, ahn-DYAH-moh, ahn-DAH-tay, VAHN-noh); Fut., andrò or anderò (ahn-DRAW, ahn-day-RAW) (essere)

go away andar via, andarsene (ahn-DAHR VEE-ah, ahn-DAHR-say-nay)

go down andar giù, scendere (SHAYN-day-ray); Past, scesi (SHAY-see); P. P., sceso (essere)

go home andare a casa (ahn-DAH-ray ah KAH-sah)

go in andar dentro, entrare (essere) (ahn-DAHR DAYN-troh, ayn-TRAH-ray)

go out andar fuori, uscire (ahn-DAHR FWAW-ree, OO-SHEE-ray) Pres.: esco, esci, esce, usciamo, uscite, escono (EHS-koh, EH-shee, EH-shay, OO-SHAH-moh, OO-SHEE-tay, EHS-koh-noh) (essere)

go shopping andare a far (delle) compere (ahn-DAH-ray ah FAHR DAYL-lay KOHM-pay-ray)

go to bed andare a letto, andare a dormire (anr-DAH-ray ah LEHT-toh, ah dohr-MEE-ray)

go up andar su, andar sopra, salire (ahn-DAHR SOO, SOH-prah, sah-LEE-ray); Pres.: salgo, sali . . . salgono (SAHL-goh, SAH-lee . . . SAHL-goh-noh) (essere)

gold l'oro (m.) (AW-roh)

good buono (BWAW-noh)

good for (valid) valido (VAH-lee-doh)

good-by arrivederci, arrivederla (ahr-ree-vay-DAYR-chee, ahr-ree-vay-DAYR-lah)

goose un'oca (AW-kah); pl. oche

grade crossing il passaggio a

livello (pahs-SAH-joh ah lee-VEHL-loh)

gram il grammo (GRAHM-moh)

grapefruit il pompelmo (pohm-PAYL-moh)

grapes l'uva (f. s.) (OO-vah)

grass l'erba (f.) (EHR-bah)

grateful grato, riconoscente (GRAH-toh, ree-koh-noh-SHEHN-tay)

gravy la salsa (SAHL-sah)

gray grigio, bigio (GREE-joh, BEE-joh)

grease (lubricate) ingrassare, lubrificare (een-grahs-SAH-ray, loo-bree-fee-KAH-ray)

Greek greco (GREH-koh); pl.: greci, m.; greche, f.

green verde (VAYR-day)

greeting il saluto, l'ossequio (sah-LOO-toh, ohs-SEH-kwyoh)

grinding la sgranatura (zgrah-nah-TOO-rah)

guide la guida (GWEE-dah)

guidebook la guida (GWEE-dah)

gum (chewing) la gomma da masticare (GOHM-mah dah mahs-tee-KAH-ray)

gums le gengive (jayn-JEE-vay)

guy il tipo (TEE-poh)

hail (noun, weather) la grandine (GRAHN-dee-nay)

hail (verb) grandinare (grahn-dee-NAH-ray)

hair i capelli (pl.) (kah-PAYL-lee)

hair bleach la tintura per i capelli (teen-TOO-rah payr ee kah-PAYL-lee)

hair lotion la lozione per i

capelli (loh-TSOYH-nay payr ee kah-PAYL-lee)

hair rinse il lavaggio ai capelli (lah-VAH-joh AH-ee kah-PAYL-lee)

hair tonic il tonico per i capelli (TAW-nee-koh payr ee kah-PAYL-lee)

hairbrush la spazzola da capelli (SPAH-tsoh-lah dah kah-PAYL-lee)

haircut (to get a . . .) farsi tagliare i capelli (FAHR-see tah-LYAH-ray ee kah-PAYL-lee)

hairnet la rete da capelli (RAY-tay dah kah-PAYL-lee)

hairpin la forcina da capelli (fohr-CHEE-nah dah kah-PAYL-lee)

half (noun) la metà (may-TAH)

half (adj.) mezzo (MEH-dzoh)

halt! ferma! stop! (FAYR-mah, STAWP)

ham il prosciutto (proh-SHOOT-toh)

hammer il martello (mahr-TEHL-loh)

hand la mano (MAH-noh); pl., le mani

hand lotion la lozione per le mani (loh-TSYOH-nay payr lay MAH-nee)

handbag la borsa, la borsetta (BOHR-sah, bohr-SAYT-tah)

handkerchief il fazzoletto (fah-tsoh-LAYT-toh)

handmade fatto a mano (FAHT-toh ah MAH-noh)

hanger (coat) un attaccapanni (aht-tahk-kah-PAHN-nee); pl., gli attaccapanni

happen accadere, avvenire, succedere (all with essere) (ahk-kah-DAY-ray, ahv-vay-NEE-ray, SOO-CHEH-day-ray); (see *to fall*, cadere, and *to come*, venire, for conjugation); succedere: Past, successi (SOO-CHEHS-see); P. P., successo (SOO-CHEHS-soh)

happy felice (fay-LEE-chay)

Happy New Year! Buon Capo d'Anno! (BWAWN KAH-poh DAHN-noh)

harbor il porto (PAWR-toh)

hard (difficult) difficile (deef-FEE-chee-lay)

hard (tough) duro (DOO-roh)

hard-boiled egg un uovo sodo (WAW-voh SAW-doh); pl., le uova sode

hat il cappello (kahp-PEHL-loh)

hat shop la cappelleria (kahp-payl-lay-REE-ah)

have avere (ah-VAY-ray); Pres.: ho, hai, ha, abbiamo, avete, hanno (AW, AH-ee, AH, ahb-BYAH-moh, ah-VAY-tay, AHN-noh); Fut., avrò (ah-VRAW); Past, ebbi (EHB-bee)

have (something) done far fare (FAHR FAH-ray); conjugate the first "fare"; the second verb, which in English appears in the past participle, appears in Italian in the infinitive: **I shall have a letter written,** farò scrivere una lettera.

have just done aver fatto proprio ora (ah-VAYR-FAHT-toh PRAW-pryoh OH-rah)

have to dovere (doh-VAY-ray); Pres.: devo or debbo, devi . . .

devono or debbono; Fut.
dovrò (doh-VRAW)
hazelnut la nocciuola (noh-CHWAW-lah)
he egli, lui (AY-lyee, LOO-ee)
head la testa, il capo (TEHS-tah, KAH-poh)
headache il dolor di testa, il mal di capo (doh-LOHR dee TEHS-tah, MAHL dee KAH-poh)
headlight il fanale (fah-NAH-lay)
headwaiter il capo cameriere (KAH-poh kah-may-RYEH-ray)
health la salute (sah-LOO-tay)
hear sentire, udire (sayn-TEE-ray, OO-DEE-ray); Pres.: odo, odi, ode, udiamo, udite, odono (AW-doh, AW-dee, AW-day, OO-DYAH-moh, OO-DEE-tay, AW-doh-noh)
hear from aver notizie di (ah-VAYR noh-TEE-tsyay dee)
heart il cuore (KWAW-ray)
heat il caldo, il calore (KAHL-doh, kah-LOH-ray)
heaven il cielo (CHEH-loh)
heavy pesante (pay-SAHN-tay)
Hebrew ebraico (ay-BRAH-ee-koh)
hectogram un ettogrammo, un etto (ayt-toh-GRAHM-moh, EHT-toh)
heel (of foot) il tallone (tahl-LOH-nay)
heel (of shoe) il tacco (TAHK-koh); pl., i tacchi
hell un inferno (een-FEHR-noh)
hello! ciao! (CHAH-oh); (on telephone) pronto! (PROHN-toh)

help aiutare (ah-yoo-TAH-ray) **may I help you?** posso servirla? (PAWS-soh sayr-VEER-lah); **help yourself** faccia or prenda pure (FAH-chah, PREHN-dah POO-ray)
her lei, la, le (LEH-ee, LAH, LAY)
here qui, qua (KWEE, KWAH)
high alto (AHL-toh)
High Mass la Messa cantata or solenne (MAYS-sah kahn-TAH-tah, soh-LEHN-nay)
highway un'autostrada (ow-toh-STRAH-dah)
him lui, lo, gli (LOO-ee, LOH, LYEE)
hip un'anca (AHN-kah)
hire affittare, prendere in affitto, prendere a nolo, noleggiare (ahf-feet-TAH-ray, PREHN-day-ray een ahf-FEET-toh, PREHN-day-ray ah NAW-loh, noh-lay-JAH-ray)
his suo, di lui (SOO-oh, dee LOO-ee)
hold tenere, reggere (tay-NAY-ray, REEH-jay-ray); tenere: Pres.: tengo, tieni, tiene, teniamo, tenete, tengono (TEHN-goh, TYEH-nee, TYEH-nay, tay-NYAH-moh, tay-NAY-tay, TEHN-goh-noh); Fut., terrò (tayr-RAW); Past, tenni TAYN-nee); reggere: Pres.: reggo, reggi . . . reggono (REHG-goh, REH-jee . . . REHG-goh-noh); Past, ressi (REHS-see); P. P., retto (REHT-toh)
hold the wire resti all'apparecchio (REHS-tee ahl-lahp-pah-RAYK-kyoh)

172

holder (cigarette) il bocchino
(bohk-KEE-noh)
home la casa (KAH-sah); go . . .
andare a casa (ahn-DAH-ray
ah KAH-sah); be at . . . essere
in casa (EHS-say-ray een
KAH-sah)
hood (car) il cofano (KAW-fah-
noh)
hook (noun) un uncino (oon-
CHEE-noh)
hope (verb) sperare (spay-RAH-
ray)
horn (car) il clacson (KLAHK-
sohn)
hors d'oeuvre un antipasto (ahn-
tee-PAHS-toh)
horse il cavallo (kah-VAHL-loh)
horse carriage la carrozza (kahr-
RAW-tsah)
hospital un ospedale (ohs-pay-
DAH-lay)
hostel (youth) un ostello (della
gioventù) (ohs-TEHL-loh
DAYL-lah joh-vayn-TOO)
hostess (plane) la hostess (OHS-
tess)
hot caldo (KAHL-doh)
hotel un hotel, un albergo (oh-
TEHL, ahl-BEHR-goh)
hour un'ora (OH-rah); by the
. . . all'ora (ahl-LOH-rah)
house la casa (KAH-sah)
how come (KOH-may)
how far a che distanza (ah KAY
dees-TAHN-tsah)
how long per (da) quanto
tempo (payr, dah, KWAN-toh
TEHM-poh)
how many quanti (KWAHN-tee)
how much quanto (KWAHN-toh)
hundred cento (CHEHN-toh)

Hungarian ungherese (oon-gay-
RAY-say)
hungry (to be) aver fame (ah-
VAYR FAH-may)
hurry (verb) sbrigarsi, affrettarsi (zbree-GAHR-see, ahf-
frayt-TAHR-see); to be in
a . . . aver fretta (ah-VAYR
FRAYT-tah)
hurt (verb) far male a (FAHR
MAH-lay ah)
husband il marito (mah-REE-
toh)

I io (EE-oh)
ice il ghiaccio (GYAH-choh)
ice cream il gelato (jay-LAH-toh)
ice water l'acqua ghiacciata
(f.) (AHK-kwah gyah-CHAH-
tah)
identification l'identità (f.)
(ee-dayn-tee-TAH)
if se (SAY)
ignition (car) l'accensione (f.)
(ah-chayn-SYOH-nay)
ill malato (mah-LAH-toh)
illness la malattia (mah-laht-
TEE-ah)
imported importato (eem-
pohr-TAH-toh)
in in (EEN)
included incluso (een-KLOO-
soh)
indigestion un'indigestione
(een-dee-jays-TYOH-nay)
indisposed indisposto (een-dees-
PAWS-toh)
information le informazioni (f.
pl.) (een-fohr-mah-TSYOH-
nee); . . . desk, bureau un
ufficio informazioni (oof-FEE-
choh)

173

injection un'iniezione (ee-nyay-TSYOH-nay)

ink un inchiostro (een-KYAWS-troh)

inner tube una camera d'aria (KAY-may-rah DAH-ryah)

inquire domandare, chiedere (doh-mahn-DAH-ray, KYEH-day-ray); Past, chiesi (KYEH-see); P. P. chiesto (KYEHS-toh)

insect un insetto (een-SEHT-toh)

insecticide un insetticida (een-seht-tee-CHEE-dah)

inside dentro (DAYN-troh)

instead invece (di) (een-VAY-chay)

insurance un'assicurazione (ahs-see-koo-rah-TSYOH-nay)

insure assicurare (ahs-see-koo-RAH-ray)

interest un interesse (een-tay-REHS-say)

interpreter un interprete (een-TEHR-pray-tay)

intersection un incrocio (stradale), una traversa (een-KROH-choh strah-DAH-lay, trah-VEHR-sah)

into in, dentro a (EEN, DAYN-troh ah)

introduce presentare (pray-sayn-TAH-ray)

iodine l'iodio (m.) (YAW-dyoh)

iron (metal) il ferro (FEHR-roh)

iron (verb) stirare (stee-RAH-ray)

is è (EH)

it esso, lo, la (AYS-soh, LOH, LAH)

Italian italiano (ee-tah-LYAH-noh)

jack (noun, car) il cricco (KREEK-koh)

jack up sollevare col cricco (sohl-lay-VAH-ray kohl KREEK-koh)

jam la marmellata (mahr-mayl-LAH-tah)

January il gennaio (jayn-NAH-yoh)

Japanese giapponese (jahp-poh-NAY-say)

jaw la mascella (mah-SHEHL-lah)

jeweler il gioielliere (joh-yehl-LYEH-ray)

jewelry, jewelry shop la gioielleria (joh-yehl-lay-REE-ah)

Jewish ebraico, israelita (ay-BRAH-ee-koh, ees-rah-ay-LEE-tah)

journey il viaggio (VYAH-joh)

juice il succo (SOOK-koh)

July il luglio (LOO-lyoh)

June il giugno (JOO-nyoh)

keep tenere (tay-NAY-ray); Pres.: tengo, tieni, tiene, teniamo, tenete, tengono; (TEHN-goh, TYEH-nee, TYEH-nay, tay-NYAH-moh, tay-NAY-tay, TEHN-goh-noh); Fut., terrò; Past, tenni

key la chiave (KYAH-vay)

kilogram il chilogrammo, il chilo (kee-loh-GRAHM-moh, KEE-loh)

kind (noun) il genere, la specie, la sorta (JEH-nay-ray, SPEH-chay, SAWR-tah)

kind (adj.) buono, gentile (BWAH-noh, jayn-TEE-lay)

kiss (noun) il bacio (BAH-choh)

kiss (verb) baciare (bah-CHAH-ray)

kitchen la cucina (koo-CHEE-nah)

knee il ginocchio (jee-NAWK-kyoh); pl., le ginocchia

knife il coltello (kohl-TEHL-loh)

knock (verb) bussare (boos-SAH-ray)

know (fact, know how) sapere (sah-PAY-ray); Pres.: so, sai, sa, sappiamo, sapete, sanno (SAW, SAH-ee, SAH, sahp-PYAH-moh, sah-PAY-tay, SAHN-noh); Fut., saprò (sah-PRAW); Past, seppi (SAYP-pee)

know (person) conoscere (koh-NOH-shay-ray); Past, conobbi (koh-NOHB-bee)

label un'etichetta (ay-tee-KAYT-tah)

lace il merletto (mayr-LAYT-toh)

lace (shoe) il laccio da scarpa, la stringa (LAH-choh dah SKAHR-pah, STREEN-gah)

ladies' room gabinetto per signore (gah-bee-NAYT-toh payr see-NYOH-ray)

lady la signora (see-NYOH-rah)

lamb un agnello (ah-NYEHL-loh)

lamp la lampada, la lampadina (LAHM-pah-dah, lahm-pah-DEE-nah)

land (noun) la terra (TEHR-rah)

land (from ship) sbarcare (zbahr-KAH-ray)

language la lingua (LEEN-gwah)

large grande, grosso (GRAHN-day, GRAWS-soh)

last (adj.) ultimo (OOL-tee-moh)

last (verb) durare (doo-RAH-ray)

late tardi, in ritardo (TAHR-dee, een ree-TAHR-doh)

latest (at the . . .) al più tardi (ahl PYOO TAHR-dee)

laugh (verb) ridere (REE-day-ray); Past, risi (REE-see); P. P., riso

laundress la lavandaia (lah-vahn-DAH-yah)

laundry la lavanderia (lah-vahn-day-REE-ah)

lavatory il gabinetto, la ritirata, il cesso (gah-bee-NAYT-toh, ree-tee-RAH-tah, CHEHS-soh)

laxative il purgante (poor-GAHN-tay)

leak (noun) la perdita d'acqua, la fuga di gas (PEHR-dee-tah DAHK-kwah, FOO-gah dee GAHS)

leak (verb) far acqua, perdere (FAHR AHK-kwah, PEHR-day-ray); Past, persi (PEHR-see); P. P., perso or perduto (PEHR-soh, payr-DOO-toh)

lean (against) appoggiarsi a (ahp-poh-JAHR-see ah); (out) sporgersi (SPOHR-jayr-see)

learn imparare, apprendere (eem-pah-RAH-ray, ahp-PREHN-day-ray); Past, appresi, P. P., appreso

least (at . . .) almeno (ahl-MAY-noh)

leather la pelle, il cuoio (PEHL-lay, KWAW-yoh)

leave (behind) lasciare (lah-SHAH-ray)

175

leave (depart) partire, andarsene (pahr-TEE-ray, ahn-DAHR-say-nay); see *to go,* andare, for conjugation

left (opposite of right) sinistro (see-NEES-troh)

leg la gamba (GAHM-bah)

lemon il limone (lee-MOH-nay)

lemonade la limonata (lee-moh-NAH-tah)

lend prestare (pray-STAH-ray)

length la lunghezza (loon-GAY-tsah)

lens la lente (LEHN-tay)

less meno (MAY-noh)

let lasciare, permettere (lah-SHAH-ray, payr-MAYT-tay-ray); Past, permisi; P. P., permesso

let off (a conveyance) far scendere (FAHR SHAYN-day-ray)

let see far vedere (FAHR vay-DAY-ray)

letter la lettera (LAYT-tay-rah)

letterbox la buca delle lettere (BOO-kah DAYL-lay LAYT-tay-ray)

lettuce la lattuga (laht-TOO-gah)

library la biblioteca (bee-blyoh-TEH-kah)

lie (down) coricarsi (koh-ree-KAHR-see)

life la vita (VEE-tah)

life preserver il salvagente (sahl-vah-JEHN-tay); pl., i salvagente

lifeboat la scialuppa (di salvataggio) (shah-LOOP-pah dee sahl-vah-TAH-joh)

lift (verb) alzare, sollevare (ahl-TSAH-ray, sohl-lay-VAH-ray)

light (noun) la luce (LOO-chay)

light (adj., color) chiaro (KYAH-roh)

light (adj., weight) leggiero (lay-JEH-roh)

light (verb) accendere (ah-CHEHN-day-ray); Past, accesi ah-CHAY-see), P. P. acceso (ah-CHAY-soh); give me a . . . mi faccia accendere (mee FAH-chah ah-CHEHN-day-ray)

lighter (cigar) un accendisigari (ah-chehn-dee-SEE-gah-ree)

lightning il lampo (LAHM-poh)

like come (KOH-may); what is he like? com'è? (koh-MEH)

like (verb) piacere (pyah-CHAY-ray) Pres. piaccio, piaci . . . piacciono (PYAH-choh, PYAH-chee . . . PYAH-choh-noh); Past, piacqui (PYAH-kwee); the subject of the English verb is the indirect object of the Italian verb, while the object of "like" is the subject of piacere: I like them, essi mi piacciono (they are pleasing to me)

limit (speed) la velocità massima (vay-loh-chee-TAH MAHS-see-mah)

line la linea (LEE-nay-ah)

linen il lino (LEE-noh)

lip il labbro (LAHB-broh); pl., le labbra

lipstick il rossetto (per le labbra) (rohs-SAYT-toh payr lay LAHB-brah)

liqueur il cordiale, il liquore (kohr-DYAH-lay, lee-KWOH-ray)

liquor la bevanda (bibita) alcoolica (bay-VAHN-dah, BEE-bee-tah, ahl-KAW-lee-kah)

list (wine, food) la lista (LEES-tah)

listen ascoltare (ahs-kohl-TAH-ray)

liter il litro (LEE-troh)

little piccolo (PEEK-koh-loh); **a . . .** un po' (oon PAW)

live (verb) vivere (VEE-vay-ray); Fut., vivrò (vee-VRAW); Past, vissi (VEES-see); P. P., vissuto (vees-soo-toh)

liver il fegato (FAY-gah-toh)

living room il salotto (sah-LAWT-toh)

lobby un atrio (AH-tryoh)

lobster un'aragosta (ah-rah-GOHS-tah)

local phone call la telefonata urbana (tay-lay-foh-NAH-tah oor-BAH-nah)

local (train) il treno accelerato (TREH-noh ah-chay-lay-RAH-toh)

lock (noun) la serratura (sayr-rah-TOO-rah)

locksmith il magnano (mah-NYAH-noh)

long lungo (LOON-goh); **how . . .** da or per quanto tempo (DAH, PAYR, KWAHN-toh TEHM-poh)

long-distance call la telefonata interurbana (tay-lay-foh-NAH-tah een-tayr-oor-BAH-nah)

look, look at guardare (gwahr-DAH-ray)

look for cercare (chayr-KAH-ray)

look out! attento! attenzione! (aht-TEHN-toh, aht-tayn-TSYOH-nay)

lose perdere (PEHR-day-ray); Past, persi (PEHR-see); P. P., perso or perduto

lost-and-found un ufficio degli oggetti smarriti (oof-FEE-choh DAY-lyee oh-JEHT-tee zmahr-REE-tee)

lotion la lozione (loh-TSYOH-nay)

lots of molto (MOHL-toh)

lounge il vestibolo (vays-TEE-boh-loh)

louse (slang) la canaglia, il mascalzone (kah-NAH-lyah, mahs-kahl-TSOH-nay)

low basso (BAHS-soh)

lower berth la cuccetta inferiore (koo-CHAYT-tah een-fay-RYOH-ray)

luck la fortuna (fohr-TOO-nah)

lunch la (seconda) colazione (say-KOHN-dah koh-lah-TSYOH-nay); **have . . .** far colazione

lunch basket il cestino di viaggio (chays-TEE-noh dee VYAH-joh)

lung il polmone (POHL-moh-nay)

maid la cameriera (kah-may-RYEH-rah)

mail la posta (PAWS-tah)

mailbox la buca delle lettere, la cassetta postale (BOO-kah DAYL-lay LAYT-tay-ray, kahs-SAYT-tah pohs-TAH-lay)

magazine la rivista (ree-VEES-tah)

make fare (FAH-ray); see *do,* fare, for conjugation

man un uomo (WAW-moh); pl., gli uomini (WAW-mee-nee)

manager il direttore, il gerente (dee-rayt-TOH-ray, jay-REHN-tay)

manicure la manicure (mah-nee-KYOOR)

many molti (MOHL-tee)

map la carta, la pianta (KAHR-tah, PYAHN-tah)

March il marzo (MAHR-tsoh)

market il mercato (mayr-KAH-toh)

mashed mascè (mah-SHEH)

Mass la Messa (MAYS-sah); **High** . . . Messa cantata, Messa solenne (kahn-TAH-tah, soh-LEHN-nay)

massage il massaggio (mahs-SAH-joh)

match il fiammifero, il cerino (fyahm-MEE-fay-roh, chay-REE-noh)

mate (officer) un ufficiale (oof-fee-CHAH-lay)

matter (what's the . . . ?) che c'è? (KAY CHEH); **it doesn't** . . . non importa, non fa niente (nohn eem-PAWR-tah, nohn FAH NYEHN-tay)

mattress il materasso (mah-tay-RAHS-soh)

May il maggio (MAH-joh)

may (verb) potere (poh-TAY-ray); see *can,* potere, for conjugation

maybe forse, chissà (FOHR-say, kees-SAH)

me me, mi (MAY, MEE)

meal il pasto (PAHS-toh)

mean (verb) significare, voler dire (see-nyee-fee-KAH-ray, voh-LAYR DEE-ray); see *want,* volere, for conjugation

measurements la misura (mee-soo-rah)

meat la carne (KAHR-nay)

mechanic il meccanico (mayk-KAH-nee-koh)

medical medico (MEH-dee-koh)

medicine la medicina (may-dee-CHEE-nah)

medium rare a mezza cottura (ah MEH-dzah koht-TOO-rah)

meet incontrare; (socially) conoscere (een-kohn-TRAH-ray, koh-NOH-shay-ray); see *know,* conoscere, for conjugation

melon il mellone (mayl-LOH-nay)

mend rammendare (rahm-mayn-DAH-ray)

men's room il gabinetto uomini (gah-bee-NAYT-toh WAW-mee-nee)

mention (don't . . . it) prego, non c'è di che (PREH-goh, nohn CHEH dee KAY)

menu la lista delle vivande, il menù (LEES-tah DAYL-lay vee-VAHN-day, may-NOO)

merry allegro (ahl-LEH-groh)

Merry Christmas! Buon Natale! (BWAWN nah-TAH-lay)

message il messaggio, un'ambasciata (mays-SAH-joh, ahm-bah-SHAH-tah)

meter (length) il metro (MEH-troh)

meter (taxi) il tassametro (tahs-SAH-may-troh)

Mexican messicano (mays-see-KAH-noh)

middle il mezzo, il centro (MEH-dzoh, CHAYN-troh)

midnight la mezzanotte (meh-dzah-NAWT-tay)

mild leggiero (lay-JEH-roh)

milk il latte (LAHT-tay)

million il milione (mee-LYOH-nay)

mind la mente (MAYN-tay); **never . . .** non importa, non fa niente (nohn eem-PAWR-tah, nohn FAH NYEHN-tay)

mine mio (MEE-oh); m. pl., miei (MYAY)

mineral water un'acqua minerale (AHK-kwah mee-nay-RAH-lay)

minister il ministro (mee-NEES-troh)

minute il minuto (mee-NOO-toh)

mirror lo specchio (SPEHK-kyoh)

Miss la signorina (see-nyoh-REE-nah)

miss (a train) perdere (PEHR-day-ray); Past, persi (PEHR-see); P. P., perso (PEHR-soh)

missing (to be) mancare (mahn-KAH-ray)

mistake lo sbaglio, un errore (ZBAH-lyoh, ayr-ROH-ray)

monastery il monastero (moh-nah-STEH-roh)

Monday il lunedì (loo-nay-DEE)

money il danaro (dah-NAH-roh)

money order il vaglia (VAH-lyah); pl. i vaglia

month il mese (MAY-say)

monument il monumento (moh-noo-MAYN-toh)

moon la luna (LOO-nah)

more più (PYOO)

morning il mattino, la mattina, la mattinata (maht-TEE-noh, maht-tee-NAH-tah)

mosquito la zanzara (dzahn-DZAH-rah)

mosquito netting la zanzariera (dzahn-dzah-RYEH-rah)

mother la madre (MAH-dray)

motion picture il cinema (CHEE-nay-mah)

motor (of car) il motore (moh-TOH-ray)

mouth la bocca (BOHK-kah)

mouthwash il liquido per risciacquare la bocca (LEE-kwee-doh payr ree-shahk-KWAH-ray lah BOHK-kah)

move (verb) muovere (MWAW-vay-ray); Past, mossi (MAWS-see); P. P., mosso (MAWS-soh)

movie film la pellicola cinematografica (payl-LEE-koh-lah chee-nay-mah-toh-GRAH-fee-kah)

Mr. il signor(e) (see-NYOHR, see-NYOH-ray); use signor before the name

Mrs. la signora (see-NYOH-rah)

much molto (MOHL-toh)

museum il museo (moo-SEH-oh)

mushroom il fungo (FOON-goh); pl., i funghi

must dovere (doh-VAY-ray); Pres.: debbo or devo, devi, deve, dobbiamo, dovete, debbono or devono (DAYB-boh, DAY-voh, DAY-vee, DAY-vay,

dohb-BYAH-moh, doh-VAY-tay, DAYB-boh-noh, DAY-voh-noh); Fut., dovrò (doh-VRAW)
my mio (MEE-oh); m. pl., miei (MYAY)

nail (finger or toe) un'unghia (OON-gyah)
nail file la lima per le unghie (LEE-mah payr lay OON-gyay)
nail polish la lacca per le unghie (LAHK-kah payr lay OON-gyay)
name il nome (NOH-may); **my . . . is** mi chiamo (mee KYAH-moh)
napkin la salvietta, il tovagliolo (sahl-VYAYT-tah, toh-vah-LYAW-loh)
narrow stretto (STRAYT-toh)
nationality la nazionalità (nah-tsyoh-nah-lee-TAH)
nauseated (to be) aver *or* sentir nausea (ah-VAYR, sayn-TEER NOW-say-ah)
near (adj.) vicino (vee-CHEE-noh)
near (prep.) vicino a (vee-CHEE-noh ah)
nearly quasi (KWAH-see)
necessary necessario (nay-chays-SAH-ryoh)
neck il collo (KAWL-loh)
necklace la collana (kohl-LAH-nah)
necktie la cravatta (krah-VAHT-tah)
need (verb) aver bisogno di (ah-VAYR bee-SAW-nyoh dee)
needle un ago (AH-goh); pl., gli aghi

nerve il nervo (NEHR-voh); **what a . . . !** che barbaro coraggio! (KAY BAHR-bah-roh koh-RAH-joh)
net (hair) la rete (da capelli) (RAY-tay dah kah-PAYL-lee)
net (mosquito) la zanzariera (dzahn-dzah-RYEH-rah)
never mai (MAH-ee)
new nuovo (NWAW-voh)
New Year l'anno nuovo (AHN-noh NWAW-voh)
newspaper il giornale (johr-NAH-lay)
newsstand un'edicola (ay-DEE-koh-lah)
next prossimo (PRAWS-see-moh); **what . . . ?** e poi? (ay PAW-ee)
night la notte (NAWT-tay)
night club il night club
night life la vita notturna (VEE-tah noht-TOOR-nah)
night rate la tariffa notturna (tah-REEF-fah noht-TOOR-nah)
nightgown la camicia da notte (kah-MEE-chah dah NAWT-tay)
nine nove (NAW-vay)
nineteen diciannove (dee-chahn-NAW-vay)
ninety novanta (noh-VAHN-tah)
ninth nono (NAW-noh)
no (adj.) nessuno (nays-SOO-noh)
no (adv.) no (NAW)
noise il rumore (roo-MOH-ray)
noisy rumoroso (roo-moh-ROH-soh)

none, no one nessuno (nays-soo-noh)

nonsense le fandonie (fahn-DAW-nyay) (f. pl.)

noon il mezzogiorno (meh-dzoh-JOHR-noh)

north il nord, il settentrione (NAWRD, sayt-tayn-TRYOH-nay)

Norwegian norvegese (nohr-vay-JAY-say)

nose il naso (NAH-soh)

not non (NOHN)

nothing niente, nulla (NYEHN-tay, NOOL-lah); . . . **else** nient'altro (nyehn-TAHL-troh)

notice (noun) un avviso (ahv-VEE-soh)

novel (noun) il romanzo (roh-MAHN-dzoh)

November il novembre (noh-VEHM-bray)

now ora, adesso (OH-rah, ah-DEHS-soh)

number il numero (NOO-may-roh)

nurse un'infermiera (een-fayr-MYEH-rah)

nut (fruit) la noce (NOH-chay)

nut (mechanical) il dado (DAH-doh)

occupied occupato (ohk-koo-PAH-toh)

o'clock (six) le sei (lay SEH-ee)

October un ottobre (oht-TOH-bray)

oculist un oculista (oh-koo-LEES-tah); pl., gli oculisti

of di (DEE)

of course naturalmente, ben in-teso (nah-too-rahl-MAYN-tay, BEHN een-TAY-soh)

off via (VEE-ah)

office un ufficio (oof-FEE-choh); **box** . . . il botteghino (boht-tay-GHEE-noh); **exchange** . . . ufficio di cambio (oof-FEE-choh dee KAHM-byoh); **post** . . . ufficio postale (oof-FEE-choh pohs-TAH-lay)

often spesso (SPAYS-soh)

oil un olio (AW-lyoh); **castor** . . . olio di ricino (AW-lyoh dee REE-chee-noh); **olive** . . . olio d'oliva (AW-lyoh doh-LEE-vah)

O.K. bene, benissimo, sta or va bene (BEH-nay, bay-NEES-see-moh, STAH, VAH)

old vecchio (VEHK-kyoh); **how** . . . **are you?** quanti anni ha? (KWAHN-tee AHN-nee AH); **I am twenty years** . . . ho vent'anni (AW vayn-TAHN-nee)

olive un'oliva (oh-LEE-vah)

omelet la frittata (freet-TAH-tah)

on su, sopra (SOO, SOH-prah)

once una volta (OO-nah VAWL-tah); **at** . . . subito (soo-bee-toh)

one un, un', uno, una (OON, OO-noh, oo-nah)

one way (traffic) il senso unico (SEHN-soh OO-nee-koh)

onion la cipolla (chee-POHL-lah)

only solo, soltanto, solamente (SOH-loh, sohl-TAHN-toh, soh-lah-MAYN-tay) open (adj.) aperto (ah-PEHR-toh)

open (verb) aprire (ah-PREE-ray); P. P. aperto (ah-PEHR-toh)

opera un'opera (AW-pay-rah)

opera glasses il binoccolo (bee-NAWK-koh-loh)

operator (phone) la telefonista (tay-lay-foh-NEES-tah)

optician un ottico (AWT-tee-koh)

or o (OH), oppure (ohp-POO-ray)

orange un'arancia (ah-RAHN-chah)

orangeade un'aranciata (ah-rahn-CHAH-tah)

orchestra un'orchestra (ohr-KEHS-trah); (in theater) la platea (plah-TEH-ah); . . . seat la poltrona (pohl-TROH-nah)

order (noun) un'ordinazione (ohr-dee-nah-TSYOH-nay)

order (verb) ordinare, comandare (ohr-dee-NAH-ray, koh-mahn-DAH-ray)

other altro (AHL-troh)

ouch! ahi! (AH-ee)

our, ours, nostro (NAWS-troh)

out fuori (FWAW-ree)

outlet (electric) la presa di corrente (PRAY-sah dee kohr-REHN-tay)

outside fuori (FWAW-ree)

over (above) sopra, su (SOH-prah, SOO)

over (finished) finito (fee-NEE-toh)

overcoat il soprabito, il pastrano, il cappotto (soh-PRAH-bee-toh, pah-STRAH-noh, kahp-PAWT-toh)

overdone troppo cotto (TRAWP-poh KAWT-toh)

overheat (motor) riscaldare (rees-kahl-DAH-ray)

overnight fino a domani (FEE-noh ah doh-MAH-nee)

owe dovere (doh-VAY-ray); see must, dovere, for conjugation

own (verb) possedere; Pres.: possiedo or posseggo, possiedi, possiede, possediamo, possedete, possiedono or posseggono (pohs-SYEH-doh, pohs-SEHG-goh)

oyster un'ostrica (AWS-tree-kah)

pack (verb) far le valige, far i bagagli (FAHR lay vah-LEE-jay, FAHR ee bah-GAH-lyee)

package il pacco, il pacchetto (PAHK-koh, pahk-KAYT-toh)

packet il pacchetto (pahk-KAYT-toh)

page (noun) la pagina (PAH-jee-nah)

page (verb) far chiamare, far cercare (FAHR kyah-MAH-ray, FAHR chayr-KAH-ray)

pain il dolore (doh-LOH-ray)

paint (wet) la vernice fresca, verniciato di fresco (vayr-NEE-chay FRAYS-kah, vayr-nee-CHAH-toh dee FRAYS-koh)

pair il paio (PAH-yoh); pl., le paia

pajamas il pigiama (pee-JAH-mah); pl., i pigiama

palace il palazzo (pah-LAH-tsoh)

panties le mutandine (moo-tahn-DEE-nay)

pants i calzoni, i pantaloni (kahl-TSOH-nee, pahn-tah-LOH-nee)

paper la carta (KAHR-tah); **toilet** . . . carta igienica (ee-JEH-nee-kah); **wrapping** . . . carta da imballaggio (dah eem-bahl-LAH-joh); **writing** . . . carta da scrivere (dah SKREE-vay-ray)

parasol un ombrellino (ohm-brayl-LEE-noh)

parcel il pacco, il pacchetto (PAHK-koh, pahk-KAYT-toh)

parcel post il pacco postale (PAHK-koh pohs-TAH-lay)

pardon (verb) perdonare, scusare (payr-doh-NAH-ray, skoo-SAH-ray)

pardon me! scusi! (SKOO-see)

park (noun) il parco (PAHR-koh)

park (car) parcheggiare, stazionare (pahr-kay-JAH-ray, stah-tsyoh-NAH-ray)

parking (no) divieto di sosta (dee-VYEH-toh dee SAWS-tah)

part (noun) la parte (PAHR-tay)

part (verb, hair) far la divisa (FAHR lah dee-VEE-sah)

part (verb, separate) separare, dividere (say-pah-RAH-ray, dee-VEE-day-ray); Past, divisi (dee-VEE-see); P. P., diviso (dee-VEE-soh)

parts (spare) i pezzi di ricambio (PEH-tsee dee ree-KAHM-byoh)

pass (noun, permit) il permesso (payr-MAYS-soh)

pass (verb) passare (pahs-SAH-ray) (essere if intransitive)

passenger il passeggero, il viaggiatore (pahs-say-JEH-roh, vyah-jah-TOH-ray)

passport il passaporto (pahs-sah-PAWR-toh)

past passato, scorso (pahs-SAH-toh, SKOHR-soh)

pastry la pasticceria (pahs-tee-chay-REE-ah)

pay pagare (pah-GAH-ray)

pea il pisello (pee-SEHL-loh)

peach la pesca (PEHS-kah)

pear la pera (PAY-rah)

pedestrian il pedone (pay-DOH-nay)

pedicure il pedicure (pay-dee-KYOOR)

pen la penna (PAYN-nah); **fountain** . . . penna stilografica (stee-loh-GRAH-fee-kah)

pencil la matita, il lapis (mah-TEE-tah, LAH-pees); pl., i lapis

people la gente, il popolo (JEHN-tay, PAW-poh-loh)

pepper il pepe (PAY-pay)

peppers i peperoni (pay-pay-ROH-nee)

per per, a (PAYR, AH)

performance la rappresentazione (rahp-pray-sayn-tah-TSYOH-nay)

perfume il profumo (proh-FOO-moh)

perfume shop la profumeria (proh-foo-may-REE-ah)

perhaps forse, chissà (FOHR-say, kees-SAH)

permanent un'ondulazione permanente (ohn-doo-lah-TSYOH-nay payr-mah-NEHN-tay)

permit (noun) il permesso (payr-MAYS-soh)

permit (verb) permettere(payr-MAYT-tay-ray); Past, permisi (payr-MEE-see); P. P., permesso (payr-MAYS-soh)

Persian persiano (payr-SYAH-noh)

personal personale (payr-soh-NAH-lay)

pest (slang) il seccatore (sayk-kah-TOH-ray)

petticoat la sottoveste (soht-toh-VAYS-tay)

phone (noun) il telefono (tay-LEH-foh-noh)

phone (verb) telefonare (tay-lay-foh-NAH-ray)

photograph (noun) la fotografia (foh-toh-grah-FEE-ah)

photograph (verb) fotografare (foh-toh-grah-FAH-ray)

pickles i cetriolini sott'aceto, i sottaceti (chay-tryoh-LEE-nee soht-tah-CHAY-toh, soht-tah-CHAY-tee)

picnic la gita, la scampagnata (JEE-tah, skahm-pah-NYAH-tah)

picture (art) il quadro, la pittura (KWAH-droh, peet-TOO-rah)

picture (motion) la pellicola, il cinema (payl-LEE-koh-lah, CHEE-nay-mah)

pie la pizza, la torta (PEE-tsah, TOHR-tah)

piece il pezzo (PEH-tsoh)

pier il molo, la banchina (MAW-loh, bahn-KEE-nah)

pill la pillola (PEEL-loh-lah)

pillow il cuscino (koo-SHEE-noh)

pillowcase la federa (FEH-day-rah)

pilot il pilota (pee-LAW-tah); pl., i piloti

pin la spilla (SPEEL-lah); safety . . . spilla di sicurezza (dee see-koo-RAY-tsah)

pineapple un ananasso (ah-nah-NAHS-soh)

pink rosa, color rosa (RAW-sah, koh-LOHR RAW-sah)

pipe (smoking) la pipa (PEE-pah)

pitcher la caraffa (kah-RAHF-fah)

pity (what a . . . !) che peccato! (kay payk-KAH-toh)

place (noun) il posto, il luogo (PAWS-toh, LWAW-goh); pl., i luoghi

plane un aeroplano (ah-ay-roh-PLAH-noh)

plate il piatto (PYAHT-toh)

platform la piattaforma (pyaht-tah-FOHR-mah)

play (noun, theater) il dramma (DRAHM-mah); pl., i drammi

play (verb, game) giuocare (jwoh-KAH-ray)

play (verb, instrument) suonare (swoh-NAH-ray)

playing cards le carte da giuoco (KAHR-tay dah JWAW-koh)

pleasant piacevole (pyah-CHAY-voh-lay)

please! per piacere, per favore, favorisca (+ infinitive) (payr pyah-CHAY-ray, payr fah-VOH-ray, fah-voh-REES-kah)

pleasure il piacere (pyah-CHAY-ray)

pliers le tenaglie (tay-NAH-lyay)

plug (spark) la candela (kahn-DAY-lah)

plum la susina (soo-SEE-nah)

p.m. pomeridiane, del pomeriggio (poh-may-ree-DYAH-nay, dayl poh-may-REE-joh)

pocket (noun) la tasca (TAHS-kah) pl., le tasche

pocket (adj.) tascabile (tahs-KAH-bee-lay)

pocket book il portafogli (pohr-tah-FAW-lyee); pl., i portafogli

point (noun) il punto, la punta (POON-toh, POON-tah)

poison il veleno (vay-LAY-noh)

police la polizia (poh-lee-TSEE-ah)

police station la questura (kways-TOO-rah)

policeman un agente (di polizia), la guardia, il carabiniere (ah-JEHN-tay, GWAHR-dyah, kah-rah-bee-NYEH-ray)

Polish polacco (poh-LAHK-koh); m. pl., polacchi, f. pl. polacche

polish (nail) la lacca per le unghie (LAHK-kah payr lay OON-gyay)

polish remover l'acetone (m.) (ah-chay-TOH-nay)

polite cortese (kohr-TAY-say)

politeness la cortesia (kohr-tay-SEE-ah)

pomade la pomata (poh-MAH-tah)

poor povero (PAW-vay-roh)

pork il maiale, il porco, la carne suina (mah-YAH-lay, PAWR-koh, KAHR-nay soo-EE-nah)

port (harbor) il porto (PAWR-toh)

porter il facchino, il portabagagli (fahk-KEE-noh pohr-tah-bah-GAH-lyee); pl., i portabagagli

portion la porzione (pohr-TSYOH-nay)

Portuguese portoghese (pohr-toh-GAY-say)

possible possibile (pohs-SEE-bee-lay)

post card la cartolina (postale) (kahr-toh-LEE-nah pohs-TAH-lay); **picture . . .** cartolina illustrata (eel-loos-TRAH-tah)

post office la posta, l'ufficio postale (PAWS-tah, oof-FEE-choh pohs-TAH-lay)

postage la francatura (frahn-kah-TOO-rah)

potable potabile (poh-TAH-bee-lay)

potato la patata (pah-TAH-tah)

pouch (tobacco) la borsa da tabacco (BOHR-sah dah tah-BAHK-koh)

pour (rain) piovere a dirotto (**a** catinelle) (PYAW-vay-ray ah dee-ROHT-toh, ah kah-tee-NEHL-lay); Past, piovve (PYAWV-vay)

powder la polvere (POHL-vay-ray); **face . . .** la cipria (CHEE-pryah)

powder puff il piumino (pyoo-MEE-noh)

powder room il gabinetto per signore (gah-bee-NAYT-toh payr see-NYOH-ray)

prefer preferire (pray-fay-REE-ray) (-isc-)

prepare preparare (pray-pah-RAH-ray)

prescription la ricetta (ree-CHEHT-tah)

press (verb, to iron) stirare (stee-RAH-ray)

pretty grazioso, carino (grah-TSYOH-soh, kah-REE-noh)

price il prezzo, l'ammontare (m.) (PREH-tsoh, ahm-mohn-TAH-ray)

priest il prete (PREH-tay)

print (photography) la copia (KAW-pyah)

program il programma (proh-GRAHM-mah); pl., i programmi

promise (verb) promettere (proh-MAYT-tay-ray); Past, promisi (proh-MEE-see); P. P., promesso (proh-MAYS-soh)

properly bene, a modo (BEH-nay, ah MAW-doh)

Protestant protestante (proh-tays-TAHN-tay)

provide procurarsi, provvedere (proh-koo-RAHR-see, prohv-vay-DAY-ray); Past, provvidi (prohv-VEE-dee); P. P., provvisto *or* provveduto (prohv-VEES-toh, prohv-vay-DOO-toh)

prune la prugna (cotta) (PROO-nyah KAWT-tah)

pudding il budino (boo-DEE-noh)

pull (verb) tirare (tee-RAH-ray)

Pullman porter il controllore, un addetto ai vagoni letto (kohn-trohl-LOH-ray, ahd-DAYT-toh AH-ee vah-GOH-nee LEHT-toh)

pump (fuel, car) la pompa di alimentazione (POHM-pah dee ah-lee-mayn-tah-TSYOH-nay)

puncture (tire) la gomma a terra (GOHM-mah ah TEHR-rah)

purchase (noun) la compera (KOHM-pay-rah)

purchase (verb) comprare, acquistare (kohm-PRAH-ray, ahk-kwees-TAH-ray)

purple (color) viola, paonazzo (koh-LOHR VYAW-lah, pah-oh-NAH-tsoh)

purse la borsa, la borsetta (BOHR-sah, bohr-SAYT-tah)

purser il commissario (di bordo) (kohm-mees-SAH-ryoh dee BOHR-doh)

push (verb) spingere (speen-JAY-ray); Pres.: spingo, spingi . . . spingono (SPEEN-goh, SPEEN-jee . . . SPEEN-goh-noh); Past, spinsi (SPEEN-see); P. P., spinto (SPEEN-toh)

put mettere (MAYT-tay-ray); Past, misi (MEE-see); P. P., messo (MAYS-soh); . . . **on** mettersi (MAYT-tayr-see)

quarter il quarto (KWAHR-toh)

quick, quickly presto (PREHS-toh)

quiet tranquillo, quieto (trahn-KWEEL-loh, KWYEH-toh)

quinine il chinino (kee-NEE-noh)

quite ben, del tutto (BEHN, dayl TOOT-toh)

rabbi il rabbino (rahb-BEE-noh)

rack (train) la rete (RAY-tay)

radiator (car) il radiatore (rah-dyah-TOH-ray)

radiator (room) il termosifone (tehr-moh-see-FOH-nay)

radio la radio (RAH-dyoh)

radish il ravanello (rah-vah-NEHL-loh)

railroad la ferrovia (fehr-roh-VEE-ah)

railroad station la stazione ferroviaria (stah-TSYOH-nay fehr-roh-VYAH-ryah)

rain (noun) la pioggia (PYAW-jah)

rain (verb) piovere (PYAW-vay-ray) Past, piovve (PYAWV-vay)

raincoat un impermeabile (eem-payr-may-AH-bee-lay)

rare (meat) al sangue (ahl SAHN-gway)

rate (exchange) il cambio (KAHM-byoh)

rate (hourly) la tariffa (tah-REEF-fah)

rather (have) preferire (pray-fay-REE-ray) (-isc-)

rattle (car) il battito (BAHT-tee-toh)

rayon il raion (rah-YAWN)

razor il rasoio (rah-SOH-yoh); **safety** . . . rasoio di sicurezza (dee see-koo-RAY-tsah)

razor blade la lametta da rasoio (lah-MAYT-tah dah rah-SOH-yoh)

reach trovare, raggiungere (troh-VAH-ray, rah-JOON-jay-ray); Past, raggiunsi (rah-JOON-see); P. P., raggiunto (rah-JOON-toh)

read leggere (LEH-jay-ray); Pres.: leggo, leggi . . . leggono (LEHG-goh, LEH-jee . . . LEHG-goh-noh); Past, lessi (LEHS-see); P. P., letto (LEHT-toh)

ready pronto (PROHN-toh)

really veramente, davvero (vay-rah-MAYN-tay, dahv-VAY-roh)

reasonable ragionevole (rah-joh-NAY-voh-lay)

receipt la ricevuta (ree-chay-VOO-tah)

receiver (on packages) destinatario (days-tee-nah-TAH-ryoh)

recommend consigliare, raccomandare (kohn-see-LYAH-ray, rahk-koh-mahn-DAH-ray)

record (phonograph) il disco (DEES-koh); pl., i dischi

recover (get back) riavere (ree-ah-VAY-ray); see *to have,* avere, for conjugation

recover (health) rimettersi (ree-MAYT-tayr-see); Past, rimisi; P. P., rimesso

red rosso (ROHS-soh)

refund (noun) il rimborso (reem-BOHR-soh)

refund (verb) rimborsare (reem-bohr-SAH-ray)

regards saluti, ossequi (sah-LOO-tee, ohs-SEH-kwee)

registered (mail) raccomandata (rahk-koh-mahn-DAH-tah)

registration blank il modulo, il registro (MAW-doo-loh, ray-JEES-troh)

registry window lo sportello lettere raccomandate (spohr-

TEHL-loh LAYT-tay-ray rahk-koh-mahn-DAH-tay)

regular (ordinary) ordinario (ohr-dee-NAH-ryoh); . . .
stop (bus) fermata obbligatoria (fayr-MAH-tah ohb-blee-gah-TAW-ryah)

remedy il rimedio(ree-MEH-dyoh)

remember ricordare, rammentare (ree-kohr-DAH-ray, rahm-mayn-TAH-ray)

rent (noun) un affitto, la pigione (ahf-FEET-toh, pee-JOH-nay)

rent (verb) affittare, prendere in affitto (ahf-feet-TAH-ray, PREHN-day-ray een ahf-FEET-toh); **for . . .** affittasi (ahf-FEET-tah-see)

repair riparare, accomodare (ree-pah-RAH-ray, ahk-koh-moh-DAH-ray)

repairs le riparazioni (ree-pah-rah-TSYOH-nee)

repeat ripetere (ree-PEH-tay-ray)

reply (noun) la risposta (rees-PAWS-tah)

reply (verb) rispondere (rees-pohn-DAH-ray); Past, risposi; P. P., risposto

reservation la prenotazione (pray-noh-tah-TSYOH-nay)

reserve prenotare (pray-noh-TAH-ray)

reserved seat posto prenotato, posto riservato (PAWS-toh pray-noh-TAH-toh, ree-sayr-VAH-toh)

rest (verb) riposarsi (ree-poh-SAHR-see)

rest room il gabinetto, la ritirata,

il cesso (gah-bee-NAYT-toh, ree-tee-RAH-tah, CHEHS-soh)

restaurant il ristorante, la trattoria (rees-toh-RAHN-tay, traht-toh-REE-ah)

return (give back) restituire (-isc-), rendere (rays-tee-too-EE-ray, REHN-day-ray); Past, resi (RAY-see); P. P., reso (RAY-soh)

return (go back) tornare, ritornare (essere)

rib la costola (KAWS-toh-lah)

ribbon il nastro (NAHS-troh)

rice il riso (REE-soh)

rich ricco (REEK-koh); m. pl., ricchi, f. pl. ricche

ride (noun) la gita (JEE-tah)

ride (verb) andare in (name conveyance) (ahn-DAH-ray een)

right (all . . .) va *or* sta bene (VAH, STAH BEH-nay)

right (opposite of left) destro (DEHS-troh)

right now proprio adesso, proprio ora, subito (PRAW-pryoh ah-DEHS-soh, OH-rah, soo-bee-toh)

right (to be) aver ragione (ah-VAYR rah-JOH-nay); see *to have,* avere, for conjugation

ring (on finger) un anello (ah-NEHL-loh)

ring (verb) suonare (il campanello) (swoh-NAH-ray eel kahm-pah-NEHL-loh)

rinse (hair) lavare i capelli (lah-VAH-ray ee kah-PAYL-lee)

river il fiume (FYOO-may)

road la via, la strada, un'autostrada (VEE-ah, STRAH-dah, ow-toh-STRAH-dah)

road map la carta stradale (KAHR-tah strah-DAH-lay)

roast arrosto, arrostito (ahr-RAWS-toh, ahr-rohs-TEE-toh)

roast beef il rosbif (rohs-BEEF)

rob rubare (roo-BAH-ray)

robe la veste da camera, un accappatoio (VEHS-tay dah KAH-may-rah, ahk-kahp-pah-TOH-yoh)

roll (bread) il panino (pah-NEE-noh)

roll (film) il rotolo (RAW-toh-loh)

room la stanza, la camera (STAHN-tsah, KAH-may-rah)

root la radice (rah-DEE-chay)

rope la corda (KAWR-dah)

rouge il rossetto (rohs-SAYT-toh)

round rotondo (roh-TOHN-doh)

round trip il viaggio d'andata e ritorno (VYAH-joh dahn-DAH-tah ay re-TOHR-noh)

row (theater) la fila (FEE-lah)

royal reale (ray-AH-lay)

rubber la gomma (GOHM-mah)

rubbers le soprascarpe (soh-prah-SKAHR-pay)

rug il tappeto (tahp-PAY-toh)

Rumanian rumeno (roo-MEH-noh)

run (verb) correre (KOHR-ray-ray); Past, corsi (KOHR-see); P. P., corso (KOHR-soh) (essere)

running water l'acqua corrente (f.) (AHK-kwah kohr-REHN-tay)

runway (plane) la pista (PEES-tah)

Russian russo (ROOS-soh)

safe (strongbox) la cassaforte (kahs-sah-FAWR-tay)

safety pin la spilla di sicurezza (SPEEL-lah dee see-koo-RAY-tsah)

safety razor il rasoio di sicurezza (rah-SOH-yoh dee see-koo-RAY-tsah)

sail (verb) salpare, partire (sahl-PAH-ray, pahr-TEE-ray)

sake (for heaven's . . .) per carità! (payr kah-ree-TAH)

salad un'insalata (een-sah-LAH-tah)

salami il salame (sah-LAH-may)

sale (bargain) la vendita d'occasione (VAYN-dee-tah dohk-kah-SYOH-nay)

salon (beauty) il salone di bellezza (sah-LOH-nay dee bayl-LAY-tsah)

saloon il bar, la mescita, un'osteria (BAHR, MAY-shee-tah, ohs-tay-REE-ah)

salt il sale (SAH-lay)

salty salato (sah-LAH-toh)

same stesso, medesimo (STAYS-soh, may-DAY-see-moh)

sand la sabbia, l'arena (f.) (SAHB-byah, ah-RAY-nah)

sandal il sandalo (SAHN-dah-loh)

sandwich il panino imbottito, il sandwich (pah-NEE-noh eem-boht-TEE-toh, sahn-GWEECH)

sardine la sardina (sahr-DEE-nah)

Saturday il sabato (SAH-bah-toh)

sauce la salsa (SAHL-sah)

saucer il piattino, la sottocoppa (pyaht-TEE-noh, soht-toh-KAWP-pah)

sausage la salsiccia (sahl-SEE-chah)

say dire (DEE-ray); Pres.: dico, dici, dice, diciamo, dite, dicono (DEE-koh, DEE-chee, DEE-chay, dee-CHAH-moh, DEE-tay, DEE-koh-noh); Fut., dirò (dee-RAW); Past, dissi (DEES-see); P. P., detto (DAYT-toh)

scalp massage il massaggio al cuoio capelluto (mahs-SAH-joh ahl KWAW-yoh kah-payl-LOO-toh)

scarf la sciarpa (SHAHR-pah)

school la scuola (SKWAW-lah)

scissors le forbici (FAWR-bee-chee)

scram! (slang) se ne vada! vada via! fuori! (say nay VAH-dah, VAH-dah VEE-ah, FWAW-ree)

screwdriver il cacciavite (kah-chah-VEE-tay)

sea il mare (MAH-ray)

seafood il pesce, il frutto di mare (PAY-shay, FROOT-toh dee MAH-ray)

seal (noun) il sigillo (see-JEEL-loh)

seal (verb) sigillare (see-jeel-LAH-ray)

search (a person) perquisire (payr-kwee-SEE-ray) (-isc-)

search (for) cercare (chayr-KAH-ray)

seasickness il mal di mare (MAHL dee MAH-ray)

season la stagione (stah-JOH-nay)

seasoned condito (kohn-DEE-toh)

seat (in conveyance) il posto (PAWS-toh)

second secondo (say-KOHN-doh)

secretary il segretario, la segretaria (say-gray-TAH-ryoh)

see vedere (vay-DAY-ray); Fut. vedrò (vay-DRAW); Past, vidi (VEE-dee); P. P.; visto or veduto (VEES-toh,vay-DOO-toh)

seem sembrare, parere (saym-BRAH-ray, pah-RAY-ray); Pres.: paio, pari . . . paiono (PAH-yoh, PAH-ree . . . PAH-yoh-noh); Fut., parrò (pahr-RAW); Past, parvi (PAHR-vee); P. P., parso (PAHR-soh) (essere)

select (verb) scegliere (SHAY-lyay-ray); Pres.: scelgo, scegli . . . scelgono (SHAYL-goh, SHAY-lyee . . . SHAYL-goh-noh); Past, scelsi (SHAYL-see); P. P., scelto (SHAYL-toh)

sell vendere (VAYN-day-rah)

send mandare, inviare, spedire (-isc-) (mahn-DAH-ray, een-vee-AH-ray, spay-DEE-ray)

send for (person or thing) mandare a cercare (mahn-DAH-ray ah chayr-KAH-ray); (thing only) mandare a prendere (PREHN-day-ray); (person only) far venire (FAHR vay-NEE-ray)

sender (on mail) il mittente (meet-TEHN-tay)

September il settembre (sayt-TEHM-bray)

serve servire (sayr-VEE-ray)

service il servizio (sayr-VEE-tsyoh); **at your . . .** ai suoi ordini (AH-ee SWOY OHR-dee-nee)

set (hair) mettere in piega (MAYT-tay-ray een PYEH-gah)

seven sette (SEHT-tay)

seventeen diciassette (dee-chahs-SEHT-tay)

seventh settimo (SEHT-tee-moh)

seventy settanta (sayt-TAHN-tah)

several parecchi, diversi (pah-RAYK-kee, dee-VEHR-see)

shade (in the . . .) all'ombra (ahl-LOHM-brah)

shade (window) la tendina, la cortina (tayn-DEE-nah, kohr-TEE-nah)

shall use future tense to indicate futurity, dovere for obligation (see *must*, dovere, for conjugation)

shampoo lo shampoo (shahm-POO); pl., gli shampoo

shave (verb) radere, far la barba (use reflexive forms if shaving yourself) (RAH-day-ray, FAHR lah BAHR-bah); Past, rasi (RAH-see); P. P., raso

shaving brush il pennello da barba (payn-NEHL-loh dah BAHR-bah)

shaving cream la crema da barba (KREH-mah dah BAHR-bah)

shawl lo scialle (SHAHL-lay)

she ella, essa, lei (AYL-lah, AYS-sah, LEH-ee)

sheet il lenzuolo (layn-TSWAW-loh); pl., le lenzuola

shine (shoes) lucidare (loo-chee-DAH-ray)

shine (stars) brillare, splendere (breel-LAH-ray, SPLEHN-day-ray)

ship (noun) la nave, il piroscafo, il vapore, il bastimento (NAH-vay, pee-RAWS-kah-foh, vah-POH-ray, bahs-tee-MAYN-toh)

ship (verb) spedire (-isc-), inviare, mandare (spay-DEE-ray, een-vee-AH-ray, mahn-DAH-ray)

shirt la camicia (kah-MEE-chah)

shoe la scarpa (SKAHR-pah)

shoe lace il laccio da scarpe, la stringa (LAH-choh dah SKAHR-pay, STREEN-gah)

shoestore la calzoleria (kahl-tsoh-lay-REE-ah)

shop il negozio, il magazzino (nay-GAW-tsyoh, mah-gah-DZEE-noh)

shopping (go) andar a far compere (ahn-DAHR ah FAHR KOHM-pay-ray)

short corto (KOHR-toh); (person) basso (BAHS-soh)

shorts i calzoncini, i pantaloncini, le mutande, le mutandine (kahl-tsohn-CHEE-nee, pahn-tah-lohn-CHEE-nee, moo-TAHN-day, moo-tahn-DEE-nay)

should use conditional of verb, or conditional of dovere (dov-rei)

shoulder la spalla (SPAHL-lah)

show (verb) mostrare, far

191

vedere (mohs-TRAH-ray, FAHR vay-DAY-ray)

showcase la vetrina, la mostra (vay-TREE-nah, MOHS-trah)

shower la doccia (DOH-chah)

shrimp il gambero, lo scampo (GAHM-bay-roh, SKAHM-poh)

shrine il santuario (sahn-too-AH-ryoh)

shut chiudere (KYOO-day-ray); Past, chiusi (KYOO-see); P. P., chiuso

shutter un'imposta (eem-PAWS-tah)

sick malato, ammalato (mah-LAH-toh, ahm-mah-LAH-toh)

sickness la malattia (mah-laht-TEE-ah)

side (of body) il fianco (FYAHN-koh); (direction) il lato, la parte (LAH-toh, PAHR-tay)

sidewalk il marciapiede (mahr-chah-PYEH-day)

sight-seeing la visita ai luoghi d'interesse (VEE-see-tah AH-ee LWAW-ghee deen-tay-REHS-say)

sign (noun) un'insegna, un avviso (een-SAY-nyah, ahv-VEE-soh)

sign (verb) firmare, apporre la firma (feer-MAH-ray, ahp-POHR-ray lah FEER-mah); Pres.: appongo, apponi . . . appongono; Past, apposi, P. P., apposto

signal stop la fermata facoltativa (fayr-MAH-tah fah-kohl-tah-TEE-vah)

silk la seta (SAY-tah)

silver l'argento (m.) (ahr-JEHN-toh)

since da, da quando (DAH, dah KWAHN-doh)

sing cantare (kahn-TAH-ray)

single room la stanza (camera) a un letto (STAHN-tsah, KAH-may-rah ah oon LEHT-toh)

sink (noun) il lavandino (lah-vahn-DEE-noh)

sir il signore (see-NYOH-ray)

sister la sorella (soh-REHL-lah)

sit (down) sedersi (say-DAYR-see); Pres.: seggo or siedo, siedi . . . seggono or siedono (SAYG-goh, SYEH-doh, SYEH-dee . . . SAYG-goh-noh)

sitting (to be) essere or stare seduto (EHS-say-ray, STAH-ray say-DOO-toh)

six sei (SEH-ee)

sixteen sedici (SAY-dee-chee)

sixth sesto (SEHS-toh)

sixty sessanta (says-SAHN-tah)

size la misura, la grandezza (mee-SOO-rah, grahn-DAY-tsah)

skin la pelle (PEHL-lay)

skirt la veste, la gonna (VEHS-tay, GAWN-nah)

sky il cielo (CHEH-loh)

sleep dormire (dohr-MEE-ray)

sleeping car il vagone letto (vah-GOH-nay LEHT-toh)

sleepy (to be) aver sonno (ah-VAYR SAWN-noh)

sleeve la manica (MAH-nee-kah); pl., le maniche

slip (petticoat) la sottoveste (soht-toh-VEHS-tay)

slippers le pantofole (pahn-TAW-foh-lay)

slow lento (LEHN-toh); the watch is . . . l'orologio va

addietro (loh-roh-LAW-joh VAH ahd-DYEH-troh)

slowly lentamente, piano, adagio (layn-tah-MAYN-tay, PYAH-noh, ah-DAH-joh)

small piccolo, piccino (PEEK-koh-loh, pee-CHEE-noh)

smelling salts i sali aromatici (SAH-lee ah-roh-MAH-tee-chee)

smoke fumare (foo-MAH-ray)

snow (noun) la neve (NAY-vay)

snow (verb) nevicare (nay-vee-KAH-ray)

so così (koh-SEE)

soap il sapone (sah-POH-nay)

soccer il calcio, il futbol (KAHL-choh, foot-BAWL)

socks i calzini, i pedali (kahl-TSEE-nee, pay-DAH-lee)

soda (bicarbonate) il bicarbonato (di soda) (bee-kahr-boh-NAH-toh dee SAW-dah)

sofa il sofà (soh-FAH); pl., i sofà

soft morbido, soffice (MAWR-bee-doh, SAWF-fee-chay)

soft drink la bibita non alcoolica (BEE-bee-tah nohn ahl-KAW-lee-kah)

sole (shoe) la suola (SWAW-lah)

some qualche, alcuno, di (+ definite article) (KWAHL-kay, ahl-KOO-noh, dee)

someone qualcuno (kwahl-KOO-noh)

something qualche cosa, niente (KWAHL-kay KAW-sah, NYEHN-tay)

sometimes qualche volta, a volte (KWAHL-kay VAWL-tah, ah VAWL-tay)

son il figlio (FEE-lyoh)

song la canzone (kahn-TSOH-nay)

soon presto, tra poco (PREHS-toh, trah PAW-koh)

sore throat il mal di gola (MAHL dee GOH-lah)

sorry dispiacente, addolorato (dees-pyah-CHEHN-tay, ahd-doh-loh-RAH-toh); I am . . . mi dispiace, mi rincresce (mee dees-PYAH-chay, reen-KRAY-shay)

soup la minestra (mee-NEHS-trah)

soup dish la scodella (skoh-DEHL-lah)

sour acre, agro, acido (AH-kray, AH-groh, AH-chee-doh)

south il sud, il meridione, il mezzogiorno (SOOD, may-ree-DYOH-nay, MEH-dzoh-JOHR-noh)

souvenir il ricordo (ree-KAWR-doh)

Spanish spagnuolo (spah-NYWAW-loh)

spare tire la gomma di ricambio (GOHM-mah de ree-KAHM-byoh)

spark plug la candela (kahn-DAY-lah)

sparkling wine lo spumante (spoo-MAHN-tay)

speak parlare (pahr-LAH-ray)

special speciale (spay-CHAH-lay); . . . delivery espresso (ays-PREHS-soh); today's . . . il piatto del giorno (PYAHT-toh dayl JOHR-noh)

speed limit la velocità massima

(vay-loh-chee-TAH MAS-see-mah)

spend (time) passare (pahs-SAH-ray); (money) spendere (SPEHN-day-ray); Past, spesi (SPAY-see); P. P., speso (SPAY-soh)

spinach gli spinaci (m. pl.) (spee-NAH-chee)

spitting forbidden vietato sputare (vyay-TAH-toh spoo-TAH-ray)

spoon il cucchiaio (kook-KYAH-yoh)

spoonful il cucchiaio, la cucchiaiata (kook-KYAH-yoh, kook-kyah-YAH-tah)

sprain (noun) la slogatura (zloh-gah-TOO-rah)

sprain (verb) slogare (zloh-GAH-ray)

spray spruzzare (sproo-TSAH-ray)

spring (mechanical) la molla (MAWL-lah)

spring (season) la primavera (pree-mah-VEH-rah)

square (noun) la piazza (PYAH-tsah)

square (adj.) quadrato (kwah-DRAH-toh)

squeak (noun) il cigolio, lo scricchiolio (chee-goh-LEE-oh, skreek-kyoh-LEE-oh)

stairs la scala, le scale (SKAH-lah, SKAH-lay)

stall (car) arrestarsi (ahr-rays-TAHR-see)

stamp (postage) il francobollo (frahn-koh-BOHL-loh)

stand (verb) stare (in piedi) (STAH-ray een PYEH-dee);

Pres.: sto, stai, sta, stiamo, state, stanno (STAW, STAH-ee, STAH, STYAH-moh, STAH-tay, STAHN-noh); Past, stetti, stesti, etc. (STAYT-tee); ... in line far la coda (FAHR lah KOH-dah)

star la stella (STAYL-lah)

starch (noun) l'amido (m.) (AH-mee-doh)

starch (verb) inamidare (ee-nah-mee-DAH-ray)

start (verb, begin) cominciare (koh-meen-CHAH-ray); (moving) mettersi in moto (MAYT-tayr-see een MAW-toh)

starter (car) l'avviamento (m.) (ahv-vyah-MAYN-toh)

stateroom la cabina (kah-BEE-nah)

station (R.R.) la stazione (stah-TSYOH-nay); (gas) la pompa, il distributore di benzina (POHM-pah, dees-tree-boo-TOH-ray dee bayn-DZEE-nah)

stationery store la cartoleria (kahr-toh-lay-REE-ah)

stationmaster il capostazione (kah-poh-stah-TSYOH-nay)

stay (noun) il soggiorno, la permanenza (soh-JOHR-noh, payr-mah-NEHN-tsah)

stay (verb) restare (essere), rimanere (essere), trattenersi (rays-TAH-ray, ree-mah-NAY-ray, traht-tay-NAYR-see); for trattenersi see hold, tenere; for rimanere: Pres.: rimango, rimani ... rimangono (ree-MAHN-goh, ree-MAH-nee ... ree-MAHN-goh-noh); Fut., rimarrò (ree-mahr-RAW);

Past, rimasi (ree-MAH-see);
P. P., rimasto (ree-MAHS-toh)
steak la bistecca (bees-TEHK-kah)
steal rubare (roo-BAH-ray)
steel l'acciaio (m.) (ah-CHAH-yoh)
steep ripido (REE-pee-doh)
steering wheel il volante (voh-LAHN-tay)
stew un umido (oo-mee-doh)
steward (deck) il cameriere di coperta (kah-may-RYEH-ray dee koh-PEHR-tah)
stewardess (plane) la hostess (OHS-tess)
stocking la calza (KAHL-tsah)
stomach lo stomaco (STAW-mah-koh); pl., gli stomachi; . . . ache il mal di stomaco (MAHL dee STAW-mah-koh)
stop (bus or car, noun) la fermata (fayr-MAH-tah)
stop light il semaforo (say-MAH-foh-roh)
stop over (train) fare una fermata intermedia (FAH-ray oo-nah fayr-MAH-tah een-tayr-MEH-dyah)
store il negozio, lo spaccio (nay-GAW-tsyoh, SPAH-choh)
straight dritto, diritto (DREET-toh, dee-REET-toh)
strap la cinghia (CHEEN-gyah)
straw la paglia (PAH-lyah)
strawberry la fragola (FRAH-goh-lah)
street la strada, la via (STRAH-dah, VEE-ah)
streetcar il tram, il tranvai (TRAHM, trahn-VAH-ee); pl., i tram, tranvai
string lo spago (SPAH-goh)

string bean il fagiolino (fah-joh-LEE-noh)
strong forte (FAWR-tay)
style la moda, lo stile, alla— (MAW-dah, STEE-lay, AHL-lah)
sudden improvviso, brusco (eem-prohv-VEE-soh, BROOS-koh)
suddenly all'improvviso (ahl-leem-prohv-VEE-soh)
sugar lo zucchero (TSOOK-kay-roh)
suit (noun) un abito, il vestito (AH-bee-toh, vays-TEE-toh)
suitcase la valigia (vah-LEE-jah)
summer un'estate (ays-TAH-tay)
sun il sole (SOH-lay)
Sunday la domenica (doh-MAY-nee-kah); pl., le domeniche
sunglasses gli occhiali da sole (ohk-KYAH-lee dah SOH-lay)
sunny assolato, pieno di sole (ahs-soh-LAH-toh, PYEH-noh dee SOH-lay)
sun-tan ointment un unguento contro il sole (oon-GWEHN-toh KOHN-troh eel SOH-lay)
supper la cena (CHAY-nah)
sure sicuro, certo (see-KOO-roh, CHEHR-toh)
surgeon il chirurgo (kee-ROOR-goh)
suspenders le bretelle (bray-TEHL-lay)
sweater il maglione (mah-LYOH-nay)
Swedish svedese (zvay-DAY-say)
sweet dolce (DOHL-chay)
swell (verb) gonfiare (gohn-FYAH-ray)
swim nuotare (nwoh-TAH-ray)

swimming pool la piscina (pee-SHEE-nah)

Swiss svizzero (ZVEE-tsay-roh)

switch (electric) un interruttore (een-tayr-root-TOH-ray)

swollen gonfio (GOHN-fyoh)

synagogue la sinagoga (see-nah-GAW-gah)

syrup (cough) lo sciroppo per la tosse (shee-RAWP-poh payr lah TOHS-say)

table la tavola, il tavolo (TAH-voh-lah, TAH-voh-loh)

table d'hote a prezzo fisso (ah PREH-tsoh FEES-soh)

tablecloth la tovaglia (toh-VAH-lyah)

tablespoon il cucchiaio (kook-KYAH-yoh)

tablespoonful il cucchiaio, la cucchiaiata (kook-kyah-YAH-tah)

tablet la pastiglia (pahs-TEE-lyah)

tail light (car) il fanalino posteriore (fah-nah-LEE-noh pohs-tay-RYOH-ray)

tailor il sarto (SAHR-toh)

take (carry) portare (pohr-TAH-ray)

take (person) condurre (kohn-DOOR-ray); Pres.: conduco, conduci . . . conducono (kohn-DOO-koh, kohn-DOO-chee . . . kohn-DOO-koh-noh); Past, condussi (kohn-DOOS-see); P. P., condotto (kohn-DOHT-toh)

take (thing) prendere (PREHN-day-ray); Past, presi (PRAY-see); P. P., preso (PRAY-soh)

take off (garment) togliersi (TAW-lyayr-see); Pres.: tolgo, togli . . . tolgono (TAWL-goh, TAW-lyee . . . TAWL-goh-noh); Past, tolsi (TAWL-see); P. P., tolto (TAWL-toh)

take time volerci (voh-LAYR-chee); **it will take time** ci vorrà tempo

taken (occupied) preso, occupato (PRAY-soh, ohk-koo-PAH-toh)

talcum powder la polvere di talco (POHL-vay-ray dee TAHL-koh)

tall alto (AHL-toh)

talk parlare, chiacchierare (pahr-LAH-ray, kyahk-kyay-RAH-ray)

tan (color) color caffellatte (koh-LOHR kahf-fayl-LAHT-tay)

tangerine il mandarino (mahn-dah-REE-noh)

tank (car) il serbatoio (di benzina) (sayr-bah-TOH-yoh dee bayn-DZEE-nah)

tap (noun) il rubinetto (roo-bee-NAYT-toh)

tape (adhesive) il nastro adesivo (NAHS-troh ah-day-SEE-voh)

tasty gustoso, saporito (goos-TOH-soh, sah-poh-REE-toh)

tax la tassa (TAHS-sah)

taxi il tassì (tahs-SEE)

tea il tè (TEH)

teaspoon, teaspoonful il cucchiaino (kook-kyah-EE-noh)

telegram il telegramma (tay-lay-GRAHM-mah); pl., i telegrammi

telegraph (noun) il telegrafo (tay-LEH-grah-foh)

telegraph (verb) telegrafare (tay-lay-grah-FAH-ray)

telephone (noun) il telefono (tay-LEH-foh-noh)

telephone (verb) telefonare (tay-lay-foh-NAH-ray)

tell dire (DEE-ray); Pres.: dico, dici, dice, diciamo, dite, dicono (DEE-koh, DEE-chee, DEE-chay, dee-CHAH-moh, DEE-tay, DEE-koh-noh); Fut., dirò (dee-RAW); Past, dissi (DEES-see); P. P., detto (DAYT-toh)

teller (bank) il cassiere, un impiegato (kahs-SYEH-ray, eem-pyay-GAH-toh)

temporarily temporaneamente (taym-poh-rah-nay-ah-MAYN-tay)

ten dieci (DYEH-chee)

tension (high- ... wires) fili ad alta tensione (FEE-lee ah DAHL-tah tayn-SYOH-nay)

tenth decimo (DEH-chee-moh)

terminal (bus, plane) il capolinea (kah-poh-LEE-nay-ah); pl., i capolinea

thank ringraziare (reen-grah-TSYAH-ray); ... you grazie (GRAH-tsyay)

that (demonstrative) quello (KWAYL-loh)

that (conjunction) che (KAY)

the il, la, lo, l', i, gli, le (eel, lah, loh, ee, lyee, lay)

theater il teatro (tay-AH-troh)

their(s) il loro (eel LOH-roh)

them li, le, loro (lee, lay, LOH-roh)

there là, lì (LAH, LEE)

there is (are) ecco (EHK-koh)

thermometer il termometro (tayr-MAW-may-troh)

these questi (KWAYS-tee)

they essi, esse, loro (AYS-see, AYS-say, LOH-roh)

thick spesso, denso (SPAYS-soh, DEHN-soh)

thief il ladro (LAH-droh)

thigh la coscia (KAW-shah)

thing la cosa (KAW-sah)

think pensare (payn-SAH-ray)

third terzo (TEHR-tsoh)

thirsty (to be) aver sete (ah-VAYR SAY-tay)

thirteen tredici (TRAY-dee-chee)

thirty trenta (TREHN-tah)

this questo (KWAYS-toh)

thoroughfare (no) divieto di transito (dee-VYEH-toh dee TRAHN-see-toh)

those quelli (KWAYL-lee)

thousand mille (MEEL-lay)

thread il filo (FEE-loh)

three tre (TRAY); ... times tre volte (TRAY VAWL-tay)

throat la gola (GOH-lah)

through per, attraverso, da (PAYR, aht-trah-VEHR-soh, DAH)

thumb il pollice (PAWL-lee-chay)

thunder (noun) il tuono (TWAW-noh)

thunder (verb) tuonare (twoh-NAH-ray)

Thursday il giovedì (joh-vay-DEE)

ticket il biglietto (bee-LYAYT-toh)

ticket office lo sportello biglietti (spohr-TEHL-loh bee-LYAYT-tee); (theater) il botteghino (boht-tay-GHEE-noh)

tie (neck) la cravatta (krah-VAHT-tah)

tighten (car, brakes) aggiustare (ah-joos-TAH-ray)

till fino a, finchè (FEE-noh ah, feen-KAY)

time il tempo (TEHM-poh); **on . . . a** tempo; **at what . . .?** a che ora? (ah KAY OH-rah)

timetable un orario (oh-RAH-ryoh)

tint (hair) tingere (TEEN-jay-ray); Past, tinsi (TEEN-see); P. P., tinto

tip (gratuity) la mancia (MAHN-chah)

tire (car) la gomma (GOHM-mah)

tired stanco (STAHN-koh); m. pl., stanchi, f. pl. stanche

tissue paper la carta velina (KAHR-tah vay-LEE-nah)

to a (AH)

toast (bread) il pane tostato (PAH-nay tohs-TAH-toh)

toast (drink) il brindisi (BREEN-dee-see)

tobacco il tabacco (tah-BAHK-koh); pl., i tabacchi

today oggi (AW-jee)

toe il dito del piede (DEE-toh dayl PYEH-day); pl., le dita

together insieme (een-SYEH-may)

toilet il gabinetto, la ritirata, il cesso (gah-bee-NAYT-toh, ree-tee-RAH-tah, CHEHS-soh)

toilet paper la carta igienica (KAHR-tah ee-JEH-nee-kah)

token (bus or phone) il gettone (jayt-TOH-nay)

tomato il pomodoro (poh-moh-DAW-roh)

tomorrow domani (doh-MAH-nee)

tongue la lingua (LEEN-gwah)

tonic (hair) il tonico (per i capelli) (TAW-nee-koh payr ee kah-PAYL-lee)

tonight stasera, questa sera (stah-SAY-rah, KWAYS-tah SAY-rah)

too anche, pure (AHN-kay, POO-ray); **. . . bad!** peccato! (payk-KAH-toh); **. . . much** troppo (TRAWP-poh)

tooth il dente (DEHN-tay)

toothache il mal di denti (MAHL dee DEHN-tee)

toothbrush la spazzolino per i denti (spah-tsoh-LEE-noh payr ee DEHN-tee)

toothpaste la crema dentifricia (KREH-mah dayn-tee-FREE-chah)

top la cima (CHEE-mah); **at the . . . of** in cima a (een CHEE-mah ah)

touch (verb) toccare (tohk-KAH-ray)

tough (meat) duro (DOO-roh)

tour (noun) il giro (JEE-roh)

tourist il or la turista (too-REES-tah); pl., i turisti

tow (car) prendere a rimorchio (PREHN-day-ray ah ree-MAWR-kyoh); see *take*, prendere, for conjugation

toward verso (VEHR-soh)

towel un asciugamani (ah-shoo-gah-MAH-nee); pl., gli asciugamani

town la città (cheet-TAH)

track (R.R.) il binario (bee-NAH-ryoh)

traffic light il semaforo (say-MAH-foh-roh)

train il treno (TREH-noh)

transfer (noun), transfer point la coincidenza (koh-een-chee-DEHN-tsah)

translate tradurre (trah-DOOR-ray); Pres.: traduco, traduci . . . traducono (trah-DOO-koh, trah-DOO-chee . . . trah-DOO-koh-noh); Past, tradussi (trah-DOOS-see); P. P., tradotto (trah-DOHT-toh)

travel viaggiare (vyah-JAH-ray)

travel insurance un'assicurazione di viaggio (ahs-see-koo-rah-TSYOH-nay dee VYAH-joh)

traveler il viaggiatore (vyah-jah-TOH-ray); f., la viaggiatrice (vyah-jah-TREE-chay)

traveler's check un assegno di viaggio (ahs-SAY-nyoh dee VYAH-joh)

tree un albero (AHL-bay-roh)

trespassing (no) divieto di transito (passaggio) (dee-VYEH-toh de TRAHN-see-toh, pahs-SAH-joh)

trip (noun) il viaggio (VYAH-joh)

trolley car il tram, il tranvai (TRAHM, trahn-VAH-ee); pl., i tram, tranvai

trouble (be in) trovarsi in guai (difficoltà) (troh-VAHR-see een GWAH-ee, deef-fee-kohl-TAH); don't . . . yourself non si scomodi, non si dis-

turbi (nohn see SKAW-moh-dee, dees-TOOR-bee)

trousers i calzoni, i pantaloni (kahl-TSOH-nee, pahn-tah-LOH-nee)

truck il camion, un autocarro (KAH-myohn, ow-toh-KAHR-roh)

true vero (VAY-roh)

trunk il baule (BAH-oo-lay)

trunk compartment (car) il portabagagli (pohr-tah-bah-GAH-lyee)

try on provarsi (proh-VAHR-see)

try to cercare di, provarsi a (chayr-KAH-ray dee, proh-VAHR-see ah)

tube (inner) la camera d'aria (KAH-may-rah DAH-ryah)

Tuesday il martedì (mahr-tay-DEE)

Turkish turco (TOOR-koh); m. pl. turchi, f. pl. turche

turn (noun) la voltata (vohl-TAH-tah)

turn (verb) voltare, girare (vohl-TAH-ray, jee-RAH-ray)

tuxedo lo smoking, un abito da sera (da società) (SMOH-king, AH-bee-toh dah SAY-rah, soh-chay-TAH)

twelve dodici (DOH-dee-chee)

twenty venti (VAYN-tee)

twice due volte (DOO-ay VAWL-tay)

twin beds due letti (DOO-ay LEHT-tee)

two due (DOO-ay)

ugly brutto (BROOT-toh)

umbrella un ombrello (ohm-BREHL-loh)

uncle lo zio (TSEE-oh)
uncomfortable scomodo (SKAW-moh-doh)
under sotto (SOHT-toh)
undershirt la maglia (MAH-lyah)
understand capire (-isc-), comprendere (kah-PEE-ray, kohm-PREHN-day-ray); see *take*, prendere, for conjugation
underwear la biancheria (intima) (byahn-kay-REE-ah EEN-tee-mah)
university un'università (oo-nee-vayr-see-TAH)
until fino a, finchè (FEE-noh ah, feen-KAY)
up su (SOO)
upon sopra, su (SOH-prah, SOO)
upper superiore (soo-pay-RYOH-ray)
upstairs sopra, di sopra (SOH-prah, dee SOH-prah)
us ce, ci, noi (CHAY, CHEE, NOH-ee)
U.S.A. gli Stati Uniti d'America (STAH-tee oo-NEE-tee dah-MEH-ree-kah)
use (noun) un uso, un impiego (OO-soh, eem-PYEH-goh)
use (verb) usare, impiegare (oo-SAH-ray, eem-pyay-GAH-ray)
usher (theater) la maschera (MAHS-kay-rah)

valet il cameriere (kah-may-RYEH-ray)
valise la valigia (vah-LEE-jah)
vaudeville il varietà (vah-ryay-TAH)
veal il vitello (vee-TEHL-loh)
vegetables le verdure, i legumi, il contorno (vayr-DOO-ray,

lay-GOO-mee, kohn-TOHR-noh)
velvet il velluto (vayl-LOO-toh)
very molto (MOHL-toh)
vest il panciotto, il gilet (pahn-CHAWT-toh, jee-LEH)
veterinarian il veterinario (vay-tay-ree-NAH-ryoh)
view la vista, la veduta, la visuale (VEES-tah, vay-DOO-tah, vee-soo-AH-lay)
vinegar un aceto (ah-CHAY-toh)
visit (noun) la visita (VEE-see-tah)
visit (verb) visitare (vee-see-TAH-ray)
visitor il visitatore (vee-see-tah-TOH-ray); f., la visitatrice (vee-see-tah-TREE-chay)

waist la vita, la cintola (VEE-tah, CHEEN-toh-lah)
wait aspettare, attendere (ahs-payt-TAH-ray, aht-TEHN-day-ray); Past, attesi (aht-TAY-see); P. P., atteso (aht-TAY-soh)
waiter il cameriere (kah-may-RYEH-ray); head . . . il capo cameriere (KAH-poh kah-may-RYEH-ray)
waiting room la sala d'aspetto (SAH-lah dahs-PEHT-toh)
waitress la cameriera (kah-may-RYEH-rah)
wake up svegliarsi, destarsi (zvay-LYAHR-see, days-TAHR-see)
walk (take a) fare una passeggiata (FAH-ray OO-nah pahs-say-JAH-tah)

wall il muro (MOO-roh); pl., for walls of a city, le mura

wallet il portafogli (pohr-tah-FAW-lyee); pl., i portafogli

want volere (voh-LAY-ray); Pres.: voglio, vuoi, vuole, vogliamo, volete, vogliono (VAW-lyoh, VWAW-ee, VWAW-lay, voh-LYAH-moh, voh-LAY-tay, VAW-lyoh-noh); Fut., vorrò (vohr-RAW); Past, volli (VAWL-lee)

warm caldo (KAHL-doh)

was ero, era, fui, fu (EH-roh, EH-rah, FOO-ee, FOO)

wash (verb) lavare (lah-VAH-ray); use in the reflexive for washing oneself

washroom il gabinetto (gah-bee-NAYT-toh)

watch guardare (gwahr-DAH-ray); . . . out! attento! attenzione! (aht-TEHN-toh, aht-tayn-TSYOH-nay)

water un'acqua (AHK-kwah)

watermelon il cocomero (koh-KOH-may-roh)

wave (finger) la messa in piega (MAYS-sah een PYEH-gah)

way la via, il modo, la direzione, la parte (VEE-ah, MAW-doh, dee-ray-TSYOH-nay, PAHR-tay); by . . . of (per) via (di) (payr VEE-ah dee); **one** . . . senso unico (SEHN-soh OO-nee-koh); **this** . . . (direction) di qua, da questa parte (dee KWAH, dah KWAYS-tah PAHR-tay); **this** . . . (fashion) così, in questo modo (koh-SEE, een KWAYS-toh MAW-doh); **that** . . .

(direction) di là, da quella parte (dee LAH, dah KWAYL-lah PAHR-tay); **that** . . . (fashion) in quel modo (een KWAYL MAW-doh); **wrong** . . . senso vietato (SEHN-soh vyay-TAH-toh)

we noi, noialtri (NOH-ee, noh-YAHL-tree)

weak debole (DAY-boh-lay)

wear portare, indossare (pohr-TAH-ray, een-dohs-SAH-ray)

weather il tempo (TEHM-poh)

Wednesday il mercoledì (mayr-koh-lay-DEE)

week la settimana (sayt-tee-MAH-nah)

weigh pesare (pay-SAH-ray)

weight il peso (PAY-soh)

welcome il benvenuto (behn-vay-NOO-toh); **to make** . . . dare il benvenuto (DAH-ray eel behn-vay-NOO-toh); **you're** . . . (in reply to "thank you") prego, niente, non c'è di che (PREH-goh, NYEHN-tay, nohn CHEH dee KAY)

well (adv.) bene (BEH-nay)

well done (steak) ben cotto (BEHN KAWT-toh)

were eri, eravamo, eravate, erano, fosti, fummo, foste, furono (EH-ree, ay-rah-VAH-moh, ay-rah-VAH-tay, EH-rah-noh, FOHS-tee, FOOM-moh, FOHS-tay, FOO-roh-noh)

west l'ovest (m.), il ponente, l'occidente (m.), (AW-vehst, poh-NEHN-tay, oh-chee-DEHN-tay)

wet umido, bagnato (OO-mee-doh, bah-NYAH-toh); . . .

paint vernice fresca, verniciato di fresco (vayr-NEE-
chay FRAYS-kah, vayr-nee-
CHAH-toh dee FRAYS-koh)

what che, cosa, che cosa (KAY,
KAW-sah, KAY KAW-sah)

wheel la ruota (RWAW-tah);
steering . . . il volante (voh-
LAHN-tay)

when quando (KWAHN-doh)

where dove (DOH-vay)

which quale (KWAH-lay)

whisky il whiskey (WEES-kee)

white bianco (BYAHN-koh);
m. pl., bianchi, f. pl. bian-
che

who chi (KEE)

whom chi, cui (KEE, KOO-ee)

whose di chi, di cui (dee KEE,
dee KOO-ee)

why perchè (payr-KAY)

wide largo (m. pl. larghi, f. pl.
larghe), ampio (LAHR-goh,
AHM-pyoh)

width la larghezza (lahr-GAY-
tsah)

wife la moglie, la signora (MOH-
lyay, see-NYOH-rah); **your**
. . . la Sua Signora (lah
SOO-ah see-NYOH-rah)

will (verb) to indicate futurity,
use future of verb; to indicate
determination, use volere, *to
want*

wind il vento (VEHN-toh)

window la finestra (fee-NEHS-
trah); **train window** il finestrino (fee-nehs-TREE-noh);
post-office or bank window lo
sportello (spohr-TEHL-loh)

windshield il paravento, il
cristallo, il vetro (pah-rah-

VEHN-toh, krees-TAHL-loh,
VAY-troh); . . . **wiper** il
tergicristallo (terh-jee-krees-
TAHL-loh)

windy ventoso (vayn-TOH-soh);
it is . . . tira vento (TEE-
rah VEHN-toh)

wine il vino (VEE-noh; . . .
list la lista dei vini (LEES-tah
day VEE-nee)

winter un inverno (een-VEHR-
noh)

wiper (windshield) il tergicristallo (tehr-jee-krees-TAHL-
loh)

wire (high-tension) il filo ad
alta tensione (FEE-loh ah-
DAHL-tah tayn-SYOH-nay);
hold the . . . resti all'apparecchio (REHS-tee ahl-lahp-
pah-RAYK-kyoh)

wish (verb) desiderare, augurare (day-see-day-RAH-ray,
ow-goo-RAH-ray)

wishes (best) cordiali saluti,
tanti auguri (kohr-DYAH-lee
sah-LOO-tee, TAHN-tee ow-
GOO-ree)

with con (KOHN)

without senza (SEHN-tsah)

woman la donna (DAWN-nah)

wood il legno (LAY-nyoh)

wool la lana (LAH-nah)

word la parola (pah-RAW-lah)

work (noun) il lavoro, un'opera
(lah-VOH-roh, AW-pay-rah)

work (verb) lavorare (lah-voh-
RAH-ray)

worry preoccuparsi (pray-ohk-
koo-PAHR-see); **don't** . . .
non si preoccupi (nohn see
pray-AWK-koo-pee)

worse peggiore, peggio (pay-JOH-ray, PEH-joh)

worst il peggiore (eel pay-JOH-ray)

worth (to be) valere (vah-LAY-ray); Pres.: valgo, vali . . . valgono (VAHL-goh, VAH-lee . . . VAHL-goh-noh); Fut., varrò (vahr-RAW); Past, valsi (VAHL-see); P. P., valso (VAHL-soh)

would use conditional of verb

wound la ferita (fay-REE-tah)

wounded ferito (fay-REE-toh)

wrap up incartare, avvolgere (een-kahr-TAH-ray, ahv-VAWL-jay-ray); Past, avvolsi (ahv-VAWL-see), P. P., avvolto (ahv-VAWL-toh)

wrapping paper la carta da imballaggio (KAHR-tah dah eem-bahl-LAH-joh)

wrench la chiave inglese (KYAH-vay een-GLAY-say)

wrist il polso (POHL-soh); . . . **watch** un orologio da polso (oh-roh-LAW-joh dah POHL-soh)

write scrivere (SKREE-vay-ray); Past, scrissi (SKREES-see), P. P., scritto (SKREET-toh)

writing paper la carta da scrivere (KAHR-tah dah SKREE-vay-ray)

wrong (to be) aver torto (ah-VAYR TAWR-toh)

X-ray la radioscopia (rah-dyoh-skoh-PEE-ah)

year un anno (AHN-noh)

yellow giallo (JAHL-loh)

yes sì (SEE)

yesterday ieri (YEH-ree)

yet ancora (ahn-KOH-rah)

you Lei, tu, voi, voialtri, la, ti, te, vi, ve, le, (LEH-ee, TOO, VOH-ee, voh-YAHL-tree, LAH, TEE, TAY, VEE, VAY, LAY)

young giovane (JOH-vah-nay)

your, yours Suo, tuo, vostro, Loro (soo-oh, TOO-oh, VAWS-troh, LOH-roh)

youth hostel un ostello della gioventù (ohs-TEHL-loh DAYL-lah joh-vayn-TOO)

Yugoslav jugoslavo (yoo-goh-SLAH-voh)

zipper la chiusura lampo (kyoo-soo-rah LAHM-poh)

zoo il giardino zoologico (jahr-DEE-noh dzoh-LAW-jee-koh)

V ITALIAN-ENGLISH VOCABULARY

This section, without transcription, lists words which the tourist is most likely to encounter in written form. For pronunciation, most of the words will be found in the English-Italian vocabulary with a transcription.

a to, at, in (the form *ad* frequently appears when the next word begins with a vowel)

abbastanza enough

abitare to live, dwell

abito dress, suit; **. . . da sera** *or* **da società** evening clothes

accelerato local (train)

accendere to light

accettare to accept

acciaio steel

accomodare to fix, adjust; **accomodarsi** to sit down, make oneself comfortable *or* at home

acconto deposit, advance payment

aceto vinegar

acetone nail polish remover

acido acid, sour; **. . . borico** boric acid

acqua water; **. . . di Colonia** Cologne water

ad see *a*

adagio slowly

addetto employe assigned to a particular task

addietro back, backward

addio good-by, farewell

adesso now

aeroplano airplane

aeroporto airport

affettato cold cuts

affisso notice, poster; **vietati gli affissi** post no bills

affittare to rent, let, hire; **affittasi** for rent

affitto rent

affrettarsi to hasten, hurry

agente agent; **. . . di polizia** policeman, detective

aggiustare to fix, adjust, repair

ago needle

agosto August

aiutare to help, aid

aiuto help, aid, assistance

ala wing

albergo hotel, inn

albero tree

alcool alcohol

alcoolico alcoholic

alla . . . in the . . . style

almeno at least

alto high, tall

altro other

alzare to lift, raise; **alzarsi** to get up, rise

ambasciata embassy, message

americano American

amica, amico friend (f. and m.)

amido starch

ammobiliato furnished

ammontare amount, total, bill, cost, price

ancora yet, still

andare to go; **. . . via, andarsene** to go away

andata going, one-way (trip); **andata e ritorno** round (return) trip

anello ring (finger)

anno year

antimeridiano a.m., in the morning

antipasto hors d'oeuvre, appetizers

aperitivo apéritif

aperto open

apparecchio apparatus, instrument, phone; **resti all' . . .** hold the wire

appartamento apartment

apprendere to learn, hear, find out

aprile April

aprire to open

aragosta lobster

arancia, arancio orange

aranciata orangeade

arena sand

arenoso sandy

argento silver

aria air, aria

arioso airy, arioso

armadio closet

arrivare to arrive, reach, get to

arrivo arrival; **treno in . . .** incoming train

arrosto, arrostito roast

articolo article, item

ascensore elevator, lift

asciugamani towel

asciugare to dry, wipe, wipe off

asciutto dry

ascoltare to listen, listen to

aspettare to wait, wait for, expect

aspetto aspect, appearance, waiting; **sala d' . . .** waiting room

assegno check; **. . . di viaggio** traveler's check

assicurare to insure, assure

assicurazione insurance, assurance

atrio lobby (hotel)

attaccapanni hanger, coat hanger

attaccare to attach, hang up, attack

attendere to wait, wait for, expect

attento attentive, careful; **Attento! Look out! Watch out! Beware!**

attenzione attention, care; **Attenzione! Look out! Watch out! Beware!**

atterraggio landing (airplane)

atterrare to land

attraversare to cross, go across

attraverso across, through

augurare to wish (someone something)

Auguri! best wishes!

autista driver, taxi driver, chauffeur

autobus bus

autocarro truck

autorimessa garage

autostrada automobile highway

autunno autumn, fall

avanti forward, ahead, before

aviolinea airline

avvertimento notice, warning, caution
avvisare to advise, notify, warn
avviso notice, warning
azzurro blue

baciare to kiss
bacio kiss
badare to heed, pay attention, watch out
baffi mustache
bagagliaio baggage room, baggage car
bagaglio baggage
bagnare to wet; **bagnarsi** to get wet
bagnato wet
bagno bath; **fare un . . . to** take a bath
baia bay, gulf
ballare to dance
ballo dance, ball
bambino child, baby
banca, banco bank
banchina pier, wharf
barattolo can, container
barba beard; **far** or **farsi la barba** to shave
barberia barber shop
barbiere barber
basilica cathedral, basilica
basso low, short, base
basta enough; **Basta!** or **Basta così!** That's enough!
bastare to suffice, be sufficient, be enough
battello boat
battere to beat
baule trunk
bellezza beauty
bello beautiful, handsome, lovely

bene well; **benissimo** very well, all right, O.K.
benvenuto welcome
benzina gasoline, benzine
bere to drink
berretto cap, beret
bevanda drink, beverage
biancheria linen, laundry; . . . **intima** underwear
bianco white
bibita drink, beverage
biblioteca library
bicchiere (drinking) glass
bigio gray
biglietteria ticket office
biglietto ticket, bank note; . . . **da cento** 100-lira bill; . . . **da visita** visiting card
bimbo child, infant, baby
binario track (R.R. or streetcar)
binoccolo opera glasses, field glasses
birra beer
birreria beer saloon
bisognare to be necessary, need, must, have to
bisogno need; **aver . . . di** to need
bocca mouth
boccone mouthful, bite; **mangiare un . . . to** have or get a bite
bolla bubble, pimple, blister
bollente boiling
bollire to boil
bollito boiled, boiled beef
bontà goodness, kindness
bordo board (ship only); **a . . .** on board
borsa, borsetta purse, handbag
bottega store, shop
botteghino box office (theater)

206

bottiglia bottle

bottiglieria wine shop, tavern, saloon

bottone button

braccialetto bracelet

braccio arm

breve brief, short

brindisi (drinking) toast

buca hole, box; . . . **da** *or* **per le lettere** letter box

buono good; **a buon mercato** cheap; **di buon'ora** early

burro butter

bussare to knock

busta envelope

buttare to throw; . . . **via** to throw away

cabina cabin, stateroom, booth; . . . **telefonica** phone booth

cacio cheese

cadere to fall

caduta (a) fall

caffè coffee; . . . **e latte** coffee with milk; . . . **espresso** *or* **nero** black coffee

calcio kick, soccer, association football

caldo warm, hot, heat, warmth

calma calm; **Calma!** Keep cool! Take it easy! Don't get excited!

calmare to calm, quiet down

calore heat, warmth

calza stocking

calzature hosiery

calzini socks

calzolaio shoemaker

calzoleria shoeshop

cambiare to change, exchange

cambiavalute exchange man, exchange office

cambio exchange, change, exchange rate

camera room; . . . **d'aria** inner tube

cameriera maid, chambermaid, waitress

cameriere waiter, valet, bellboy

camicetta blouse

camicia shirt

camion truck

campagna country (outside city)

campana bell (large, church, etc.)

campanello bell (small, door, etc.)

cancellare to cancel, erase

cancello gate

candeggio bleach

candela candle, spark plug

cane dog

canocchiale field glasses, spyglass

cantare to sing (criminal slang: to squeal, rat)

canto song, singing, canto

cantone canton, corner

canzone song

capelli hair (of head)

capire to understand

capitano captain

capo head, chief

capolinea terminal (bus, R.R., plane)

capostazione stationmaster

cappelleria hatstore

cappello hat

carabiniere state trooper, military policeman

caraffa pitcher, carafe

carico loaded, laden, cargo

carità charity; **per . . . !** for Heaven's sake!

carne meat, flesh; . . . **fredda** cold cuts

caro dear, expensive

carrozza coach, carriage, railroad car

carta paper, card, map; . . . **automobilistica** *or* **stradale** road map; . . . **copiativa** carbon paper; . . . **igienica** toilet paper; . . . **da giuoco** playing card; . . . **da imballaggio** wrapping paper; . . . **da scrivere** writing paper;

cartellone poster, notice, ad

cartolaio stationer

cartoleria stationery, stationery store

cartolina card, post card; . . . **illustrata** picture post card; . . . **postale** post card

casa house, home; **andare a** . . . to go home; **essere in** . . . to be at home

casalingo home style

caso case, chance

cassa cashier's desk, packing case, box

cassaforte strongbox, safe

cassetta small box; . . . **postale** letter box

cassiere cashier, teller

castello castle, hilltop town

catena chain

cattolico Catholic

cautela caution

cavallo horse

celere swift

celeste blue, light blue, sky blue, heavenly, celestial

cena supper

cenare to have supper

centinaio about a hundred

cento a *or* one hundred

centro center, middle

cera wax

cercare to seek, look for

cerino wax match

cerotto court plaster

certamente certainly

certo certain, certainly, sure, surely

cesso toilet, rest room

cesta basket

cestino small basket; . . . **di viaggio** traveler's lunch basket, peddled at railroad stations

chiamare to call; **chiamarsi** to be called, one's name is

chiamata call

chiaro light-colored, clear

chiave key; . . . **inglese** wrench

chiesa church

chilo, chilogrammo kilogram

chincaglieria knicknacks

chinino quinine

chirurgo surgeon

chissà perhaps, maybe, who knows?

chiudere to close, shut

chiuso closed, shut

chiusura closing; . . . **lampo** zipper

ciao hello, hi, bye-bye

cielo heaven, sky

cinema movie house, movie show

cinghia belt

cinquanta fifty

cinque five

cintura belt; . . . **di salvataggio** life preserver

cioccolata, cioccolato chocolate

cioccolatino chocolate candy, bonbon
cipria face powder
città city, town
classe class
cocchiere coachman
cognome second name, family name
coincidenza transfer, transfer point, point of change (R.R. or bus)
colazione breakfast, lunch; prima . . . breakfast; seconda . . . lunch
collana necklace
colletto collar
collo neck, piece of baggage
colore color
coltelleria cutlery
coltello knife
comandare to order, command
come as, how, like
cominciare to begin, start
commissariato (di polizia) police station
commissario commissioner, official; . . . di bordo ship's purser
comodo comfortable, ease
compagnia company
compartimento compartment
compera purchase
comperare, comprare to purchase, buy
completo complete, full (on busses: full; no more passengers)
comprendere to understand
compreso understood, included
comunicazione communication, message, connection (on phone)

con with
concerto concert
condire to season, dress (food)
conducente motorman (on streetcar)
condurre to conduct, lead, take (a person)
conduttore conductor
conoscenza knowledge, acquaintance
conoscere to know, make acquaintance of
consegna delivery
consegnare to deliver, hand over
consigliare to advise, recommend, counsel
consiglio advice, recommendation, counsel
consolato consulate
console consul
contagoccie dropper
contanti cash, ready money
contare to count
conto account, bill, check (restaurant)
contorno garnish, vegetables served with a dish of meat
contravvenzione violation, fine; essere in . . . to be guilty of a violation
contro against
controllo control, check, check point
controllore controller, conductor (train)
convenire to agree
coperta blanket, deck; sopra . . . on deck
coperto covered, cover, cover charge
copia copy, print (of photograph)

copiare to copy
corda rope
cordiale cordial, hearty, heart-felt, liqueur
corpo body
corrente current, running, inst. (in business letters), draft (of air)
correre to run
corsa run, trip, fare
cortese courteous, polite
cortesia courteousness, polite-ness
cortile courtyard
cosa thing, what?
così so, thus, this way
costare to cost
costo cost, price
cotoletta cutlet, chop
cotone cotton
cotto cooked, done
cravatta necktie
credenza credit
credere to believe, think
crema cream
cristallo crystal, windshield
cuccetta berth, bunk
cucina kitchen, cooking, cuis-ine
cucinare to cook
cuoio leather
cuore heart
cura care, attention, cure
curva curve
cuscino pillow, cushion

da from, by, at the house or business place of
danaro money
dare to give
data date (calendar only)
davanti before, in front of

davvero really, truly, indeed, in fact
dazio customs duty
debole weak, feeble
decimo tenth
decollare to take off (plane)
decollo flight, take-off
denso thick, dense, heavy (oil)
dentale dental
dente tooth
dentiera denture
dentista dentist
dentro inside, within
deposito deposit; . . . bagagli baggage room
desiderare to wish, desire
destinatario receiver (on pack-age or letter)
destro right, right-hand, adroit
deviazione deviation, curve on highway
diavolo devil
dicembre December
dichiarare to declare, state
dichiarazione declaration, state-ment
diciannove nineteen
diciassette seventeen
diciotto eighteen
dieci ten
dietro behind, back of, after
diletto pleasure, amusement
dipinto painting, painted
dire to say, tell
diretto direct, express (train)
direttore director, manager
diritto straight, right, upright
disco disk, phonograph record
dispiacente sorry
dispiacere sorrow, displeasure
distante distant, away, far away
distanza distance

distributore (**di benzina**) gas pump, gas station

disturbare to disturb, bother; **Non si disturbi.** Don't bother, don't stand up.

disturbo trouble, bother; **Scusi il disturbo.** Pardon me for troubling you.

dito finger; . . . **del piede** toe

ditta firm, company, concern

diverso different, varied; **diversi** several

dizionario dictionary

doccia shower

documento document, paper

dodici twelve

dogana customs, custom house

dolce sweet, dessert; **dolci** sweets, candy

dolceria confectionery, sweets shop

dolore pain, ache

domanda question, request, inquiry

domandare to ask, ask for, request, inquire

domani tomorrow

domenica Sunday

donna woman; . . . **di servizio** maid, domestic worker

dono gift

dopo after, afterward

dopodomani day after tomorrow

dopopranzo afternoon

dormire to sleep

dottore doctor

dove where

dozzina dozen

dritto straight

drogheria grocery store

droghiere grocer

due two

duomo cathedral

duro hard

e and (**ed** is often used before vowels)

eccedenza excess, over-

eccesso excess, over-

ecco here is, here are, there is, there are; **eccomi** here I am; **eccolo** there it is

ed see **e**

edicola newsstand

effetti effects, belongings

egli he

elettrico electric

ella she; **Ella** you, used chiefly in correspondence

entrare to enter, come in, go in

entrata entrance

erba grass, herb

esaminare to examine

escursione excursion, trip

espresso special delivery, black coffee

essere to be

est east

estate summer

estrarre to extract, draw out

estrazione extraction

etichetta label

etto, ettogrammo hectogram, 100 grams

evitare to avoid

fa ago

fabbro (**ferraio**) blacksmith

facchino porter, baggage carrier

faccia face; **in** or **di** . . . opposite

facile easy

falso false

fame hunger; **aver . . . to be
hungry**
famiglia family
fanale street lamp, headlight
farcito stuffed
fare to do, make; **far freddo,
caldo to be cold, warm; fare
un bagno, una passeggiata to
take a bath, a walk**
farina flour
farinacei food products made
with flour, e. g., spaghetti
farmacia drugstore, pharmacy
farmacista druggist, pharma-
cist
fasciare to bandage, wrap up
fasciatura bandage
fatto a mano handmade
favore favor; **per . . . please**
favorire to favor, be kind enough
to; **favorisca please, please
come in**
fazzoletto handkerchief
febbraio February
febbre fever, temperature
federa pillowcase
fegato liver
felice happy
felicitare to congratulate
felicitazioni congratulations
feltro felt
ferita wound
ferma! stop! halt!
fermare to stop, halt; **fermarsi
to stop, come to a stop**
fermata stop; **. . . facoltativa
signal stop; . . . intermedia
stop over; . . . obbligatoria
regular stop**
fermo halted, standing, motion-
less; **. . . in posta general
delivery**

ferro iron; **. . . da stiro flatiron**
ferrovia railroad
ferroviario pertaining to a railroad
festa feast, festival, holiday,
celebration
fiamma flame
fiammifero match
figlia daughter
figlio son
fila file, row
filo thread, wire; **. . . ad alta
tensione high-tension wire**
fine end
finestra window
finestrino window (train), small
window
finire to finish, end
fiore flower
firma signature; **apporre la . . .
to sign, affix one's signature**
firmare to sign
fiume river
fodera lining
fontana fountain
forbici scissors
forcina hairpin, bobbypin
forestiero foreign, foreigner
formaggio cheese
forno oven; **al . . . baked**
forse perhaps, maybe
forte strong
fortuna fortune, luck
forza strength
fotografia photograph
fra among, between, **within**
francatura postage
francese French
francobollo postage stamp
freddo cold
freno brake
fresco cool, fresh

fretta hurry; aver . . . to be in a hurry

frittata omelet

fritto fried, fry; . . . misto assorted fry

fronte front, forehead

frutto fruit; . . . di mare shell-fish, seafood

fuga flight, escape; . . . di gas gas leak

fumare to smoke

fumatore smoker

fuoco fire; fuochi d'artificio fire-works

fuori out, outside

futbol football, soccer, association football

gabinetto cabinet, toilet, rest room

galleria gallery

gamba leg

garza gauze

gelateria ice-cream store, confectionery

gelato ice cream

genere kind, sort

gennaio January

gente people

gentile kind, polite, courteous

gentilezza kindness, politeness, act of courtesy

gerente manager, director

gettare to throw; . . . via to throw away

gettone token (bus, streetcar, phone)

ghiacciata iced drink

ghiacciato iced, frozen

ghiaccio ice

giallo yellow

giardino garden

ginocchio knee

giocattolo toy, plaything

gioielleria jewelry shop

gioielliere jeweler

gioiello jewel, gem

giornale newspaper, journal

giornata, giorno day

giovane young

giovedì Thursday

girare to turn, go about; . . . un assegno to endorse a check

gita trip, excursion

giù down, downward, below

giugno June

giuocare to play (games only; not instruments)

giuoco play, game

giusto just

gli the, to him

golfo gulf

gomma gum, rubber, eraser, tire; . . . a terra flat tire

gonfio swollen

gonna skirt, gown

grammo gram

grande large, big, great

grandezza size, measure, greatness

grandine hail

gratis, gratuito free, free of charge

grazioso nice, pretty, graceful

greco Greek

grigio gray

grossezza size, width, thickness

grosso big, large, thick

guancia cheek

guanciale pillow

guanto glove

guardare to watch, look, look at

guardaroba wardrobe, check room

guardia guard, sentinel, watchman

guasto breakdown (motor), broken

guida guide, guidebook

gusto taste

gustoso tasty, savory

hostess hostess, stewardess

identità identity, identification

idrofilo absorbent; **cotone . . .** absorbent cotton

ieri yesterday

igienico hygienic; **carta igienica** toilet paper

imbarcarsi to get on a ship

imbarco embarking, getting on shipboard

imparare to learn

impermeabile waterproof, raincoat

impiegato employee, clerk, salesman, bank teller

importare to matter, import; **non importa** it does not matter, never mind

importato imported

imposta shutter, screen, tax

impostare to mail

inchiostro ink

incluso included, enclosed

incontrare to meet, encounter

incontro meeting, encounter; **all' . . .** on the contrary

incrocio crossing, crossroad

indicare to show, direct, indicate, point out

indietro back, backward

indirizzare to address

indirizzo address

indossare to wear, put on

indumenti garments, wearing apparel

inferiore lower, inferior

infermiera, infermiere nurse (hospital)

infermo ill, sick, infirm

inferno hell

informazione piece of information; **informazioni** information

inglese English

ingrandimento enlargement

ingrassare to grease, lubricate, grow fat

ingresso entrance, admission, admittance; **vietato l' . . .** no admittance

iniezione injection

inizio beginning, start

inoltrare to send on, forward

insalata salad

insegna sign (on store or inn), ensign

insegnare to teach

inserviente servant, waiter, clerk

insetticida insecticide

insetto insect

insieme together

interesse interest

interruttore electric light switch

interurbano between cities, long distance

invece instead

inviare to send

invio sending, shipment

io I

iodio iodine

la the, her; **La** you

là there

labbro lip

lacca sealing wax, nail polish

laccio (da scarpe) shoelace
ladro thief, burglar, dishonest,
  extortioner
lagnanza complaint
lagnarsi to complain
lago lake
lama, lametta blade; lametta da
  rasoio razor blade
lampada, lampadina lamp;
  lampadina tascabile flashlight
lampo lightning, lightning flash;
  treno . . . fast express
lana wool
lapis pencil
larghezza width, size
largo wide, ample
lasciare to leave (an object);
  . . . in deposito to check
lato side; da questo . . . on
  this side, this way
latte milk
latteria milk bar, dairy
lavaggio wash
lavandaia laundry woman
lavanderia laundry
lavandino sink
lavare to wash; lavarsi to wash
  oneself
lavorare to work, labor
lavoro work, labor
le the, them, to her; Le to you
leggere to read
leggero, leggiero light (in
  weight)
legno wood
lei she, her; Lei you
lentamente slowly
lente lens; . . . d'ingrandimento magnifying glass
lento slow
lenzuolo sheet, bed sheet
lettera letter

letto bed
levare to remove, raise; levarsi
  to get up
li the, them
lì there
libero free, not occupied
libraio bookseller
libreria bookshop
libro book
lima file; limetta per le unghie
  nail file
limare to file
limonata lemonade
limone lemon
linea line; . . . aerea airline
lingua tongue, language
lino linen, flax
liquore liqueur, cordial
lista list; . . . delle vivande
  menu
litro liter
loggione balcony (of theater)
lontano distant, far away
loro their, to them; Loro your,
  to you
lozione lotion
luce light
lucidare to shine (shoes)
luglio July
lui he, him
luna moon
lunedì Monday
lunghezza length
lungo long
luogo place, spot

macchina machine, automobile
macchinetta small machine;
  . . . da caffè coffee-making
  machine; . . . da capelli
  hair clippers; . . . fotografica camera

macellaio butcher
macelleria meat market, butcher shop
madre mother
magazzino department store, large store, warehouse
maggio May
maggiore greater, elder, major
magnano locksmith
mai never, ever
maiale pig, pork
malato ill, sick
malattia illness, sickness, disease
male ill, badly, poorly, sickness; mal di mare seasickness
mancare to be lacking, fail, be missing, be wanting
mancia tip, gratuity
mandare to send
mangiare to eat
manica sleeve
maniglia handle, doorhandle
mano hand; fatto a . . . handmade
manzo beef
marca brand, trade-mark
marciapiede sidewalk
mare sea
marito husband
marmellata jam, marmalade
martedì Tuesday
martello hammer
marzo March
mascè mashed (potatoes)
massaggio massage
materasso mattress
matita pencil
mattina, mattinata, mattino morning
me me
meccanico mechanic, mechanical

medesimo same
medicina medicine
medicinali medical supplies
medico physician, doctor
meglio better, best
meno less, fewer
mente mind
mercato market; a buon . . . cheap
merceria dry goods
mercoledì Wednesday
meridionale southern
merletto lace
mescita saloon, bar, cocktail lounge
mese month
Messa Mass; Messa cantata or solenne High Mass
messa in piega permanent wave
metà half
metro meter
mettere to put, place, set
mezzanotte midnight
mezzo half; mezza pensione room with breakfast and one additional meal
mezzogiorno noon, midday, south
mi me
migliore better, best
miliardo billion
milione million
minestra soup
ministro minister
minuto minute
misura measure, measurement, size
misurare to measure, fit
mittente sender (on letter or parcel)
mobili, mobilia furniture
mobiliato furnished

moda fashion, style
modista milliner
modisteria millinery shop
modulo blank, schedule
moglie wife
molo pier, wharf
molto much, a great deal, lots of; molti many, lots of
moneta coin
montagna, monte mount, mountain
monumento monument
morbido soft
morire to die
morte death
morto dead
mostrare to show, display
motore motor, engine
multa fine (legal)
municipio city hall
muovere to move, shift
muro wall
museo museum

nascere to be born
naso nose
nastro ribbon
Natale Christmas
nato born
nave ship
nazionale national, local, domestic (not imported)
nazionalità nationality
nebbia fog
nebbioso foggy
negozio store, shop
nero black
nessuno no one, none, no
neve snow
nevicare to snow
niente nothing; nient'altro nothing else

no no
noi, noialtri we, us
noleggiare to hire, rent
nolo hire; prendere a . . . to hire; automobile da nolo car for hire
nome name
non not
nono ninth
nord north
nostro our, ours
notizia news
notte night
novanta ninety
nove nine
novella short story
novembre November
nulla nothing, something, anything
numero number
nuotare to swim
nuovo new

o or (od is frequently used before vowels)
occasione occasion, chance, opportunity; d' . . . bargain
occhiali eyeglasses
occhio eye
occupato busy, taken, occupied
oculista oculist, ophthalmologist
od see o
oggetti smarriti lost and found
oggi today
olio oil; . . . d'oliva olive oil; . . . di ricino castor oil
ombrellino (da sole) parasol
ombrello umbrella
ondulazione permanente permanent wave
opera opera, work

217

oppure or, or else
ora hour, now, time
orario timetable
orchestra orchestra (group of players only)
ordinare to order
ordinario ordinary, customary, general
ordinazione, ordine order
orecchia, orecchio ear
orecchino earring
orefice goldsmith, jeweler
oreficeria goldsmith's shop, jeweler's
oro gold
orologiaio watchmaker
orologio clock, watch; . . . da polso wrist watch
oscuro dark
ospedale hospital
ossequi greetings, regards
osso bone
ostello hostel; . . . della gioventù youth hostel
osteria wineshop, tavern
ostrica oyster
ottanta eighty
ottavo eighth
ottico optician
otto eight
ottobre October
otturare to fill (a tooth)
otturazione filling (of tooth)

pacchetto pack, packet, package
pacco package; . . . postale parcel post
padre father
paesano pertaining to the country, rural, provincial, fellow townsman

paese country, nation
pagare to pay; far . . . to charge
pagina page (of book)
paglia straw
paio pair
palazzo palace
palco box (theater)
pane bread
panetteria bakery
panino roll; . . . imbottito sandwich, stuffed bun
panna cream; . . . al motore stalled motor, breakdown
panno cloth
pantofola slipper
parcheggiare to park
parcheggio parking
parco park
parere to seem
parlare to speak, talk
parola word
parrucchiere haircutter, barber
parte part, direction; da questa . . . this way
partenza departure
particolare private, special, separate, particular
partire to depart, leave, go out or away
partita game
passaggio passage, passing; . . . a livello grade crossing; divieto di . . . no thoroughfare
passaporto passport
passare to pass
passato past
passeggiata walk, promenade; fare una . . . to take a walk
passeggiero passenger
passo step, pass; veicoli a . . .

218

d'uomo vehicles no faster than a man can walk

pasta macaroni products, piece of pastry, paste; . . . **asciutta** macaroni dish

pasticceria pastry

pasto meal

patata potato

paternità father's name

pedone pedestrian

peggio, peggiore worse, worst

pelle skin

pelliccería furs, furrier's

pelliccia fur

pellicola film

pelo hair (single, from head or body)

pendenza slope; **strada in** . . . steep or sloping road

penna pen; . . . **stilografica** fountain pen

pensione boardinghouse; . . . **completa** room and board; **mezza** . . . room with breakfast and one additional meal

per for, through, by, in order to

perdere to lose

perdita loss

perdonare to forgive, pardon

pericolo danger; . . . **di morte** danger of death

pericoloso dangerous

permesso permit, pass, allowed, permitted; . . . **fumare** smoking permitted; **Permesso?** May I come in?

permettere to permit, allow

perquisire to search (a person or place)

perquisizione search (of person or place)

pesante heavy

pesare to weigh

pesce fish

peso weight

pezza cloth, piece of cloth

pezzo piece; . . . **di ricambio** spare part, replacement part

piacere pleasure, favor; **per** . . . please

piacere to please, be pleasing to, like; **egli mi piace** I like him

piano slowly, softly, gently, piano

pianta plant, city map

piatto plate, dish; . . . **del giorno** today's special

piazza square, plaza

piccolo small, little

piede foot; **a piedi** on foot

pieno full, filled; **Faccia il pieno** Fill her up!

pigione rent

pillola pill

pilota pilot

pinacoteca picture gallery, collection of paintings

pioggia rain

piovere to rain; . . . **a dirotto,** . . . **a catinelle** to pour, rain cats and dogs

pipa pipe (smoking only)

piroscafo steamer, ship, liner

piscina swimming pool

pista race track, airplane runway

pittura painting

più more

pizza pie

pizzeria pie shop

platea orchestra (in theater)

pneumatico tire

poco little, not much

poi then, afterward

polizia police
pollice thumb
pollo chicken
polmone lung
polso pulse
poltrona armchair, orchestra seat (theater)
polvere dust, powder; . . . di talco talcum powder
pomata pomade
pomeridiane p.m., of the afternoon
pomeriggio afternoon
pomodoro tomato
pompa pump, gas station
ponte bridge
porta door, gate
portabagagli porter, baggage carrier, trunk compartment
portafogli wallet, pocketbook
portare to bring, carry
portata course (in meal)
portiere doorman, gatekeeper
portone outer door
porzione portion
possedere to own, possess
possesso possession, ownership
posta mail, post; . . . aerea air mail
postale postal
posteggio parking
posto place, spot
potabile potable, drinkable
povero poor, unfortunate
pranzare to dine, have dinner
pranzo dinner
prato meadow, field, lawn
pregare to pray, beg, request; pregasi you are requested
preghiera prayer; . . . di you are requested

prendere to take (an object, without transporting it)
prenotare to reserve, make a reservation
prenotazione reservation
preparare to prepare, make ready
presa (di corrente) outlet (electric)
presentare to introduce, present
prestare to lend
prestito loan; prendere in . . . to borrow
presto early, quickly
prete priest
prezzo price; . . . fisso fixed price, table d'hôte; prezzi modici moderate prices
primavera spring
primo first
profondo deep
profumeria perfume shop
profumo perfume
programma program
proibito forbidden
pronto ready; . . . soccorso first aid; Pronto! Hello! (on telephone)
prosciutto ham
prossimo next
protestante Protestant
provvedere to provide
provvista supply, provision
prudenza prudence, caution
pulire to clean; . . . a secco to dry-clean
pulizia cleaning, cleanliness
punta point, tip
punto point, spot, dot, period
purgante laxative

qua here

220

quadrato square
quadro picture, portrait, square
qualche some, any
qualcuno someone, anyone
quale which, which one
qualsiasi any whatsoever
qualunque any, some
quando when
quanto as much, how much; **quanti** as many, how many
quaranta forty
quarto fourth, quarter
quasi almost, as though, as it were
quattordici fourteen
quattro four
quello that, that one, the one
questo this, this one
questura police station
qui here
quiete quiet, peace, tranquillity
quieto quiet, peaceful, tranquil
quindici fifteen
quinto fifth

rabbino rabbi
raccomandare to recommend, register (letter)
raccomandata registered letter
radere to shave; **radersi** to shave oneself
radioscopia X-ray
raffreddore cold (in head)
ragazza girl
ragazzo boy
ragione reason; **aver . . .** to be right
ragionevole reasonable
raion rayon
rallentare to slow down
rammendare to mend

rappresentazione performance, show
rasoio razor; **. . . di sicurezza** safety razor
reale royal, real
recapitare to deliver, forward
recapito address
reclamare to complain
reclamo complaint
regalare to present, give as a present
regalo gift, present
reggere to hold, hold up, rule
registro register
reparto section, division
respirare to breathe
restare to stay, remain
restituire to return, give back
resto remainder, rest, change (from a paid bill)
rete net
riavere to get back, have returned
ricambio spare; **gomma di . . .** spare tire; **pezzi di . . .** spare parts
ricco rich, wealthy
ricetta prescription
ricevere to receive
ricevuta receipt
ricordare, ricordarsi di to remember, recall
ricordo memory, remembrance, souvenir
ridere to laugh
riempire to fill, fill up
rimandare to put off, postpone
rimanere to remain, stay
rimborsare to refund, reimburse
rimborso refund
rimedio remedy
rimorchiare to tow

rimorchio towing; **prendere a
. . .** to tow
rincrescere to be sorry about;
mi rincresce I am sorry
ringraziamenti thanks
ringraziare to thank
rione section of a city, ward
riparare to repair, fix
riparazioni repairs
ripetere to repeat
riposare, riposarsi to rest, take a
rest
riposo rest, closing (theaters)
riscaldamento heating, heat
riscaldare to heat
riscuotere to collect, cash
riso rice, laughter
rispondere to answer, reply
risposta answer, reply
ristorante restaurant
ritardo delay, lateness; **essere in
. . .** to be late
ritirata retreat, toilet, rest room
ritornare to return, come back,
go back
ritorno return, coming back,
going back; **andata e . . .**
two-way, round-trip
rivista magazine, periodical, re-
view
romanzo novel
rompere to break
rosa rose, rose-colored, pink
rossetto rouge; **. . . per le
labbra** lipstick
rosso red
rotolo roll (of film or something
similar)
rotondo round
rotto broken
rubare to steal, rob
rubinetto tap, faucet

rumore noise
rumoroso noisy
ruota wheel
ruscello brook, small stream

sabato Saturday
sabbia sand
sabbioso sandy
sala room, large room, hall
salame salami
sale salt
salire to go up
salita rise, ascent; **strada in . . .**
rising road
salone salon, saloon, hall; **. . .
di bellezza** beauty parlor;
. . . da pranzo dining hall
salpare to sail, set sail, leave, depart (of boats)
salsa sauce, gravy
salsiccia sausage
salumeria delicatessen store
salumiere delicatessen store-
keeper
salute health; **Salute!** Good
luck! Here's to you!
salvagente life preserver, life
belt
sandalo sandal
sangue blood
santuario shrine, sanctuary
sapere to know, know how
sapone soap
sapore flavor, taste
saporito tasty
sardina sardine
sarto tailor
sartoria tailor shop
sbagliare to make a mistake, be
mistaken
sbaglio mistake, error
sbarcare to land, get off a boat

sbarco landing, pier
sbrigarsi to hasten, hurry
scala stairs, ladder
scarico discharged, unloaded, unladen
scarpa shoe
scatola box
scegliere to choose, pick, select
scendere to go down, descend
scialle shawl
scialuppa (di salvataggio) lifeboat
sciarpa scarf
sciroppo syrup
scommessa bet
scommettere to bet
scomodo uncomfortable
sconto discount
scontrino check (baggage)
scorso last, just past; l'anno . . . last year
scrivere to write
scuola school
scuro dark
scusa excuse, apology
scusare to excuse; scusarsi to apologize
se if, self, himself, herself, themselves
sè self, himself, herself, themselves
seccare to annoy, bother
secco dry
secondo second
sedere to be sitting; sedersi to sit down; seduto seated
sedia chair; . . . a sdraio deck chair
sedici sixteen
segnare to mark, jot down, register
segretaria, segretario secretary

seguire to follow
sei six
semaforo traffic light, stop light, signal
sembrare to seem, appear
sempre always, still
senso sense, direction, way; . . . vietato wrong way; . . . unico one-way
sentire to feel, hear; sentirsi to feel, with reference to health
senza without
sera evening
serbatoio reservoir, tank, gas tank
serratura lock
servire to serve
servizio service
sessanta sixty
sesto sixth
seta silk
sete thirst; aver . . . to be thirsty
seterie silk products
settanta seventy
sette seven
settembre September
settentrionale northern
settimana week
settimo seventh
si self, oneself, himself, herself, themselves, one
sì yes
sicurezza assurance, security; pubblica . . . police; rasoio di . . . safety razor
sicuro sure, certain, certainly
sigaretta cigarette
sigaro cigar
sigillare to seal
sigillo seal
significare to mean, signify

223

significato meaning

signora lady, madam, Mrs.

signore, signor gentleman, sir, Mr. (use **signor** before names)

signorina young lady, Miss

silenzio silence, quiet

sinagoga synagogue

sinistro left, left-hand, sinister

slogare to sprain

slogatura sprain

smarrire to lose, mislay; **ufficio oggetti smarriti** lost-and-found bureau

smoking tux, tuxedo, dinner jacket

smontare to get off, dismount, take apart

soccorso help, aid; **pronto . . .** first aid

soffice soft

soggetto subject, topic

soggiorno stay, sojourn

solamente only

sollevare to raise, lift

solo alone, only

soltanto only

sonno sleep, sleepiness; **aver . . .** to be sleepy

sopra above, over, on

soprabito overcoat, topcoat

soprascarpa overshoe, rubber shoe

sorella sister

sosta halt, stop, pause; **divieto di . . .** no standing, no parking

sostare to halt, pause, stop, stand

sotto under, beneath, underneath, below; **. . . pena di** under penalty of

sottoveste slip, undergarment

spaccio store, shop; **. . . di bibite alcooliche** liquor store

spazzola brush; **spazzolino da denti** toothbrush

specchio mirror, looking glass

specie kind, sort, species

spedire to send, forward, ship

spesso often, frequently, dense, thick; **olio . . .** heavy oil

spiaggia beach, shore

spiccioli loose change, pocket money

spilla, spillo pin; **. . . di sicurezza** safety pin

spingere to push

sporcizia, sporchizia dirt

sporco dirty

sporgersi to lean out; **Vietato . . . dai finestrini** Do not lean out of car windows.

sportello window (of bank or ticket office)

spumante sparkling wine

sputare to spit

stamane, stamattina this morning

stampa press

stampati printed matter

stanchezza weariness

stanco tired, weary

stanotte tonight

stanza room

stare to be, stand

stasera this evening

stazionare to station, stand, park

stazione station

stella star

stesso same; **fa lo . . .** it's all the same

stile style

stirare to iron, press

stoffa material, cloth

stomaco stomach
straniero foreign, foreigner
stretto tight, narrow, strait
strettoia narrow passage, narrow road

tabaccheria tobacco shop
tabacco tobacco
tabarin cabaret, night club
tacco heel (of shoe)
tagliare to cut
tappeto carpet, rug
tardi late
tariffa rate, fixed and regular charge
tasca pocket
tascabile pocket-
tassa tax
tassametro meter on taxi or cab
tassì taxi
tavola, tavolo table
tazza cup
te you, yourself
tè tea
teatro theater
tedesco German
tela cloth, linen
telefonare to phone
telefonata phone call
telefonista telephone operator
telegrafare to telegraph, wire
telegrafata wire, telegraph message
telegramma telegram
tempo time, weather; fa bel . . . the weather is nice
tenere to hold, keep
tergicristallo windshield wiper
termosifone radiator (in room)
terra earth, land; a . . . on land; per . . . on the ground
terzo third

testa head; mal di . . . headache
ti you, yourself
tingere to tint, dye, stain
tintoria dry-cleaning shop
tintura tincture
tirare to draw, pull, throw
tiretto drawer
toccare to touch; . . . a to be up to, be one's turn
tonico tonic
tornare to return, come back
torto wrong; aver . . . to be wrong
tosse cough
tossire to cough
tovaglia tablecloth
tovagliolo napkin
tra among, between, within; . . . breve, . . . poco in a short time
tradurre to translate
traduzione translation
tragitto crossing, passage, transit, trip over
tram streetcar
transito transit, thoroughfare; Divieto di . . . No thoroughfare, Keep out.
tranvai streetcar
tratta bank draft
trattenersi to stay, remain
trattoria restaurant
traversa crossroad, block
tre three
tredici thirteen
treno train
trenta thirty
troppo too, too much; troppi too many
trovare to find; trovarsi to be
tu you

tutto all, everything; **tutti** all, everybody, everyone

uccello bird
udire to hear
ufficiale officer, official
ufficio office, bureau, desk
ultimo last, latest
umido damp, stew
undici eleven
unghia fingernail, toenail, claw
unguento ointment
uno, una, un, un' a, an, one
uomo man
uovo egg
urbano urban, city; **vigile . . .** city policeman
uscire to go out, leave
uscita exit, going out, departure
uso use
uva grapes

vaglia money order
vagone railroad car; **. . . bagagli** baggage car; **. . . letto** sleeping car, Pullman; **. . . ristorante** dining car
valere to be worth
valido valid, good for
valigia suitcase, bag, valise
valore worth, value, valor
valuta currency; **. . . pregiata** "hard" currency
vapore steam, steamer, steamship, vapor
varietà variety, vaudeville
ve you, there
vecchio old
vedere to see
veduta view
veicolo vehicle, conveyance
veleno poison

velenoso poisonous
velluto velvet
velocità speed, velocity; **. . . massima** speed limit
vendere to sell
vendita sale; **. . . d'occasione** bargain sale
venerdì Friday
venire to come, arrive
ventaglio fan (lady's)
ventilatore fan (car or room), ventilator
vento wind; **tira . . .** it is windy
veramente really, truly
verde green
verdura green vegetables
verificare to check, verify
verità truth
vernice varnish, paint; **. . . fresca, verniciato di fresco** fresh paint
vero true, real, actual
verso toward, in the direction of, about, at about
vertigini dizziness, dizzy spells; **avere . . .** to be dizzy
veste dress, gown; **. . . da camera** dressing gown
vestiario clothing, articles of clothing
vestito dress, suit of clothes
vetrina display window, showcase
vetro glass (material)
vettura coach, horse-cab, conveyance
vetturino coachman, horse-cab driver
vi you, there
via way, street, road, away, by way of; **. . . aerea** airmail

226

viaggiare to travel
viaggiatore traveler
viaggio journey, voyage, trip
vicino near, close by, neighboring, neighbor
vietato forbidden; . . . **fumare** no smoking; . . . **l'ingresso** no admittance
vino wine
visita visit
visitare to visit
visitatore visitor
viso face
vita life
vitello veal, calf
vivere to live
voi, voialtri you
volante steering wheel
volare to fly
volentieri gladly, with pleasure, willingly

volere to want; **voler dire** to mean
volo flight
volta time, turn, curve; . . . **pericolosa** dangerous curve; **tre volte** three times
voltare to turn
voltata turn; **fare una voltata a destra** to make a turn to the right
volto face
vuoto empty

zanzara mosquito
zanzariera mosquito netting
zia aunt
zio uncle
zoologico zoological; **giardino** . . . zoo
zucchero sugar